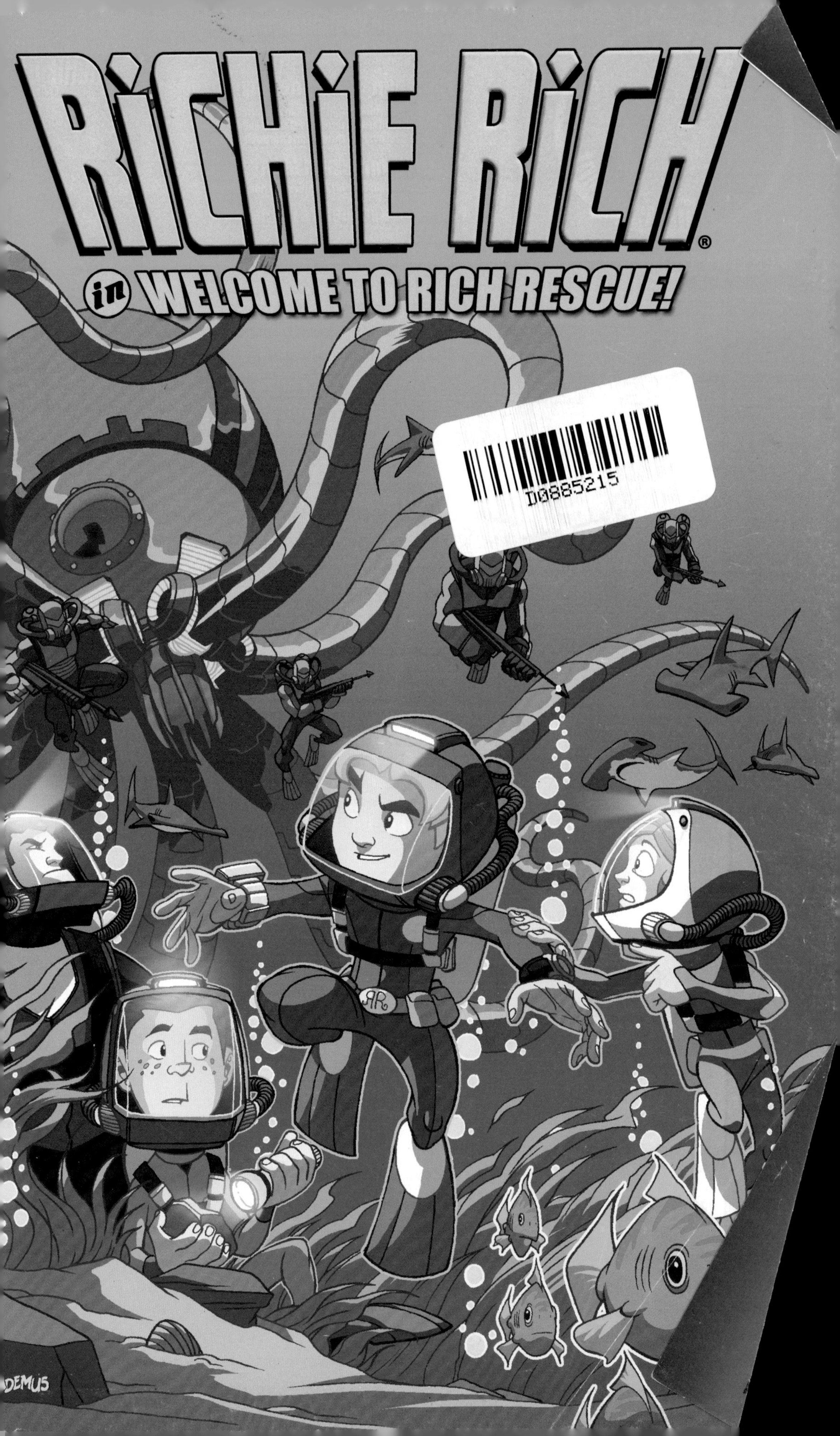
RICHIE RICH®
in WELCOME TO RICH RESCUE!
DEMUS

APE ENTERTAINMENT

David Hedgecock
CEO | Partner
DHedgecock@Ape-Entertainment.com

Brent E. Erwin
COO | Partner
BErwin@Ape-Entertainment.com

Aaron Sparrow
Editor
ASparrow@Ape-Entertainment.com

Weldon Adams
Editor
WAdams@Ape-Entertainment.com

Kevin Freeman
Editor | Special Projects
KFreeman@Ape-Entertainment.com

Brent E. Erwin
Graphic Designer
BErwin@Ape-Entertainment.com

Company Information:
Ape Entertainment
P.O. Box 7100
San Diego, CA 92167
www.ApeComics.com

For Advertising contact:
The Bonfire Agency
Ed Cato
ed.catto@bonfireagency.com
917.595.4107

APE DIGITAL COMIC SITE:
ApeComics.com
Apecmx.com

TWITTER: Twitter.com/ApeComics

FACEBOOK: Facebook.com/ApeEntertainment

YouTube: YouTube.com/user/Apecomics

ALSO AVAILABLE
DIGEST VOL. 1

All covers by: Jack Lawrence
Edited by: Aaron Sparrow

Richie Rich Introduction

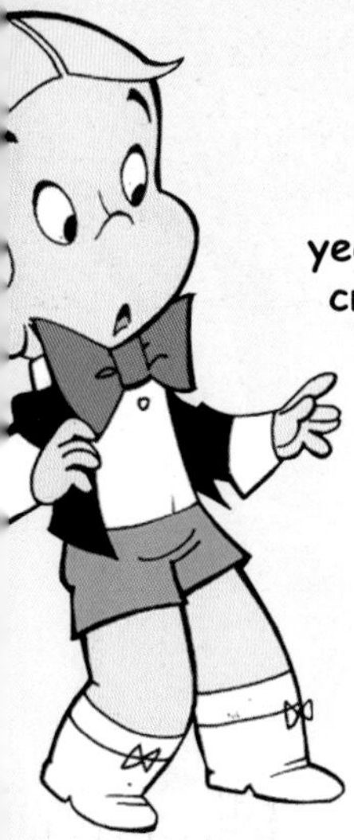

If you look at him you wouldn't know that Richie Rich is 58 years old! That smile, that golden hair, that red bow tie, that crisp white shirt and black jacket, and, yes, those blue short pants makes you think he's no more than ten years old. Forget it.

He was created by Warren Kremer and myself way back in 1953, appearing for the first time in Little Dot #1 in a story called "The Dancing Lessons." Warren and I wrote the story, and though Warren is by far the most famous artist associated with the character, the artist that time was Steve Muffatti, an animation giant in his own right.

Richie appeared in almost every issue of both Little Dot and Little Lotta books for many years. But not until November, 1960 did he enjoy his own book. Did I say "his own book?" By leaps and bounds Richie appeared in more and more and more Richie Rich titles until he had more titles carrying his name than any other comics character in history!

There was Richie Rich, Richie Rich Dollars and Cents, Richie Rich Millions, Richie Billions, Richie Rich Zillions, Richie Rich Cash, Richie Rich Diamonds, Richie Rich and Silver, Richie Rich Jackpots, etc, etc, until there was even Super Richie! A e title—four or five titles—wasn't enough for Richie's fans. More than FIFTY s existed over the years!

At the beginning, Richie was a kind of rich kid. Something we might today call "up-middle class." But that's only where he started. As issues grew and titles multiplied, became far and away the richest kid in the world! He also was surrounded by a con-gation of great characters that could fill a dozen comics titles. How about Mr. and . Rich, Reggie Van Dough, Gloria Glad, Freckles and Pee Wee, Cadbury, Bascomb, da Munny, Dollar the Dollarmatian and on and on. Then this world's richest kid was ught into TV animation, starring in several series, and then into real life filmdom with ung Macaulay Culkin starring in the role.

Sadly, when Richie Rich's publisher, Harvey Publications, closed its doors, though name Richie Rich had become part of our language, the charac-disappeared from the newsstands.

I am thrilled to find the kid is back, this time un-the auspices of Ape Entertainment. And thrilled, to play a part in his rebirth alongside Ernie n, who learned his craft and honed his fantas-tools while working with Warren Kremer.

You'll find a touch of the old Richie Rich ting for you here, but also a great deal of ew, exciting and colorful Richie that will ck your socks off—and lift you out of r shoes!

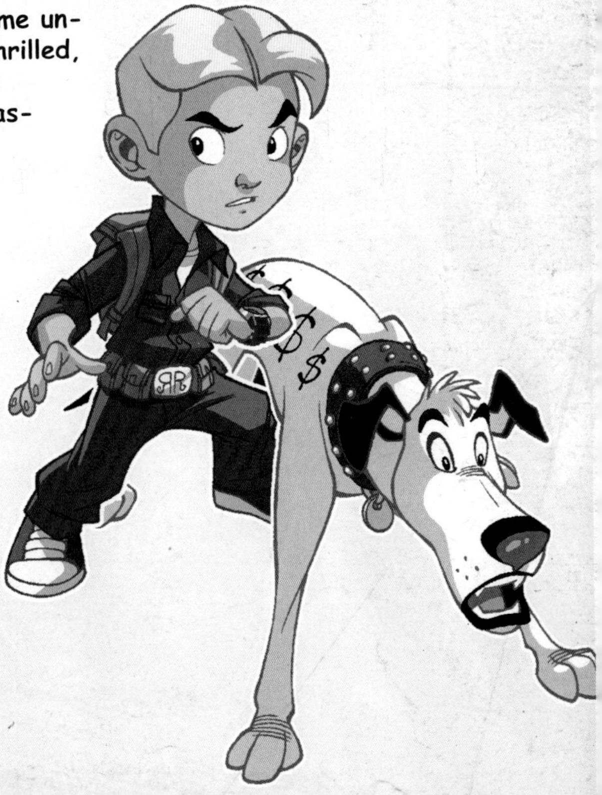

Welcome to the new Richie Rich!

Sid Jacobson
Los Angeles, CA
March, 2011

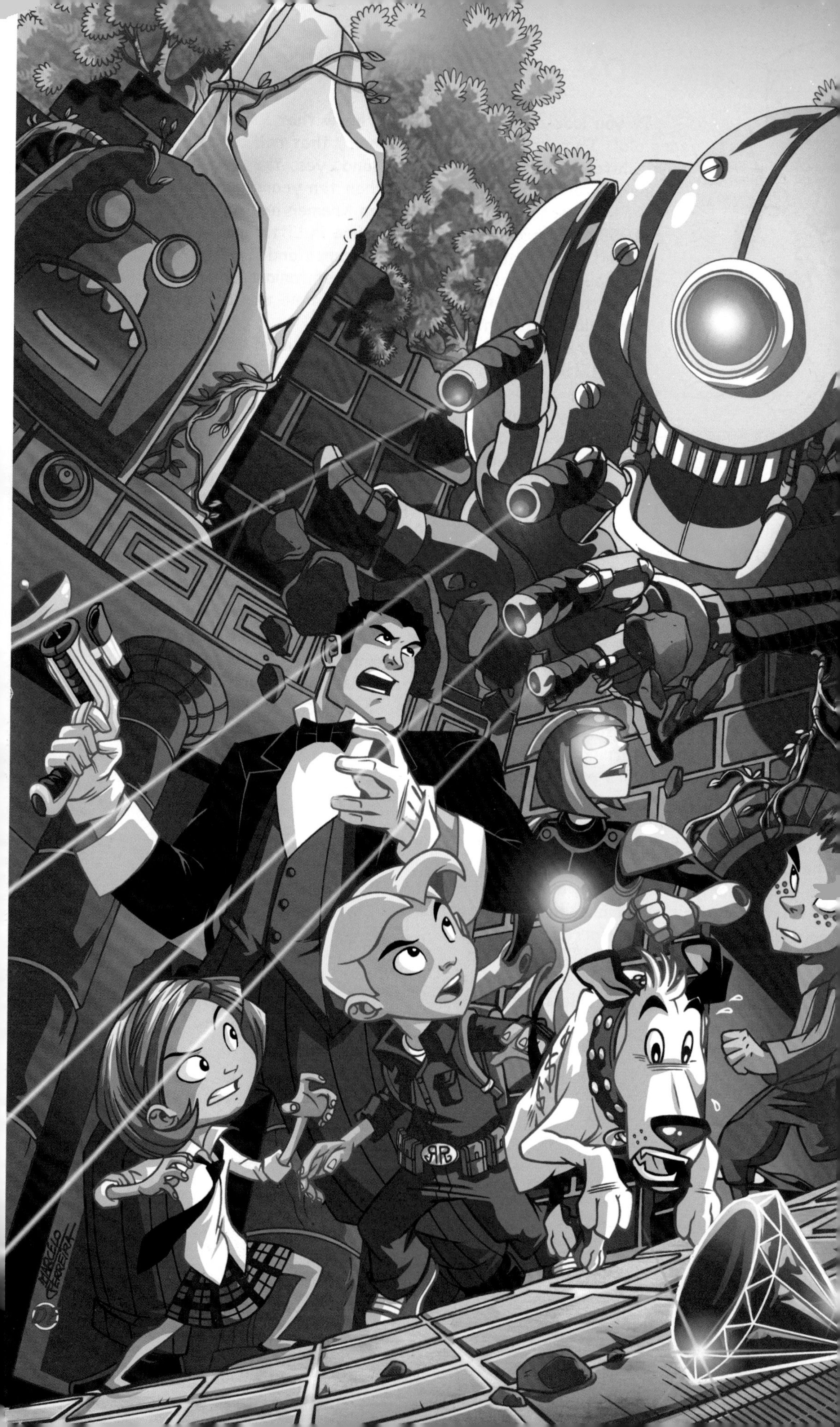
MARCELO FERREIRA

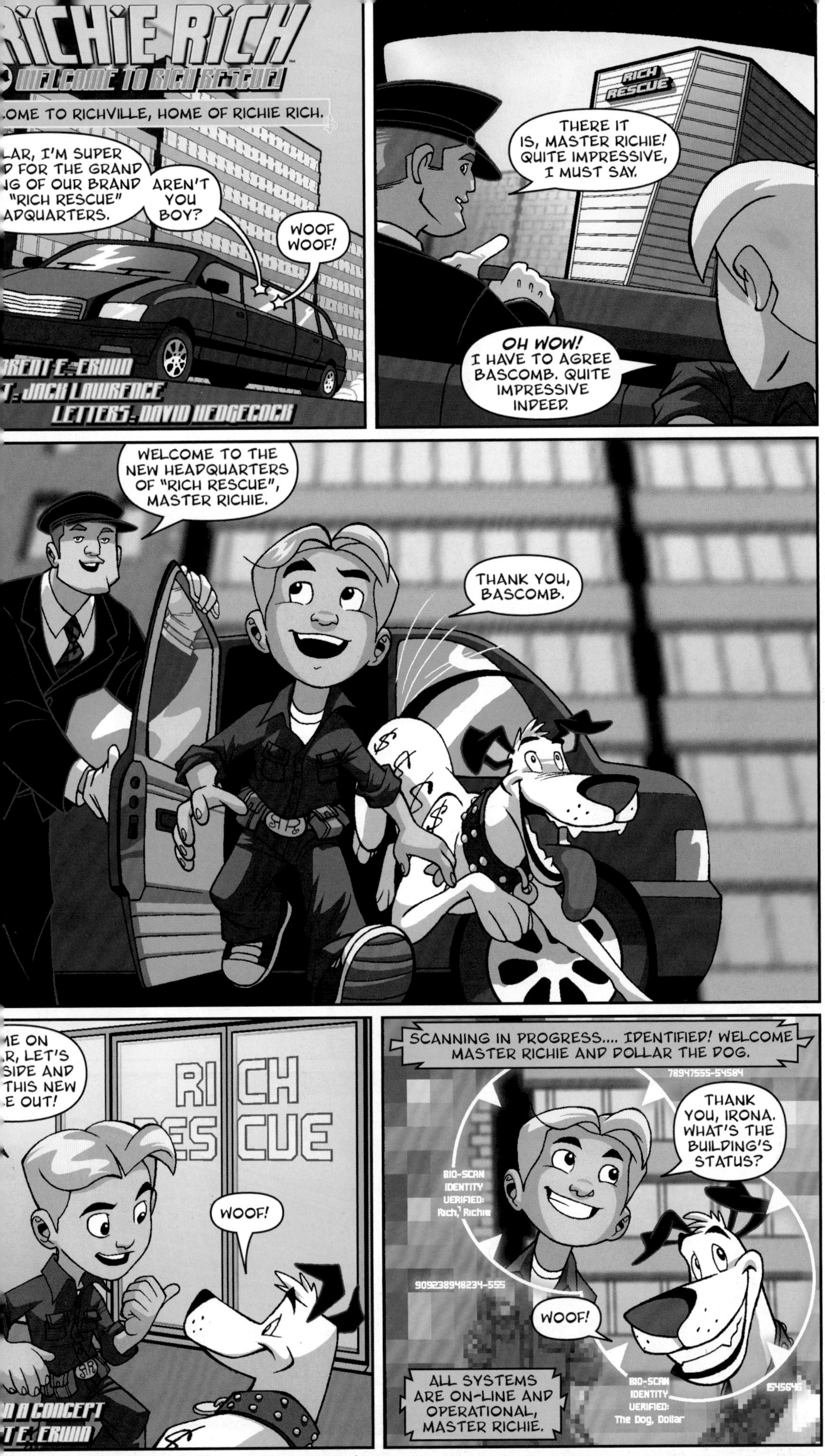

ICHIE RICH
WELCOME TO RICH RESCUE!
OME TO RICHVILLE, HOME OF RICHIE RICH.
LAR, I'M SUPER D FOR THE GRAND NG OF OUR BRAND "RICH RESCUE" ADQUARTERS.
AREN'T YOU BOY?
WOOF WOOF!
BRENT E. ERWIN
T: JACK LAWRENCE
LETTERS: DAVID HEDGECOCK
RICH RESCUE
THERE IT IS, MASTER RICHIE! QUITE IMPRESSIVE, I MUST SAY.
OH WOW! I HAVE TO AGREE BASCOMB. QUITE IMPRESSIVE INDEED.
WELCOME TO THE NEW HEADQUARTERS OF "RICH RESCUE", MASTER RICHIE.
THANK YOU, BASCOMB.
ME ON R, LET'S SIDE AND THIS NEW E OUT!
RICH RESCUE
WOOF!
N A CONCEPT
T E. ERWIN
SCANNING IN PROGRESS.... IDENTIFIED! WELCOME MASTER RICHIE AND DOLLAR THE DOG.
78947555-54584
THANK YOU, IRONA. WHAT'S THE BUILDING'S STATUS?
BIO-SCAN IDENTITY VERIFIED: Rich, Richie
909238948234-555
WOOF!
ALL SYSTEMS ARE ON-LINE AND OPERATIONAL, MASTER RICHIE.
BIO-SCAN IDENTITY VERIFIED: The Dog, Dollar
1545646

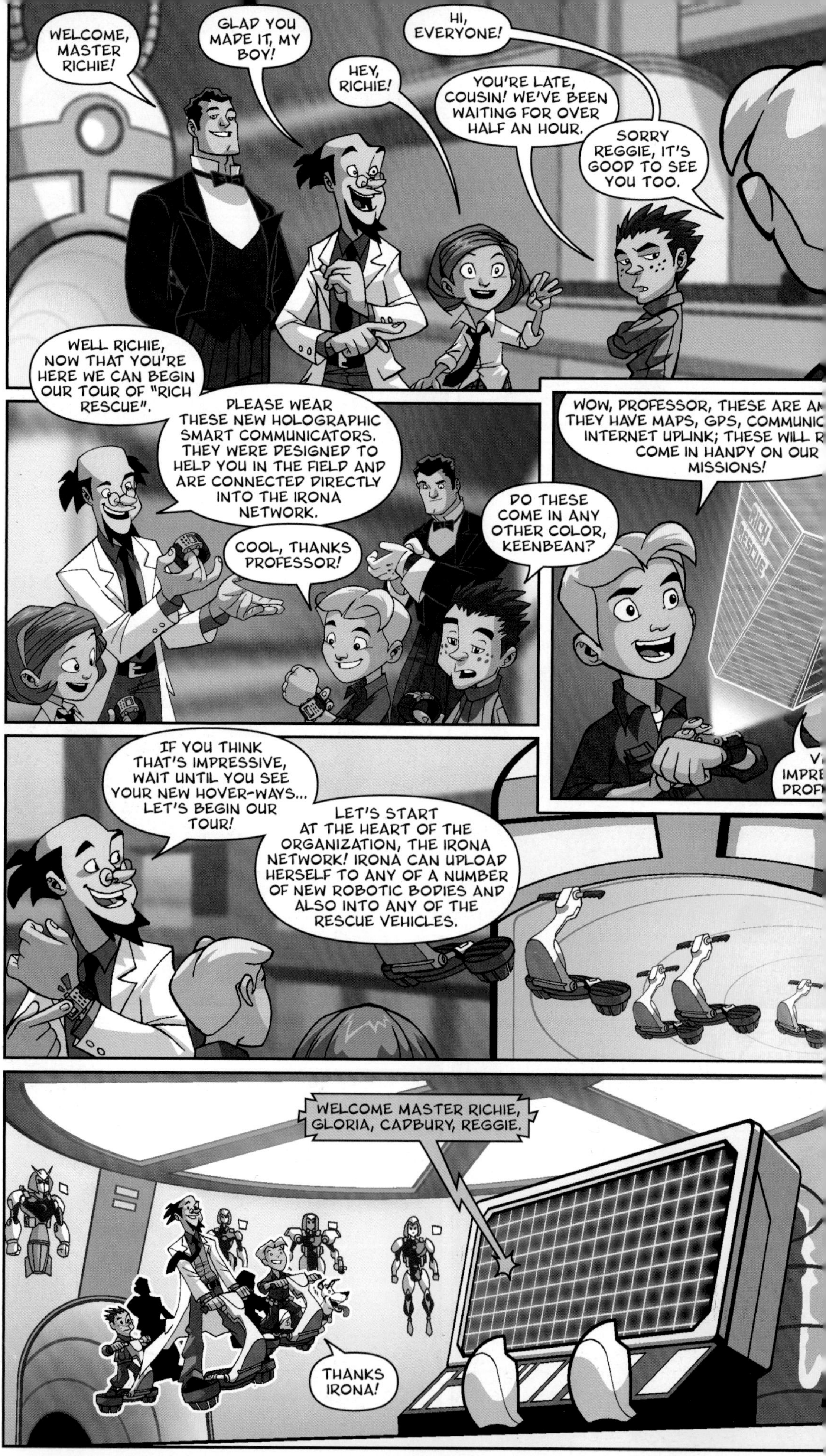
WELCOME, MASTER RICHIE!
GLAD YOU MADE IT, MY BOY!
HEY, RICHIE!
HI, EVERYONE!
YOU'RE LATE, COUSIN! WE'VE BEEN WAITING FOR OVER HALF AN HOUR.
SORRY REGGIE, IT'S GOOD TO SEE YOU TOO.
WELL RICHIE, NOW THAT YOU'RE HERE WE CAN BEGIN OUR TOUR OF "RICH RESCUE".
PLEASE WEAR THESE NEW HOLOGRAPHIC SMART COMMUNICATORS. THEY WERE DESIGNED TO HELP YOU IN THE FIELD AND ARE CONNECTED DIRECTLY INTO THE IRONA NETWORK.
COOL, THANKS PROFESSOR!
DO THESE COME IN ANY OTHER COLOR, KEENBEAN?
WOW, PROFESSOR, THESE ARE AM
THEY HAVE MAPS, GPS, COMMUNIC
INTERNET UPLINK; THESE WILL R
COME IN HANDY ON OUR
MISSIONS!
IF YOU THINK THAT'S IMPRESSIVE, WAIT UNTIL YOU SEE YOUR NEW HOVER-WAYS... LET'S BEGIN OUR TOUR!
LET'S START AT THE HEART OF THE ORGANIZATION, THE IRONA NETWORK! IRONA CAN UPLOAD HERSELF TO ANY OF A NUMBER OF NEW ROBOTIC BODIES AND ALSO INTO ANY OF THE RESCUE VEHICLES.
WELCOME MASTER RICHIE, GLORIA, CADBURY, REGGIE.
THANKS IRONA!

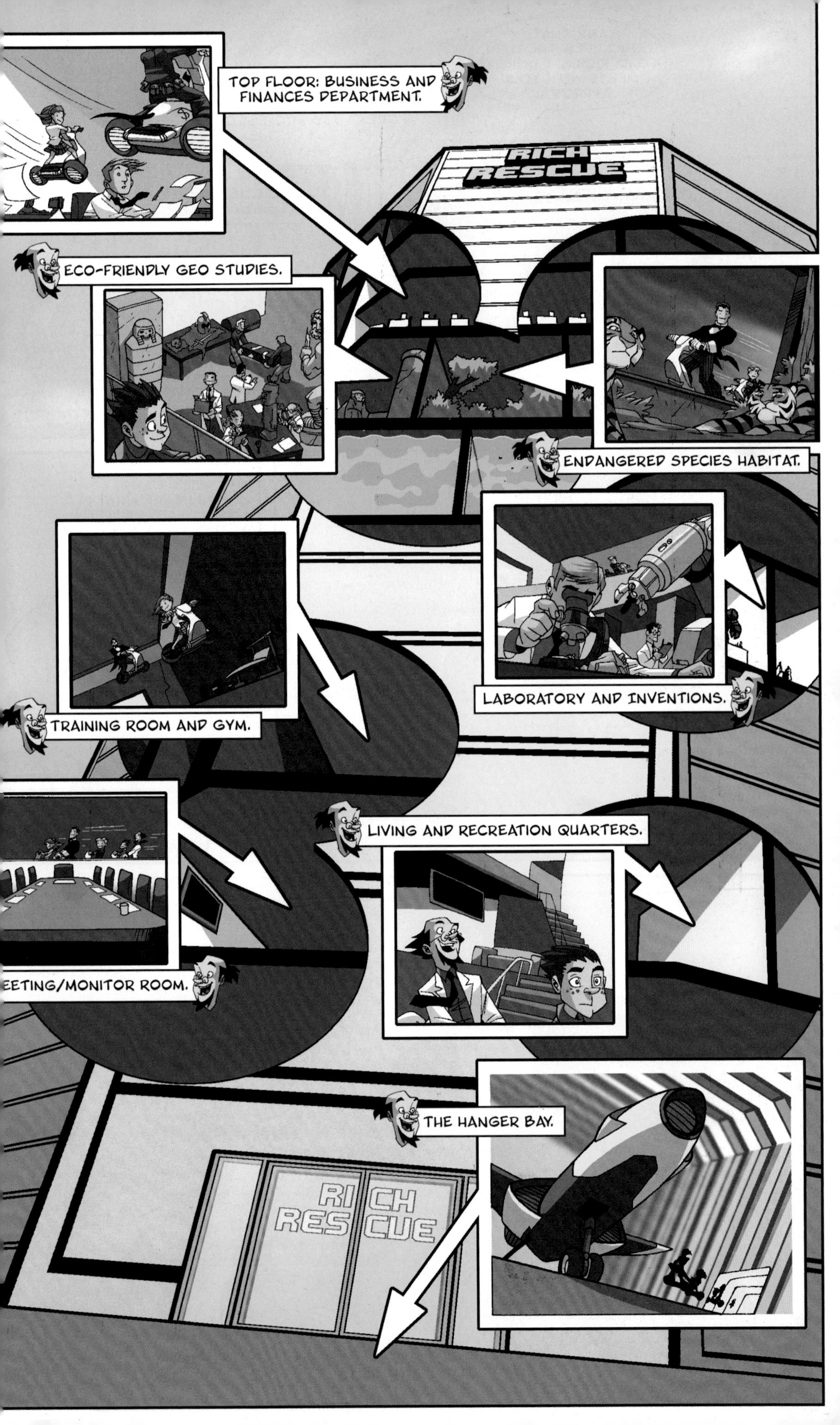
TOP FLOOR: BUSINESS AND FINANCES DEPARTMENT.
RICH RESCUE
ECO-FRIENDLY GEO STUDIES.
ENDANGERED SPECIES HABITAT.
LABORATORY AND INVENTIONS.
TRAINING ROOM AND GYM.
LIVING AND RECREATION QUARTERS.
EETING/MONITOR ROOM.
THE HANGER BAY.
RICH RESCUE

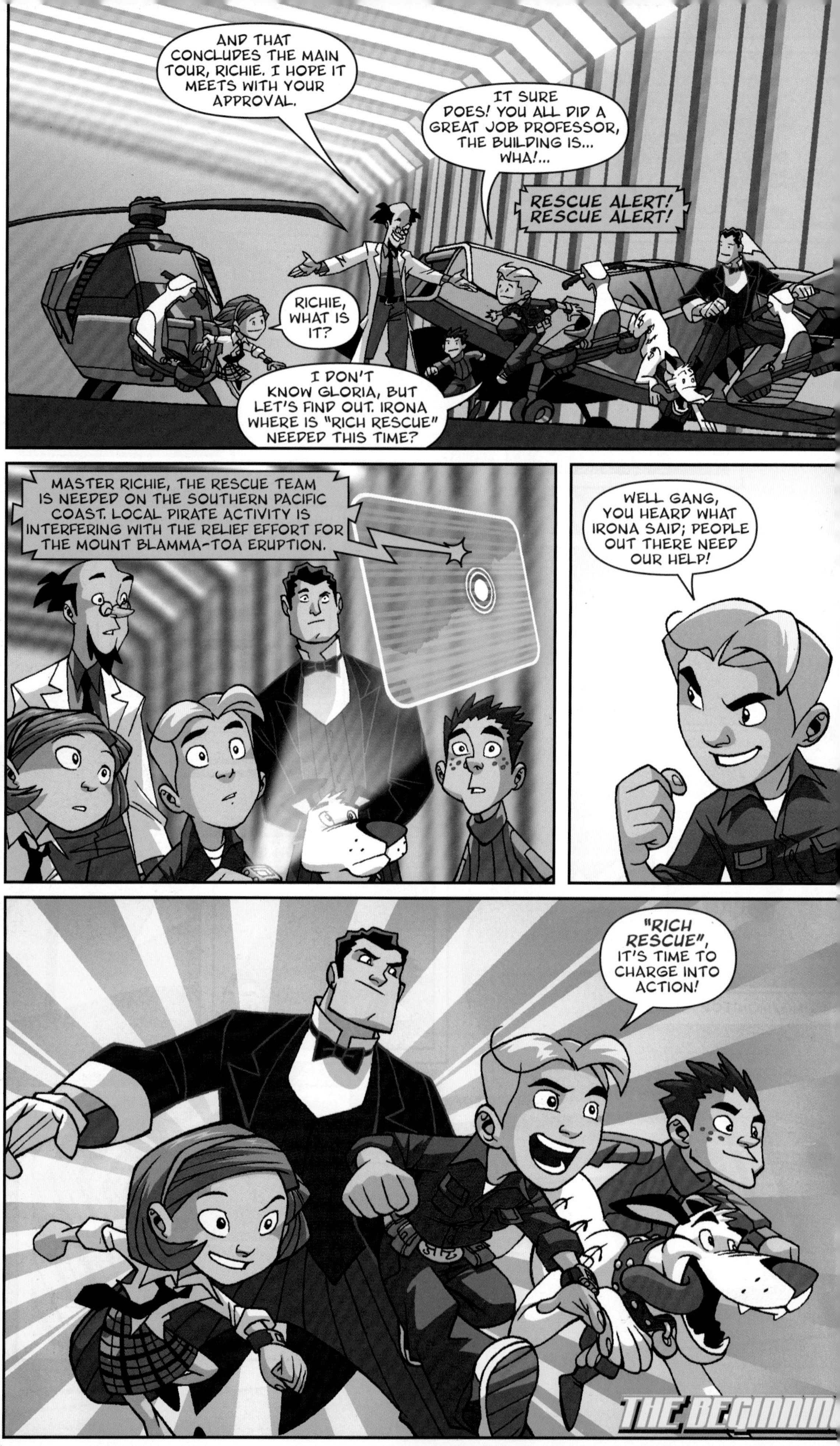
AND THAT CONCLUDES THE MAIN TOUR, RICHIE. I HOPE IT MEETS WITH YOUR APPROVAL.
IT SURE DOES! YOU ALL DID A GREAT JOB PROFESSOR, THE BUILDING IS... WHA!...
RESCUE ALERT! RESCUE ALERT!
RICHIE, WHAT IS IT?
I DON'T KNOW GLORIA, BUT LET'S FIND OUT. IRONA WHERE IS "RICH RESCUE" NEEDED THIS TIME?
MASTER RICHIE, THE RESCUE TEAM IS NEEDED ON THE SOUTHERN PACIFIC COAST. LOCAL PIRATE ACTIVITY IS INTERFERING WITH THE RELIEF EFFORT FOR THE MOUNT BLAMMA-TOA ERUPTION.
WELL GANG, YOU HEARD WHAT IRONA SAID; PEOPLE OUT THERE NEED OUR HELP!
"RICH RESCUE", IT'S TIME TO CHARGE INTO ACTION!
THE BEGINNIN

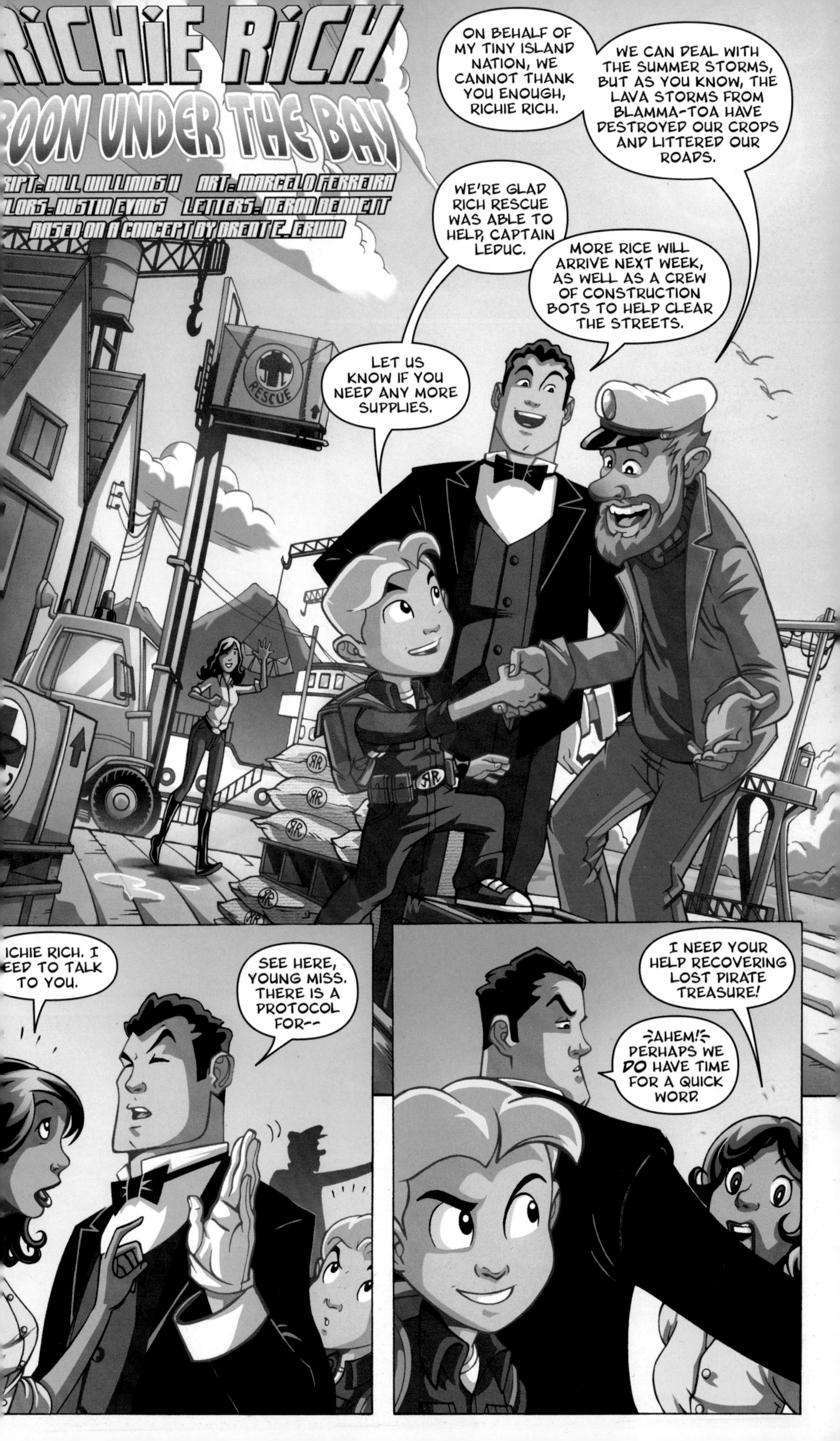
RICHIE RICH
OON UNDER THE BAY
RIPT: BILL WILLIAMS II ART: MARCELO FERREIRA
LORS: DUSTIN EVANS LETTERS: DERON BENNETT
BASED ON A CONCEPT BY BRENT E. ERWIN
ON BEHALF OF MY TINY ISLAND NATION, WE CANNOT THANK YOU ENOUGH, RICHIE RICH.
WE CAN DEAL WITH THE SUMMER STORMS, BUT AS YOU KNOW, THE LAVA STORMS FROM BLAMMA-TOA HAVE DESTROYED OUR CROPS AND LITTERED OUR ROADS.
WE'RE GLAD RICH RESCUE WAS ABLE TO HELP, CAPTAIN LEDUC.
MORE RICE WILL ARRIVE NEXT WEEK, AS WELL AS A CREW OF CONSTRUCTION BOTS TO HELP CLEAR THE STREETS.
LET US KNOW IF YOU NEED ANY MORE SUPPLIES.
RESCUE
ICHIE RICH. I EED TO TALK TO YOU.
SEE HERE, YOUNG MISS. THERE IS A PROTOCOL FOR--
I NEED YOUR HELP RECOVERING LOST PIRATE TREASURE!
AHEM! PERHAPS WE DO HAVE TIME FOR A QUICK WORD.

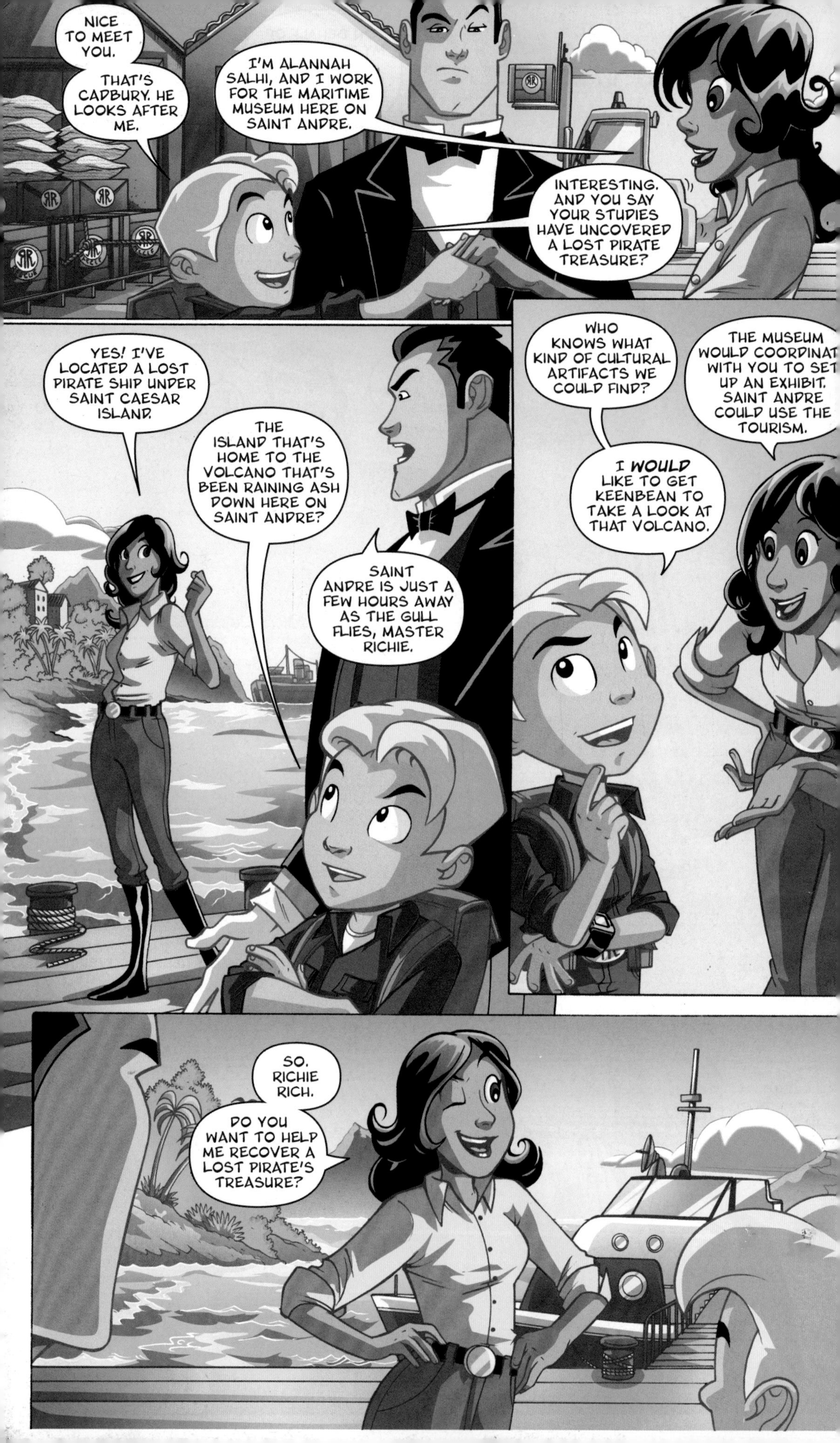
NICE TO MEET YOU.
THAT'S CADBURY. HE LOOKS AFTER ME.
I'M ALANNAH SALHI, AND I WORK FOR THE MARITIME MUSEUM HERE ON SAINT ANDRE.
INTERESTING. AND YOU SAY YOUR STUDIES HAVE UNCOVERED A LOST PIRATE TREASURE?
YES! I'VE LOCATED A LOST PIRATE SHIP UNDER SAINT CAESAR ISLAND.
THE ISLAND THAT'S HOME TO THE VOLCANO THAT'S BEEN RAINING ASH DOWN HERE ON SAINT ANDRE?
SAINT ANDRE IS JUST A FEW HOURS AWAY AS THE GULL FLIES, MASTER RICHIE.
WHO KNOWS WHAT KIND OF CULTURAL ARTIFACTS WE COULD FIND?
THE MUSEUM WOULD COORDINAT WITH YOU TO SET UP AN EXHIBIT. SAINT ANDRE COULD USE THE TOURISM.
I ***WOULD*** LIKE TO GET KEENBEAN TO TAKE A LOOK AT THAT VOLCANO.
SO. RICHIE RICH.
DO YOU WANT TO HELP ME RECOVER A LOST PIRATE'S TREASURE?

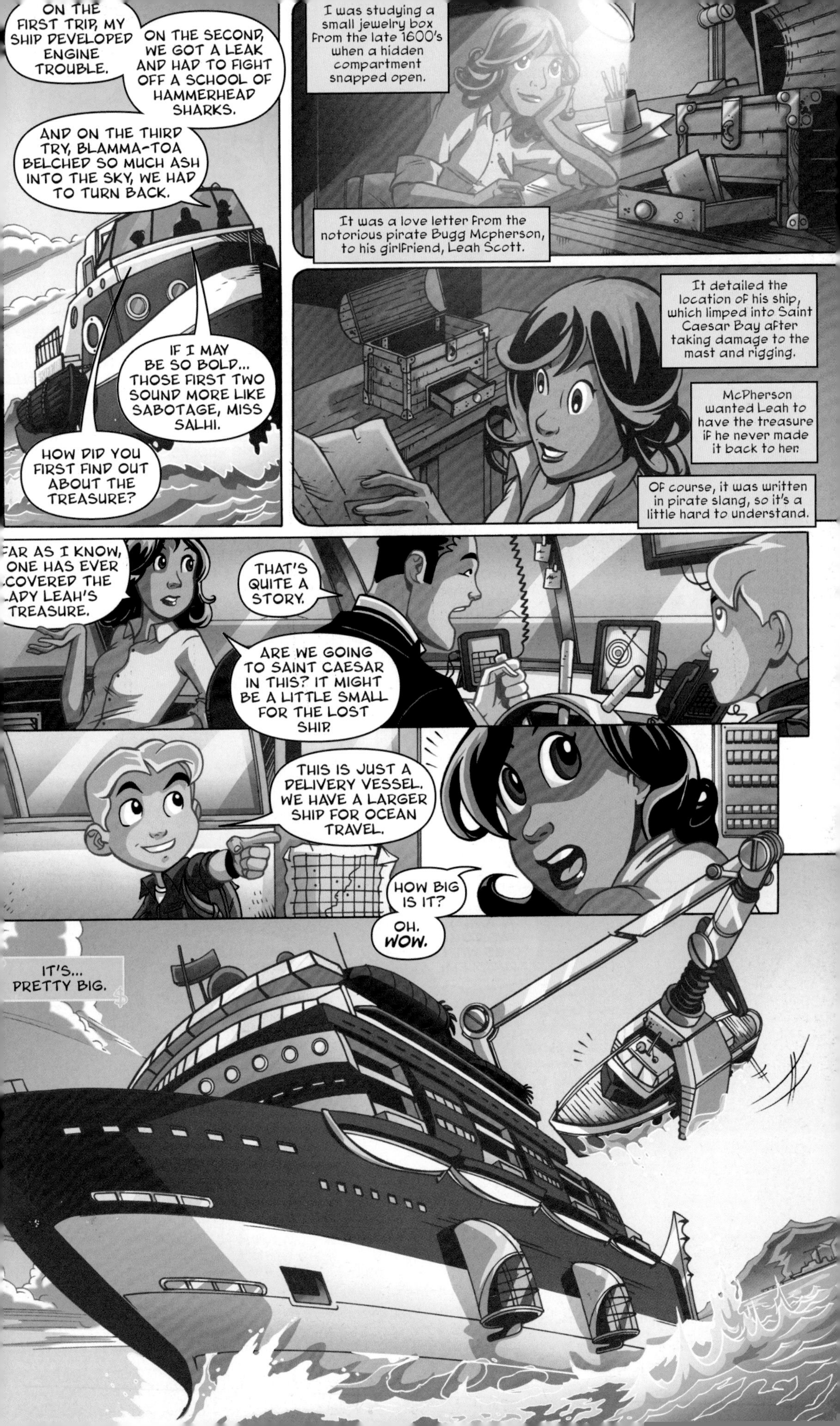
ON THE FIRST TRIP, MY SHIP DEVELOPED ENGINE TROUBLE.
ON THE SECOND, WE GOT A LEAK AND HAD TO FIGHT OFF A SCHOOL OF HAMMERHEAD SHARKS.
AND ON THE THIRD TRY, BLAMMA-TOA BELCHED SO MUCH ASH INTO THE SKY, WE HAD TO TURN BACK.
IF I MAY BE SO BOLD... THOSE FIRST TWO SOUND MORE LIKE SABOTAGE, MISS SALHI.
HOW DID YOU FIRST FIND OUT ABOUT THE TREASURE?
I was studying a small jewelry box from the late 1600's when a hidden compartment snapped open.
It was a love letter from the notorious pirate Bugg Mcpherson, to his girlfriend, Leah Scott.
It detailed the location of his ship, which limped into Saint Caesar Bay after taking damage to the mast and rigging.
McPherson wanted Leah to have the treasure if he never made it back to her.
Of course, it was written in pirate slang, so it's a little hard to understand.
AR AS I KNOW, ONE HAS EVER COVERED THE ADY LEAH'S TREASURE.
THAT'S QUITE A STORY.
ARE WE GOING TO SAINT CAESAR IN THIS? IT MIGHT BE A LITTLE SMALL FOR THE LOST SHIP.
THIS IS JUST A DELIVERY VESSEL. WE HAVE A LARGER SHIP FOR OCEAN TRAVEL.
HOW BIG IS IT?
OH. WOW.
IT'S... PRETTY BIG.

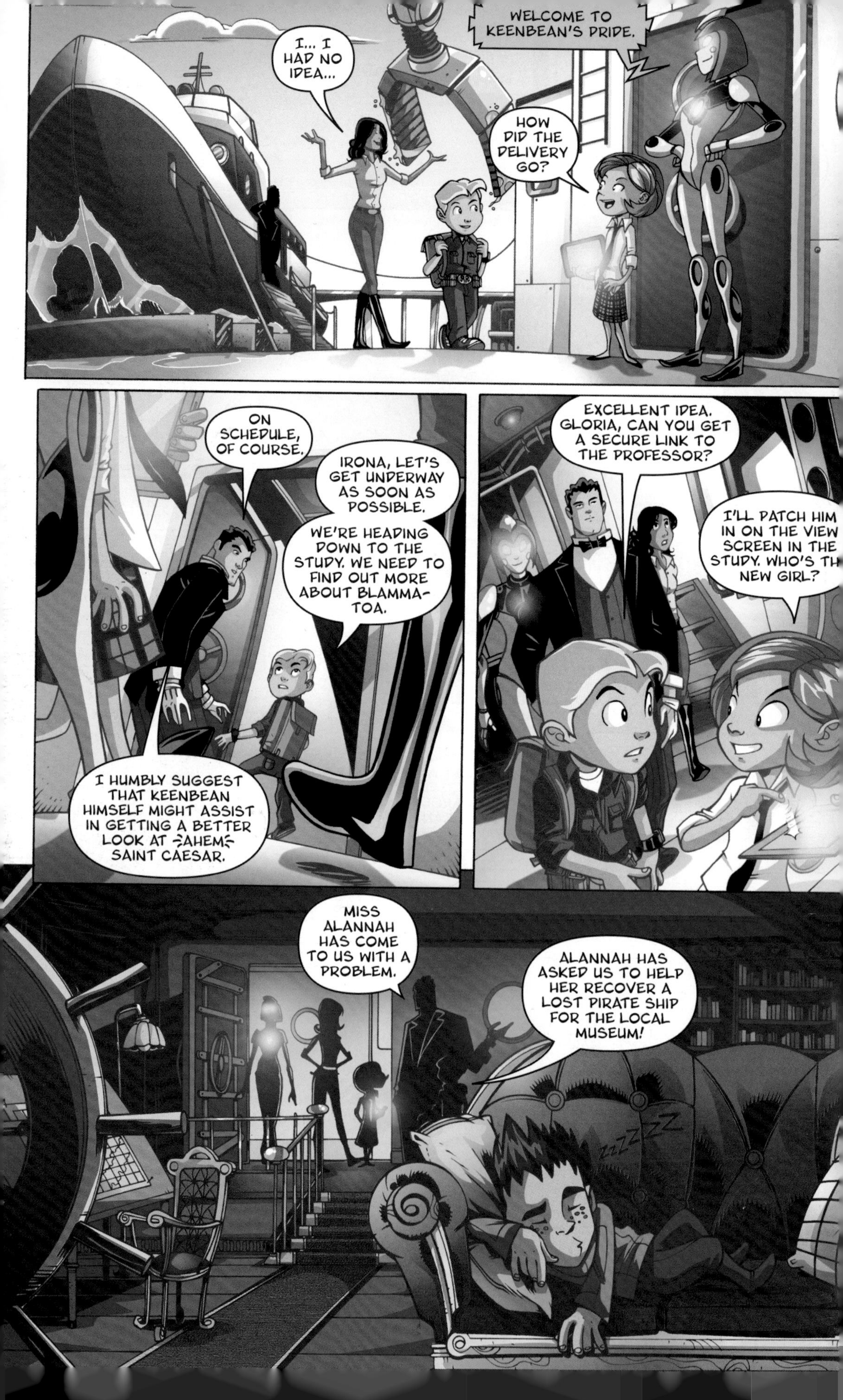
WELCOME TO KEENBEAN'S PRIDE.
I... I HAD NO IDEA...
HOW DID THE DELIVERY GO?
ON SCHEDULE, OF COURSE.
IRONA, LET'S GET UNDERWAY AS SOON AS POSSIBLE.
WE'RE HEADING DOWN TO THE STUDY. WE NEED TO FIND OUT MORE ABOUT BLAMMA-TOA.
I HUMBLY SUGGEST THAT KEENBEAN HIMSELF MIGHT ASSIST IN GETTING A BETTER LOOK AT -AHEM- SAINT CAESAR.
EXCELLENT IDEA. GLORIA, CAN YOU GET A SECURE LINK TO THE PROFESSOR?
I'LL PATCH HIM IN ON THE VIEW SCREEN IN THE STUDY. WHO'S TH NEW GIRL?
MISS ALANNAH HAS COME TO US WITH A PROBLEM.
ALANNAH HAS ASKED US TO HELP HER RECOVER A LOST PIRATE SHIP FOR THE LOCAL MUSEUM!
ZZZZZ

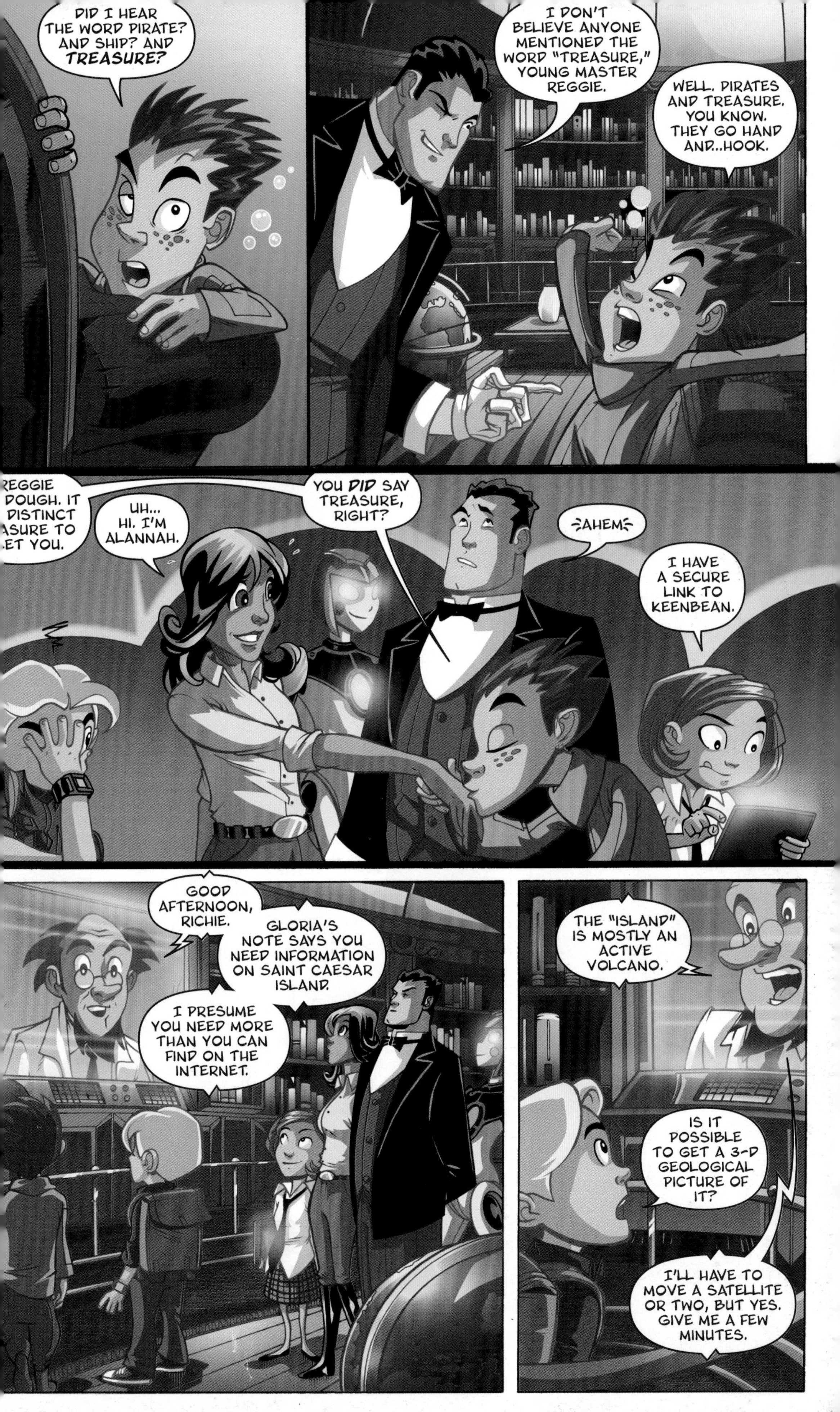
DID I HEAR THE WORD PIRATE? AND SHIP? AND **TREASURE?**
I DON'T BELIEVE ANYONE MENTIONED THE WORD "TREASURE," YOUNG MASTER REGGIE.
WELL, PIRATES AND TREASURE. YOU KNOW. THEY GO HAND AND...HOOK.
REGGIE DOUGH. IT DISTINCT ASURE TO ET YOU.
UH... HI. I'M ALANNAH.
YOU **DID** SAY TREASURE, RIGHT?
AHEM
I HAVE A SECURE LINK TO KEENBEAN.
GOOD AFTERNOON, RICHIE.
GLORIA'S NOTE SAYS YOU NEED INFORMATION ON SAINT CAESAR ISLAND.
I PRESUME YOU NEED MORE THAN YOU CAN FIND ON THE INTERNET.
THE "ISLAND" IS MOSTLY AN ACTIVE VOLCANO.
IS IT POSSIBLE TO GET A 3-D GEOLOGICAL PICTURE OF IT?
I'LL HAVE TO MOVE A SATELLITE OR TWO, BUT YES. GIVE ME A FEW MINUTES.

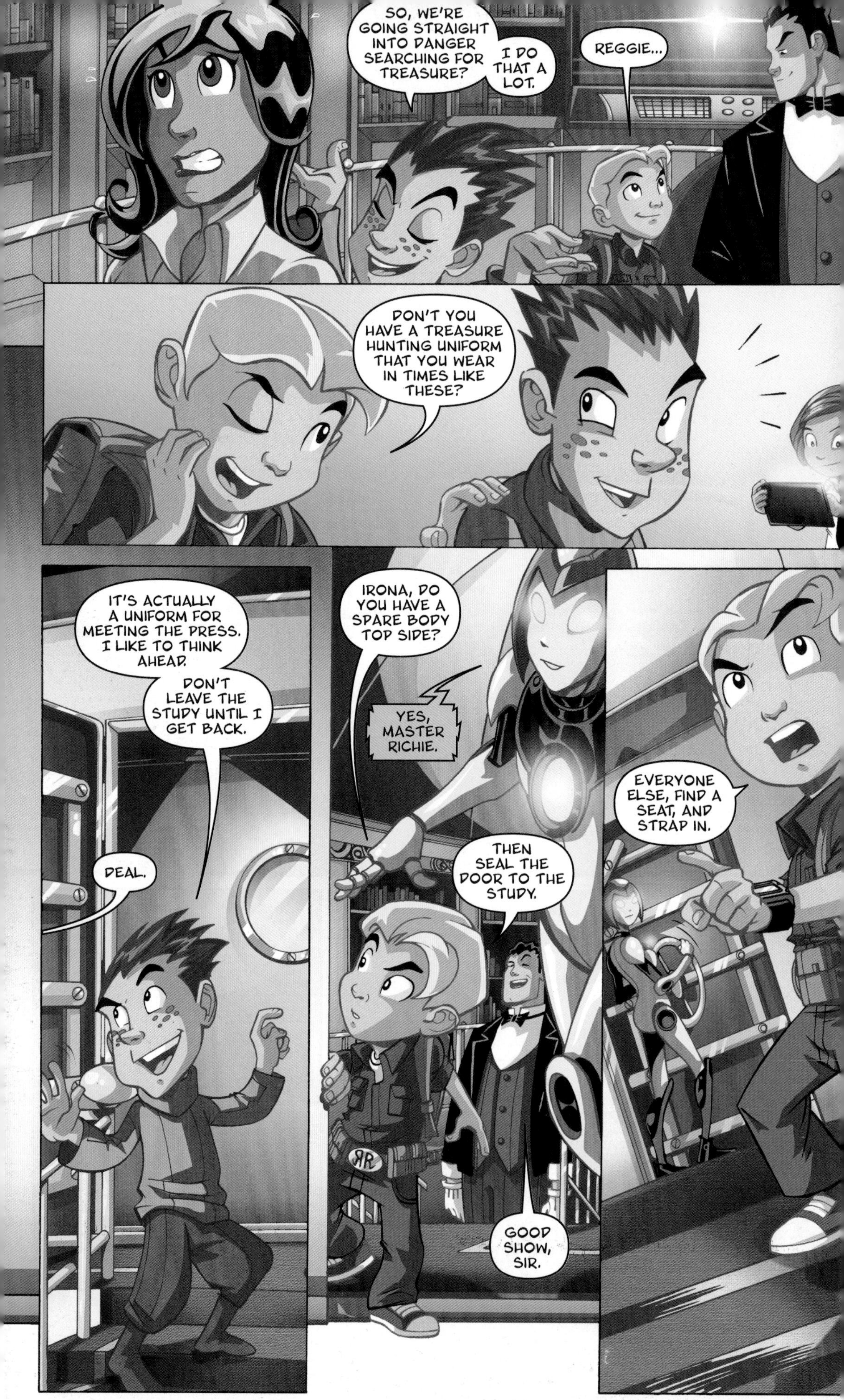
SO, WE'RE GOING STRAIGHT INTO DANGER SEARCHING FOR TREASURE?
I DO THAT A LOT.
REGGIE...
DON'T YOU HAVE A TREASURE HUNTING UNIFORM THAT YOU WEAR IN TIMES LIKE THESE?
IT'S ACTUALLY A UNIFORM FOR MEETING THE PRESS. I LIKE TO THINK AHEAD.
DON'T LEAVE THE STUDY UNTIL I GET BACK.
DEAL.
IRONA, DO YOU HAVE A SPARE BODY TOP SIDE?
YES, MASTER RICHIE.
THEN SEAL THE DOOR TO THE STUDY.
GOOD SHOW, SIR.
EVERYONE ELSE, FIND A SEAT, AND STRAP IN.

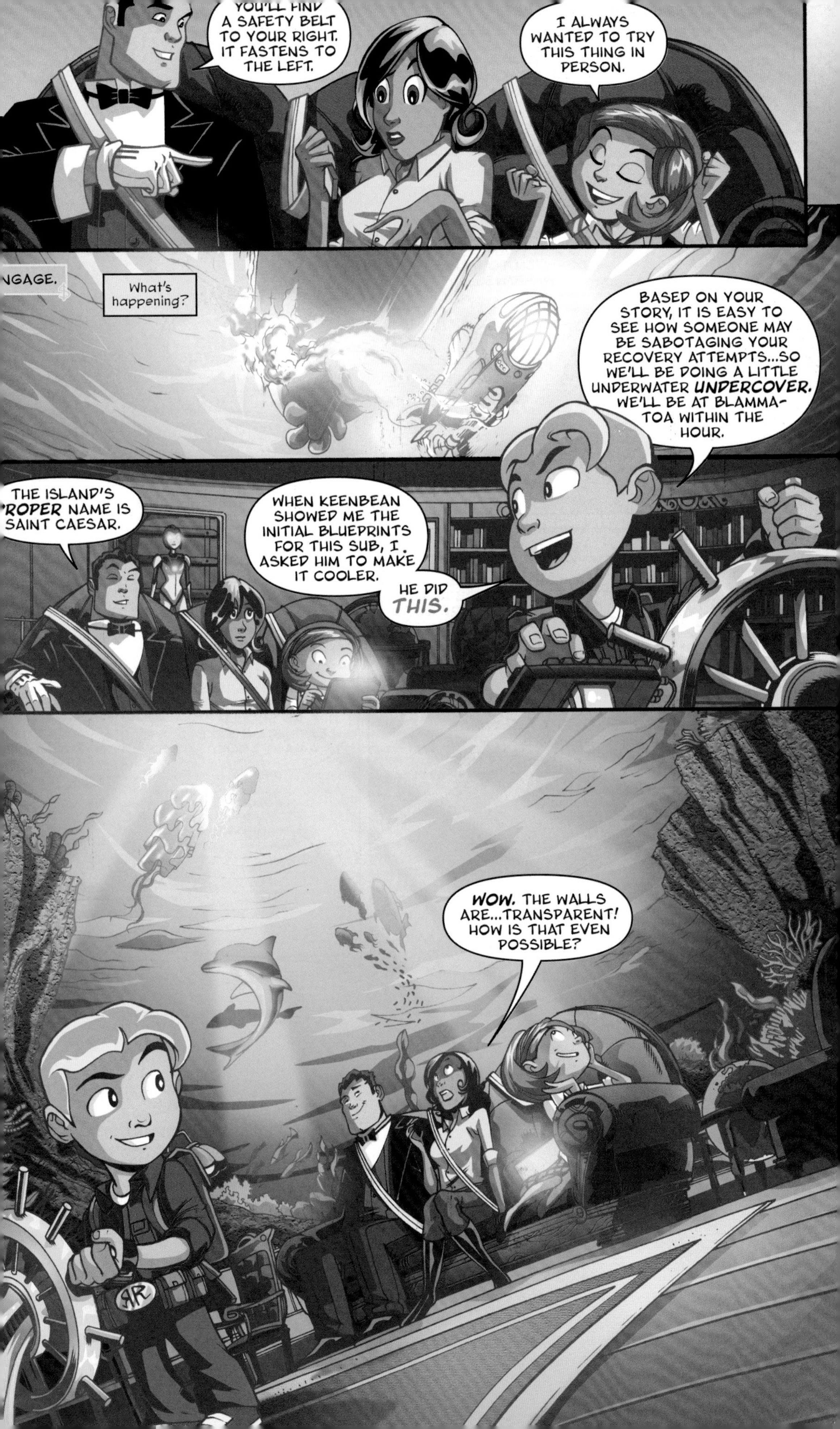
YOU'LL FIND A SAFETY BELT TO YOUR RIGHT. IT FASTENS TO THE LEFT.
I ALWAYS WANTED TO TRY THIS THING IN PERSON.
NGAGE.
What's happening?
BASED ON YOUR STORY, IT IS EASY TO SEE HOW SOMEONE MAY BE SABOTAGING YOUR RECOVERY ATTEMPTS...SO WE'LL BE DOING A LITTLE UNDERWATER UNDERCOVER. WE'LL BE AT BLAMMA-TOA WITHIN THE HOUR.
THE ISLAND'S PROPER NAME IS SAINT CAESAR.
WHEN KEENBEAN SHOWED ME THE INITIAL BLUEPRINTS FOR THIS SUB, I ASKED HIM TO MAKE IT COOLER.
HE DID THIS.
WOW. THE WALLS ARE...TRANSPARENT! HOW IS THAT EVEN POSSIBLE?

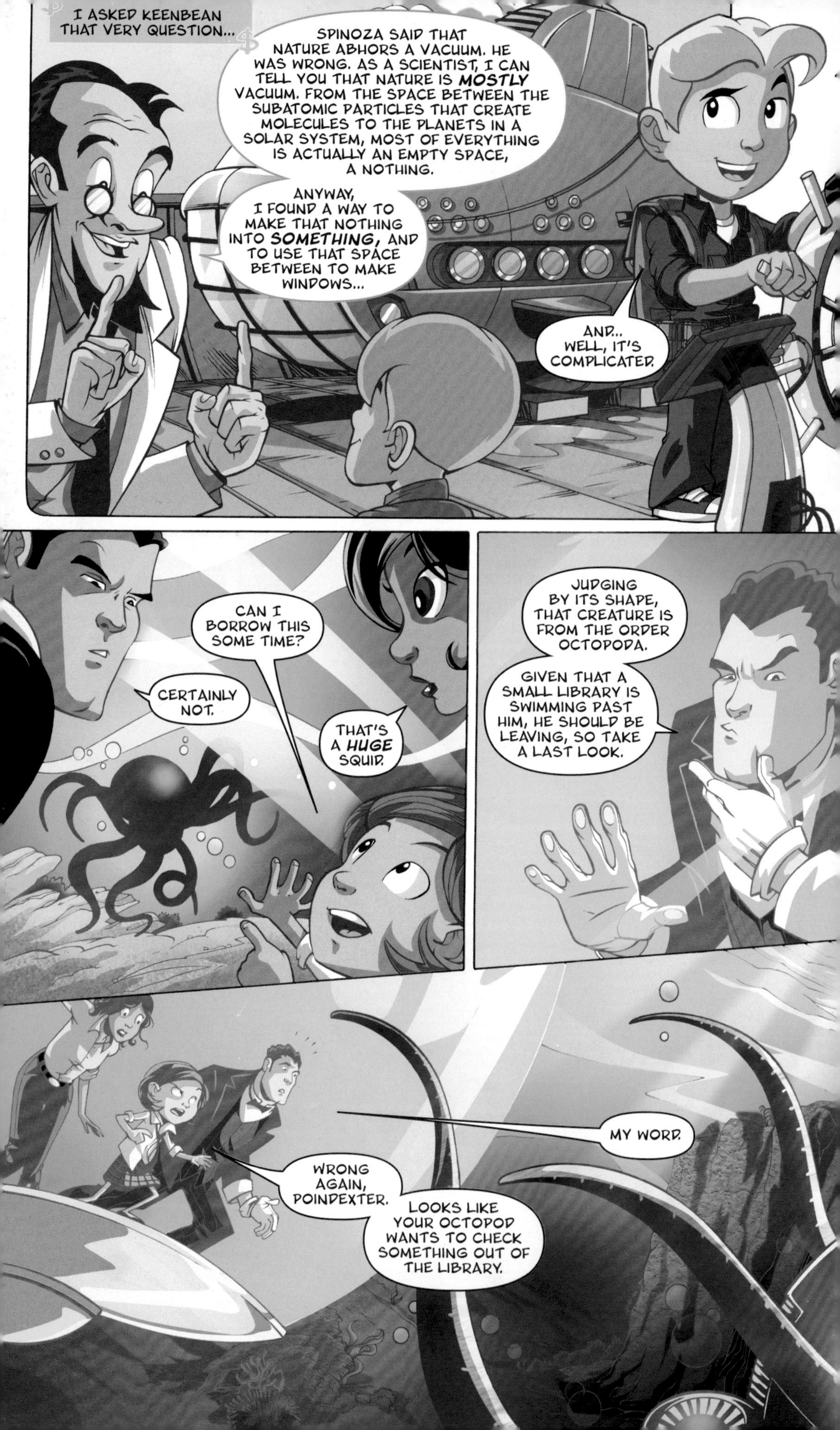
I ASKED KEENBEAN THAT VERY QUESTION...
SPINOZA SAID THAT NATURE ABHORS A VACUUM. HE WAS WRONG. AS A SCIENTIST, I CAN TELL YOU THAT NATURE IS *MOSTLY* VACUUM. FROM THE SPACE BETWEEN THE SUBATOMIC PARTICLES THAT CREATE MOLECULES TO THE PLANETS IN A SOLAR SYSTEM, MOST OF EVERYTHING IS ACTUALLY AN EMPTY SPACE, A NOTHING.
ANYWAY, I FOUND A WAY TO MAKE THAT NOTHING INTO **SOMETHING,** AND TO USE THAT SPACE BETWEEN TO MAKE WINDOWS...
AND... WELL, IT'S COMPLICATED.
CAN I BORROW THIS SOME TIME?
CERTAINLY NOT.
THAT'S A *HUGE* SQUID.
JUDGING BY ITS SHAPE, THAT CREATURE IS FROM THE ORDER OCTOPODA.
GIVEN THAT A SMALL LIBRARY IS SWIMMING PAST HIM, HE SHOULD BE LEAVING, SO TAKE A LAST LOOK.
MY WORD.
WRONG AGAIN, POINDEXTER.
LOOKS LIKE YOUR OCTOPOD WANTS TO CHECK SOMETHING OUT OF THE LIBRARY.

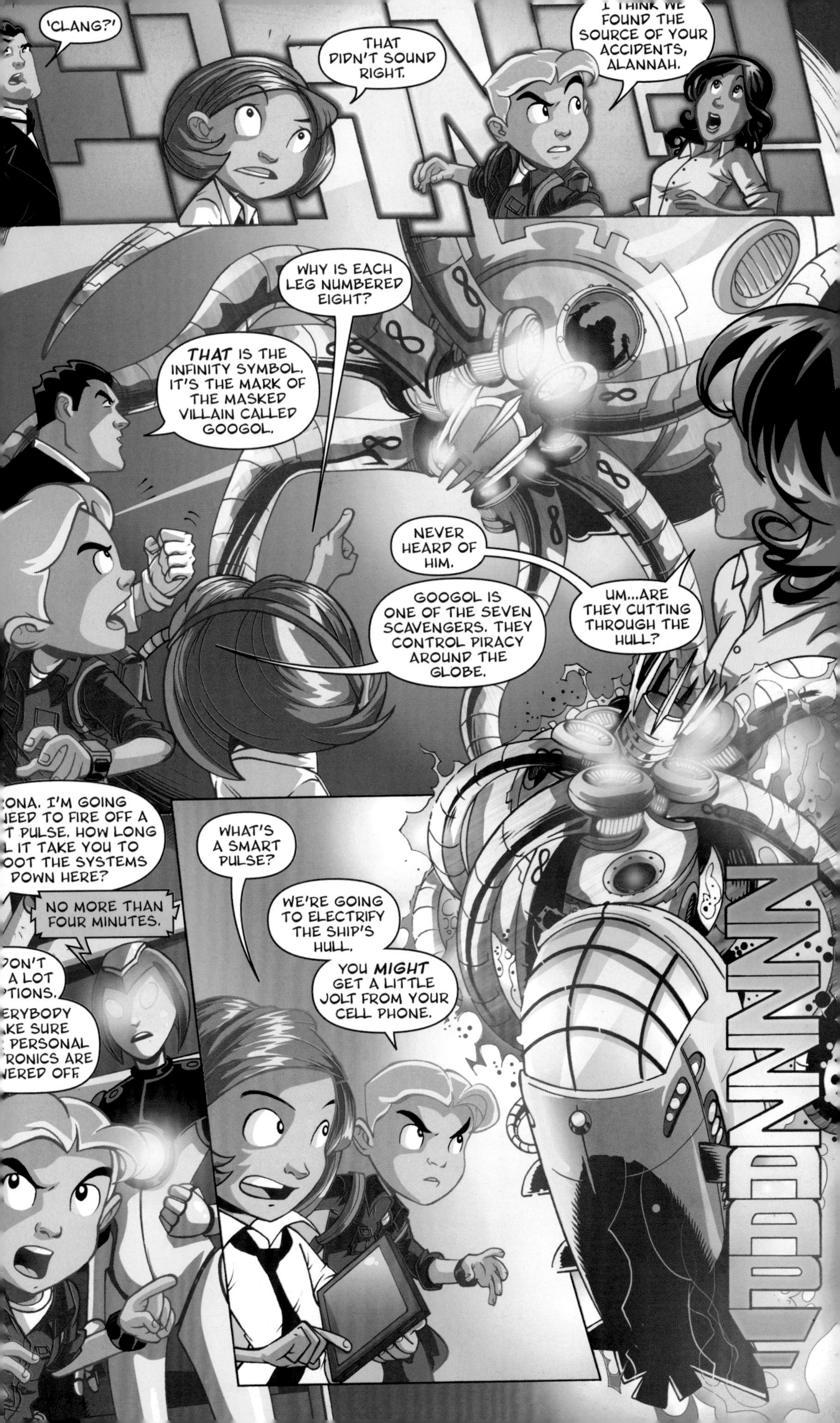
'CLANG?'
THAT DIDN'T SOUND RIGHT.
I THINK WE FOUND THE SOURCE OF YOUR ACCIDENTS, ALANNAH.
WHY IS EACH LEG NUMBERED EIGHT?
THAT IS THE INFINITY SYMBOL. IT'S THE MARK OF THE MASKED VILLAIN CALLED GOOGOL.
NEVER HEARD OF HIM.
GOOGOL IS ONE OF THE SEVEN SCAVENGERS. THEY CONTROL PIRACY AROUND THE GLOBE.
UM...ARE THEY CUTTING THROUGH THE HULL?
ONA. I'M GOING NEED TO FIRE OFF A T PULSE. HOW LONG L IT TAKE YOU TO OOT THE SYSTEMS DOWN HERE?
NO MORE THAN FOUR MINUTES.
DON'T A LOT PTIONS. ERYBODY AKE SURE PERSONAL RONICS ARE WERED OFF.
WHAT'S A SMART PULSE?
WE'RE GOING TO ELECTRIFY THE SHIP'S HULL.
YOU MIGHT GET A LITTLE JOLT FROM YOUR CELL PHONE.

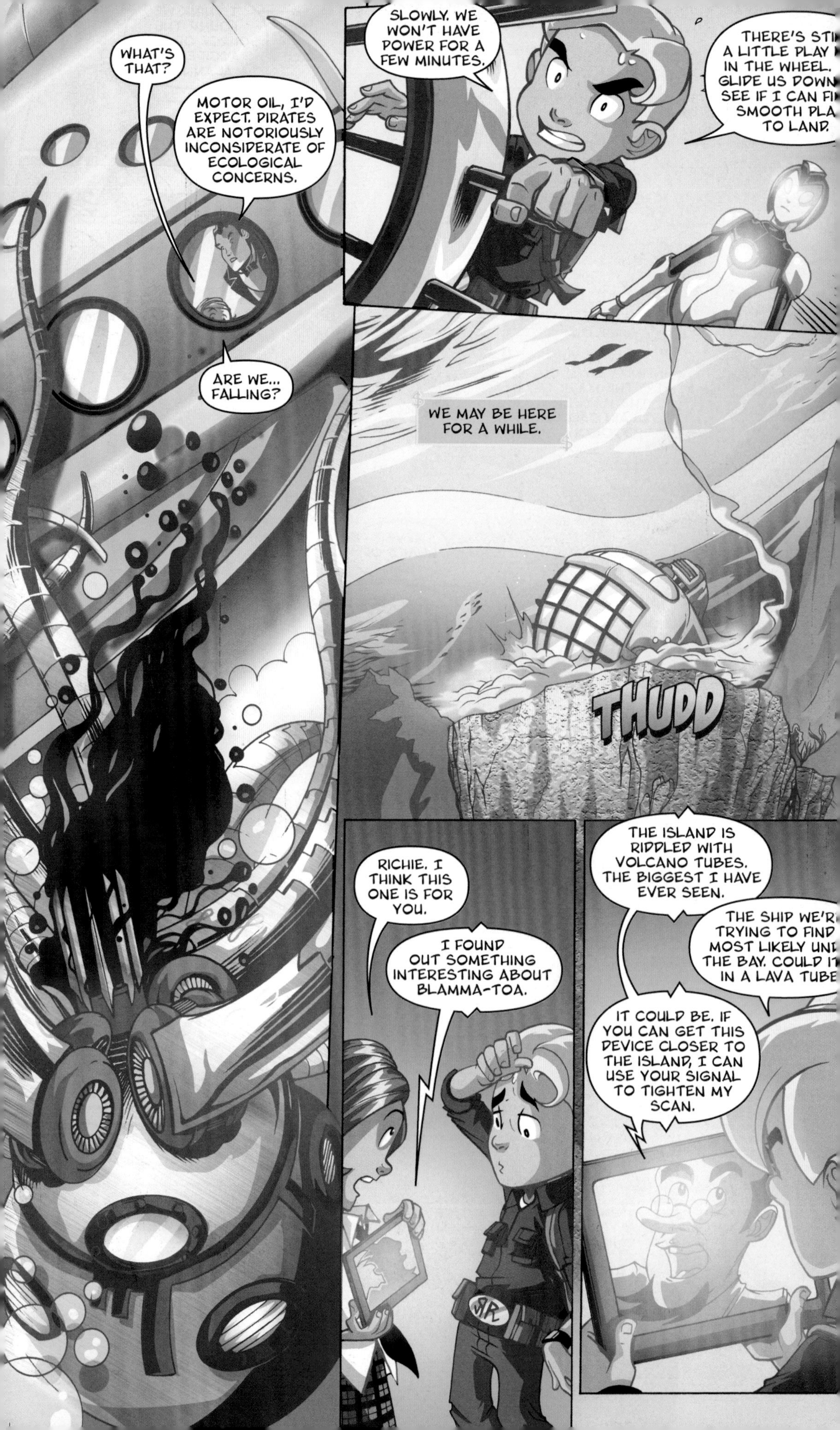
WHAT'S THAT?
MOTOR OIL, I'D EXPECT. PIRATES ARE NOTORIOUSLY INCONSIDERATE OF ECOLOGICAL CONCERNS.
ARE WE... FALLING?
SLOWLY. WE WON'T HAVE POWER FOR A FEW MINUTES.
WE MAY BE HERE FOR A WHILE.
THUDD
RICHIE. I THINK THIS ONE IS FOR YOU.
I FOUND OUT SOMETHING INTERESTING ABOUT BLAMMA-TOA.
THE ISLAND IS RIDDLED WITH VOLCANO TUBES. THE BIGGEST I HAVE EVER SEEN.
IT COULD BE. IF YOU CAN GET THIS DEVICE CLOSER TO THE ISLAND, I CAN USE YOUR SIGNAL TO TIGHTEN MY SCAN.

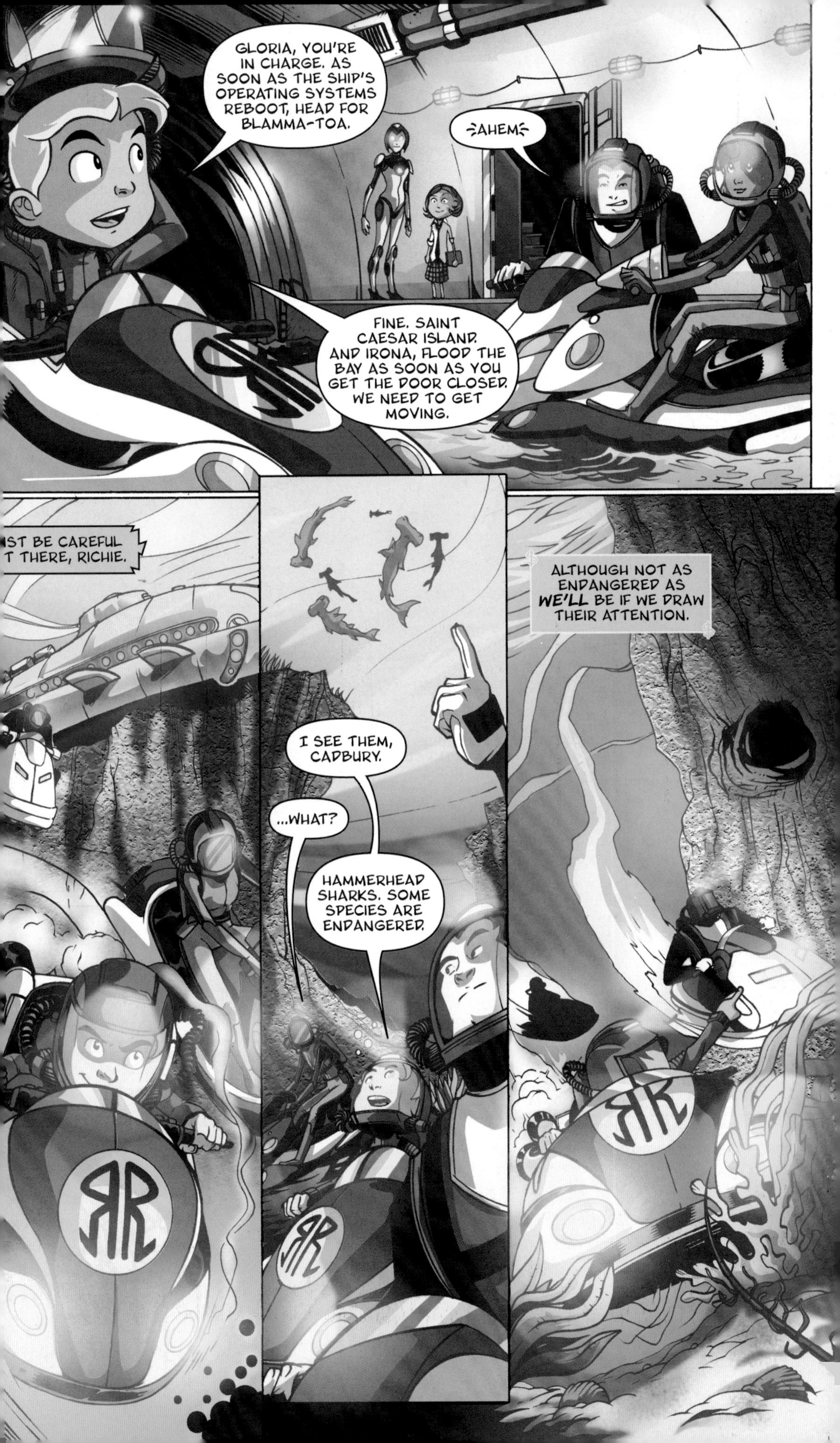
GLORIA, YOU'RE IN CHARGE. AS SOON AS THE SHIP'S OPERATING SYSTEMS REBOOT, HEAD FOR BLAMMA-TOA.
AHEM
FINE. SAINT CAESAR ISLAND. AND IRONA, FLOOD THE BAY AS SOON AS YOU GET THE DOOR CLOSED. WE NEED TO GET MOVING.
ST BE CAREFUL
T THERE, RICHIE.
I SEE THEM, CADBURY.
...WHAT?
HAMMERHEAD SHARKS. SOME SPECIES ARE ENDANGERED.
ALTHOUGH NOT AS ENDANGERED AS WE'LL BE IF WE DRAW THEIR ATTENTION.

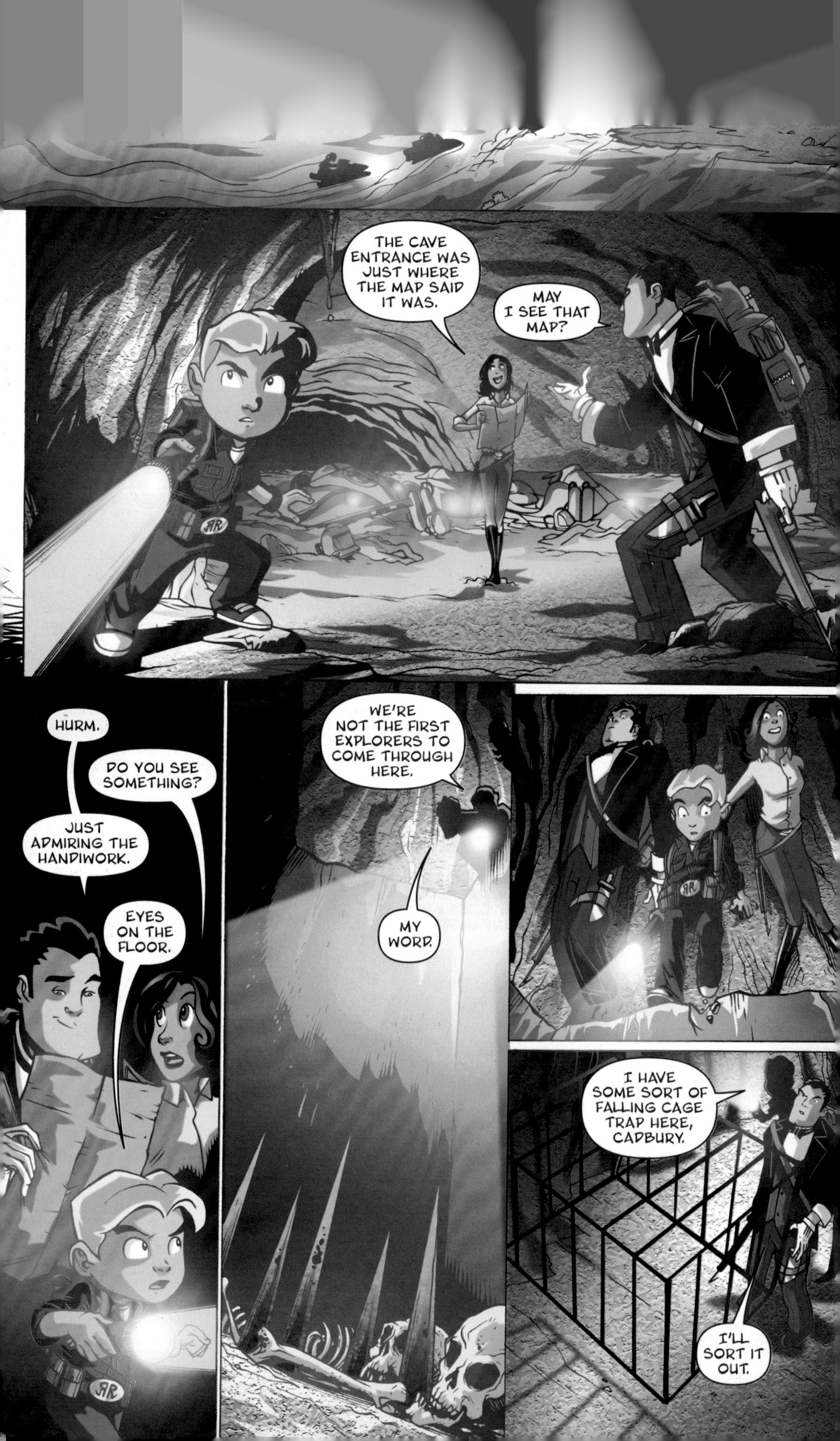
THE CAVE ENTRANCE WAS JUST WHERE THE MAP SAID IT WAS.
MAY I SEE THAT MAP?
HURM.
DO YOU SEE SOMETHING?
JUST ADMIRING THE HANDIWORK.
EYES ON THE FLOOR.
WE'RE NOT THE FIRST EXPLORERS TO COME THROUGH HERE.
MY WORD.
I HAVE SOME SORT OF FALLING CAGE TRAP HERE, CADBURY.
I'LL SORT IT OUT.

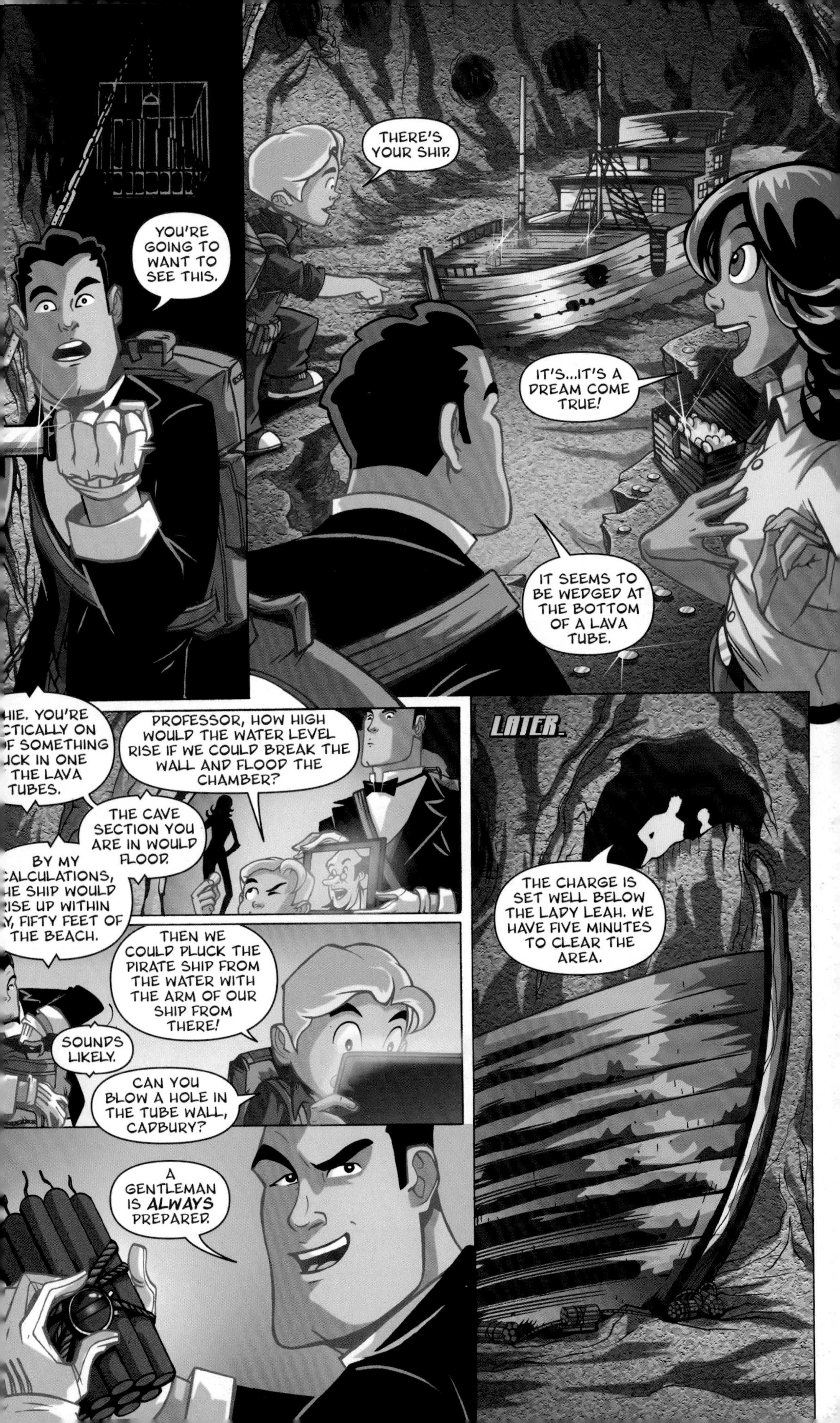

YOU'RE GOING TO WANT TO SEE THIS.
THERE'S YOUR SHIP.
IT'S...IT'S A DREAM COME TRUE!
IT SEEMS TO BE WEDGED AT THE BOTTOM OF A LAVA TUBE.
HIE. YOU'RE CTICALLY ON F SOMETHING JCK IN ONE THE LAVA TUBES.
PROFESSOR, HOW HIGH WOULD THE WATER LEVEL RISE IF WE COULD BREAK THE WALL AND FLOOD THE CHAMBER?
THE CAVE SECTION YOU ARE IN WOULD FLOOD.
BY MY CALCULATIONS, HE SHIP WOULD RISE UP WITHIN Y, FIFTY FEET OF THE BEACH.
THEN WE COULD PLUCK THE PIRATE SHIP FROM THE WATER WITH THE ARM OF OUR SHIP FROM THERE!
SOUNDS LIKELY.
CAN YOU BLOW A HOLE IN THE TUBE WALL, CADBURY?
A GENTLEMAN IS ALWAYS PREPARED.
LATER...
THE CHARGE IS SET WELL BELOW THE LADY LEAH. WE HAVE FIVE MINUTES TO CLEAR THE AREA.

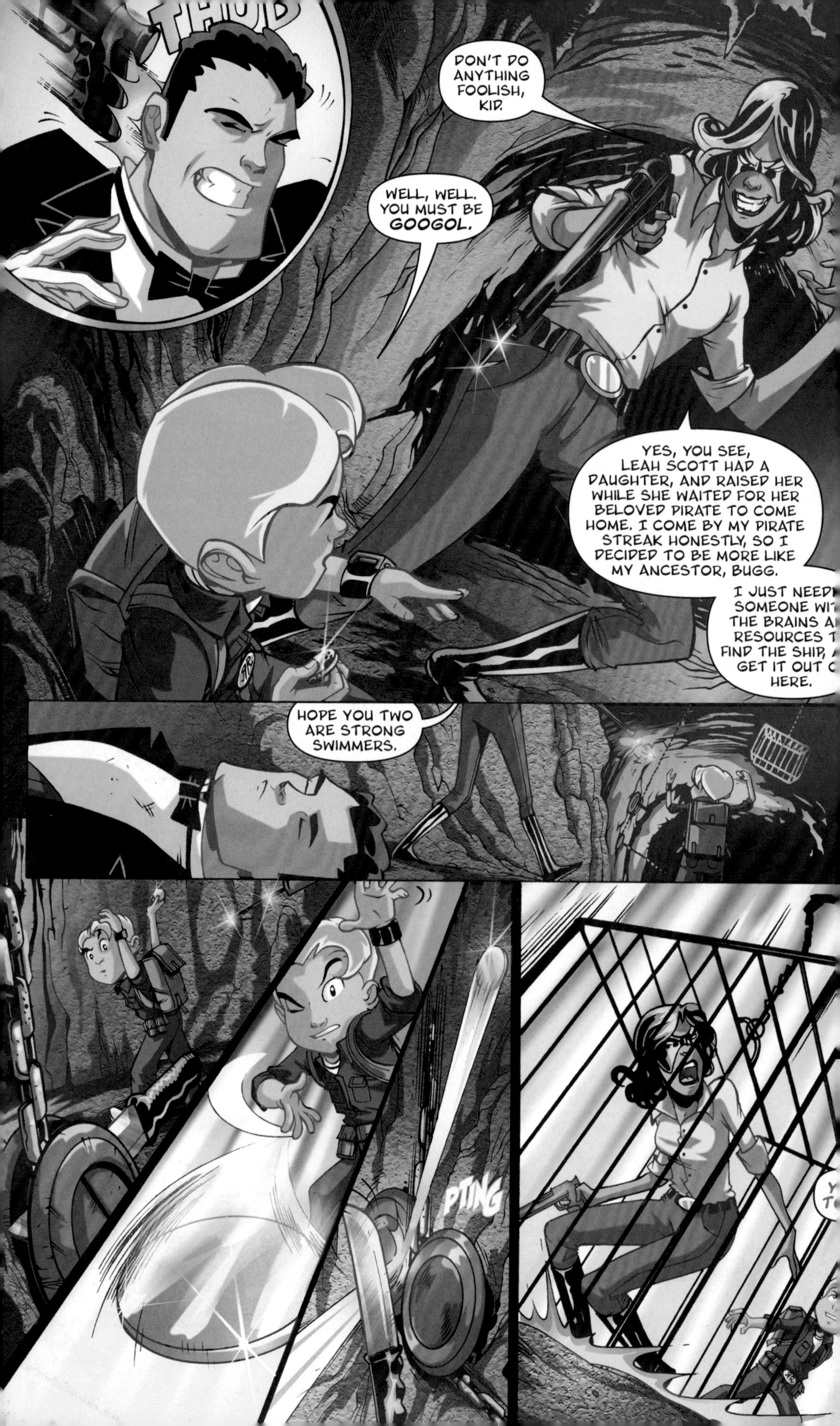
THUD
DON'T DO ANYTHING FOOLISH, KID.
WELL, WELL. YOU MUST BE GOOGOL.
YES, YOU SEE, LEAH SCOTT HAD A DAUGHTER, AND RAISED HER WHILE SHE WAITED FOR HER BELOVED PIRATE TO COME HOME. I COME BY MY PIRATE STREAK HONESTLY, SO I DECIDED TO BE MORE LIKE MY ANCESTOR, BUGG.
I JUST NEED SOMEONE WIT THE BRAINS A RESOURCES T FIND THE SHIP, A GET IT OUT O HERE.
HOPE YOU TWO ARE STRONG SWIMMERS.
PTING

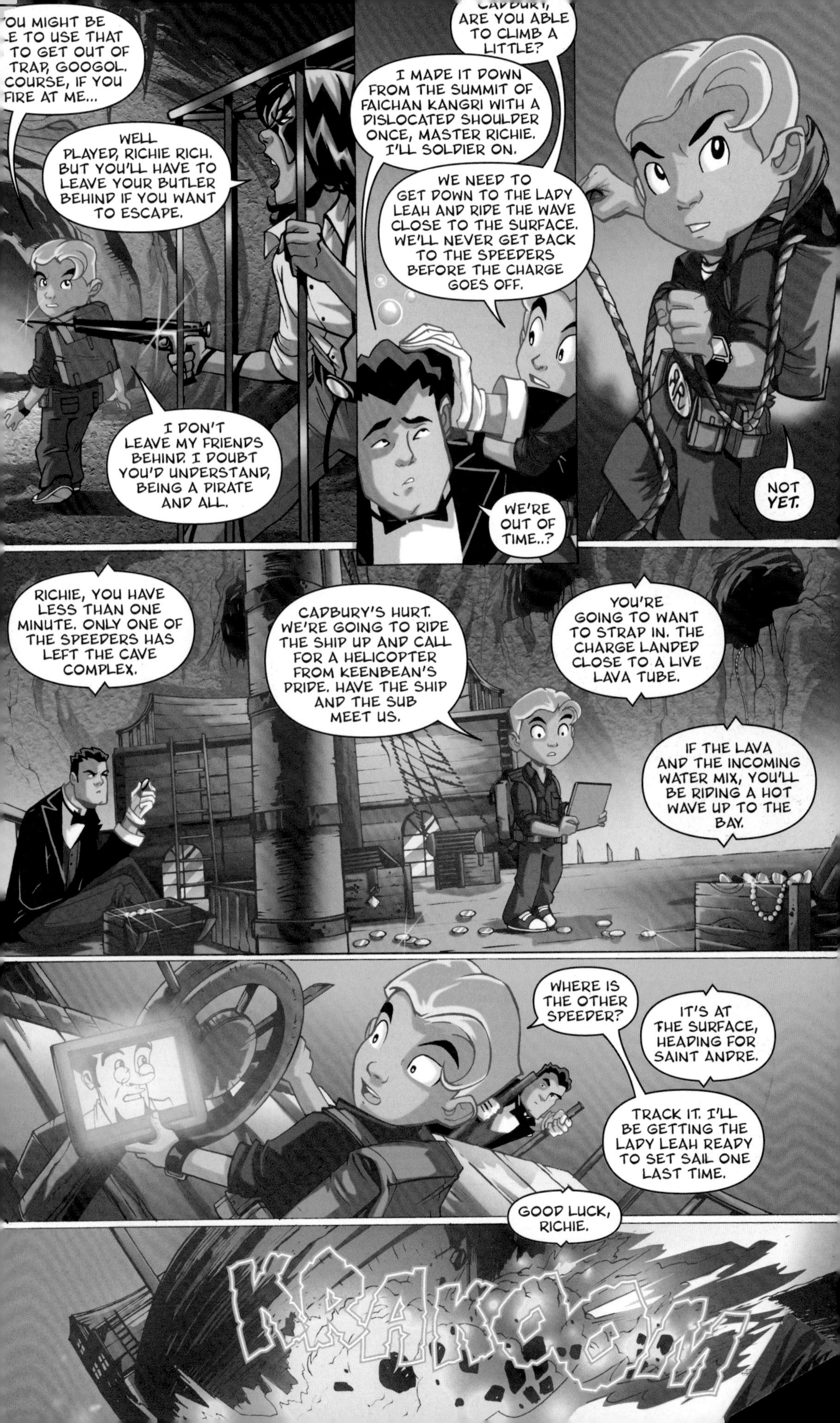
TO GET OUT OF TRAP, GOOGOL. COURSE, IF YOU FIRE AT ME...
WELL PLAYED, RICHIE RICH. BUT YOU'LL HAVE TO LEAVE YOUR BUTLER BEHIND IF YOU WANT TO ESCAPE.
I DON'T LEAVE MY FRIENDS BEHIND. I DOUBT YOU'D UNDERSTAND, BEING A PIRATE AND ALL.
ARE YOU ABLE TO CLIMB A LITTLE?
I MADE IT DOWN FROM THE SUMMIT OF FAICHAN KANGRI WITH A DISLOCATED SHOULDER ONCE, MASTER RICHIE. I'LL SOLDIER ON.
WE NEED TO GET DOWN TO THE LADY LEAH AND RIDE THE WAVE CLOSE TO THE SURFACE. WE'LL NEVER GET BACK TO THE SPEEDERS BEFORE THE CHARGE GOES OFF.
WE'RE OUT OF TIME..?
NOT YET.
RICHIE, YOU HAVE LESS THAN ONE MINUTE. ONLY ONE OF THE SPEEDERS HAS LEFT THE CAVE COMPLEX.
CADBURY'S HURT. WE'RE GOING TO RIDE THE SHIP UP AND CALL FOR A HELICOPTER FROM KEENBEAN'S PRIDE. HAVE THE SHIP AND THE SUB MEET US.
YOU'RE GOING TO WANT TO STRAP IN. THE CHARGE LANDED CLOSE TO A LIVE LAVA TUBE.
IF THE LAVA AND THE INCOMING WATER MIX, YOU'LL BE RIDING A HOT WAVE UP TO THE BAY.
WHERE IS THE OTHER SPEEDER?
IT'S AT THE SURFACE, HEADING FOR SAINT ANDRE.
TRACK IT. I'LL BE GETTING THE LADY LEAH READY TO SET SAIL ONE LAST TIME.
GOOD LUCK, RICHIE.

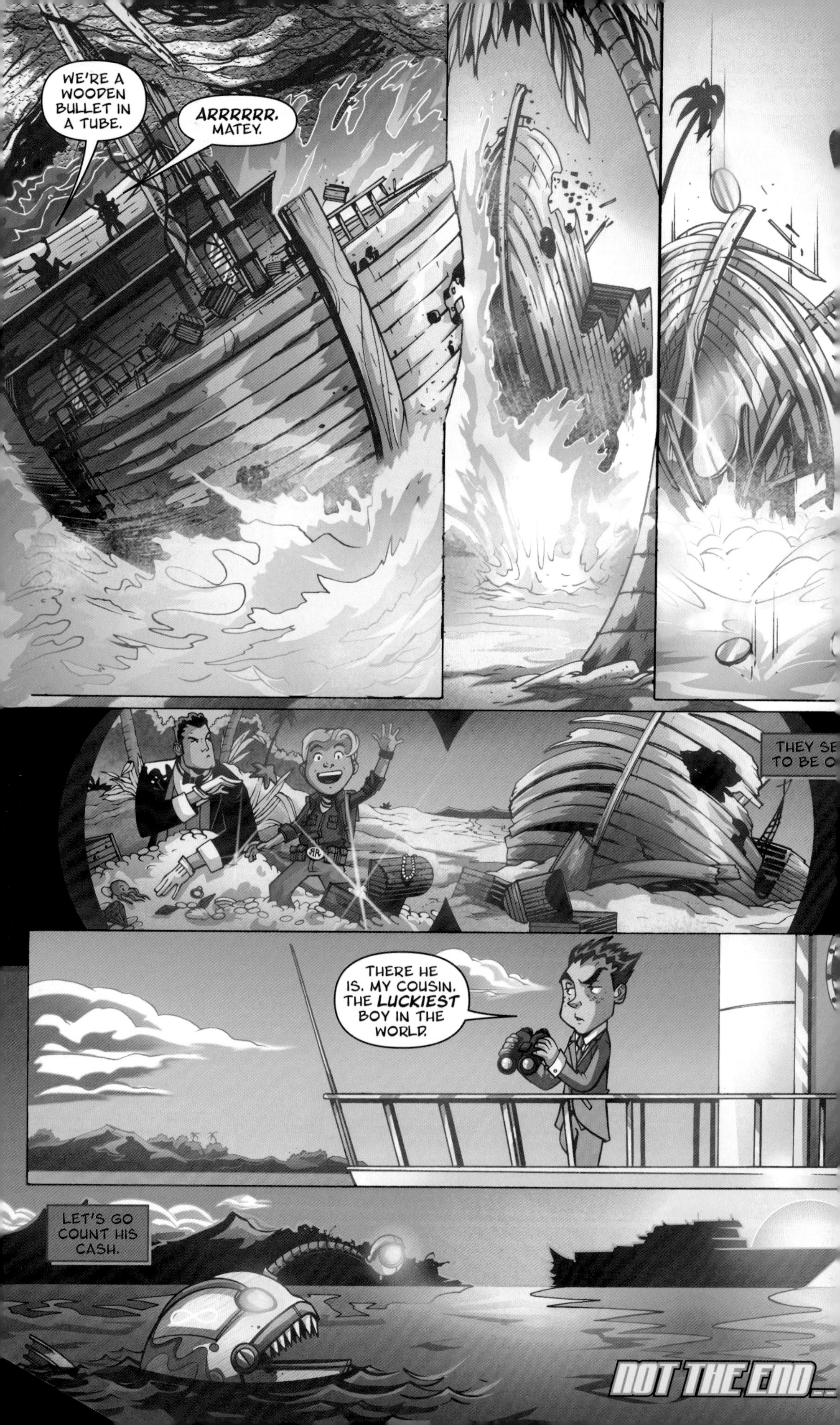
WE'RE A WOODEN BULLET IN A TUBE.
ARRRRRR. MATEY.
THEY SE TO BE C
THERE HE IS. MY COUSIN. THE LUCKIEST BOY IN THE WORLD.
LET'S GO COUNT HIS CASH.
NOT THE END...

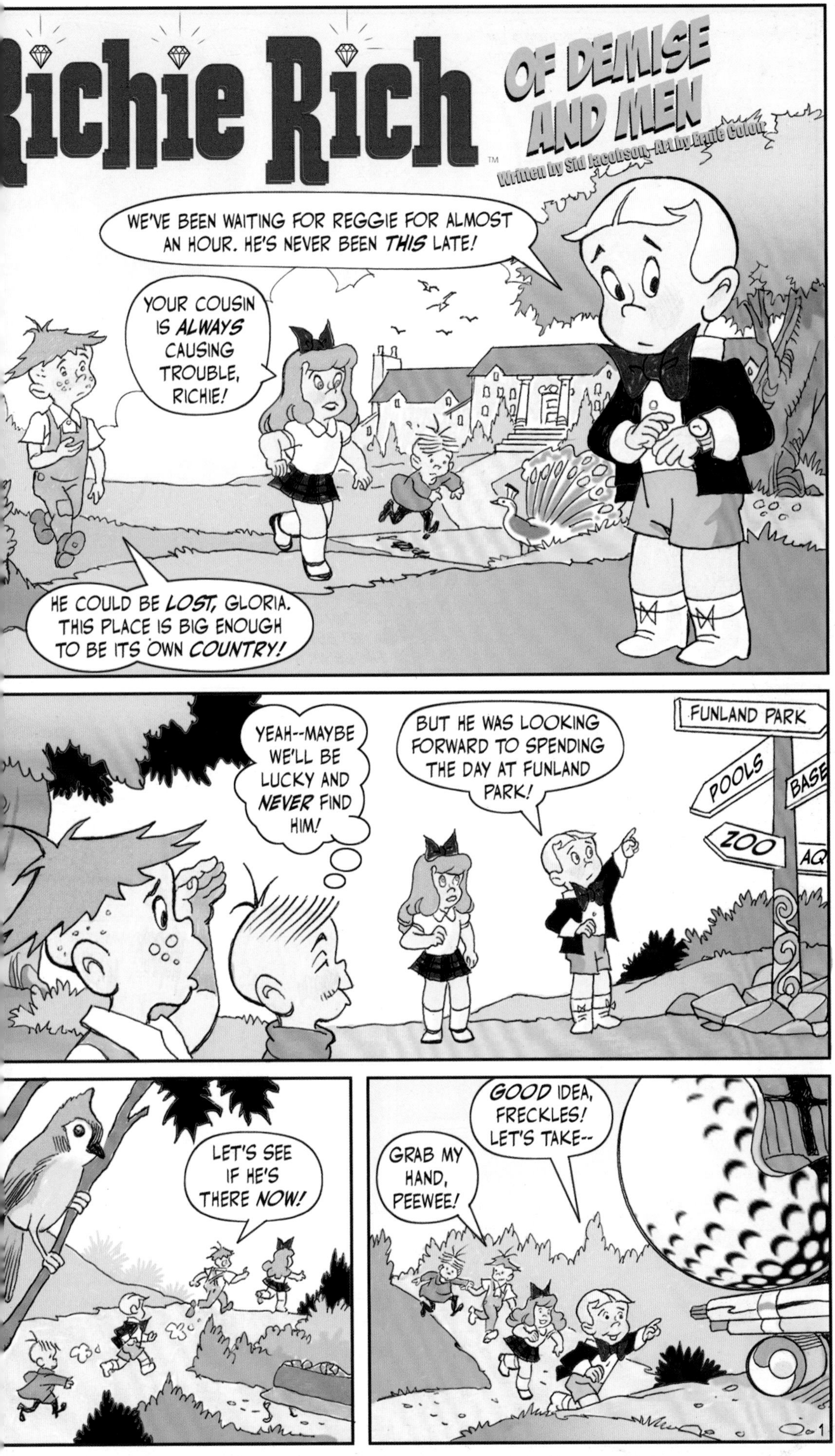

Richie Rich™
OF DEMISE AND MEN
Written by Sid Jacobson—Art by Ernie Colon
WE'VE BEEN WAITING FOR REGGIE FOR ALMOST AN HOUR. HE'S NEVER BEEN THIS LATE!
YOUR COUSIN IS ALWAYS CAUSING TROUBLE, RICHIE!
HE COULD BE LOST, GLORIA. THIS PLACE IS BIG ENOUGH TO BE ITS OWN COUNTRY!
YEAH--MAYBE WE'LL BE LUCKY AND NEVER FIND HIM!
BUT HE WAS LOOKING FORWARD TO SPENDING THE DAY AT FUNLAND PARK!
FUNLAND PARK
POOLS
BASE
ZOO
AQ
LET'S SEE IF HE'S THERE NOW!
GOOD IDEA, FRECKLES! LET'S TAKE--
GRAB MY HAND, PEEWEE!

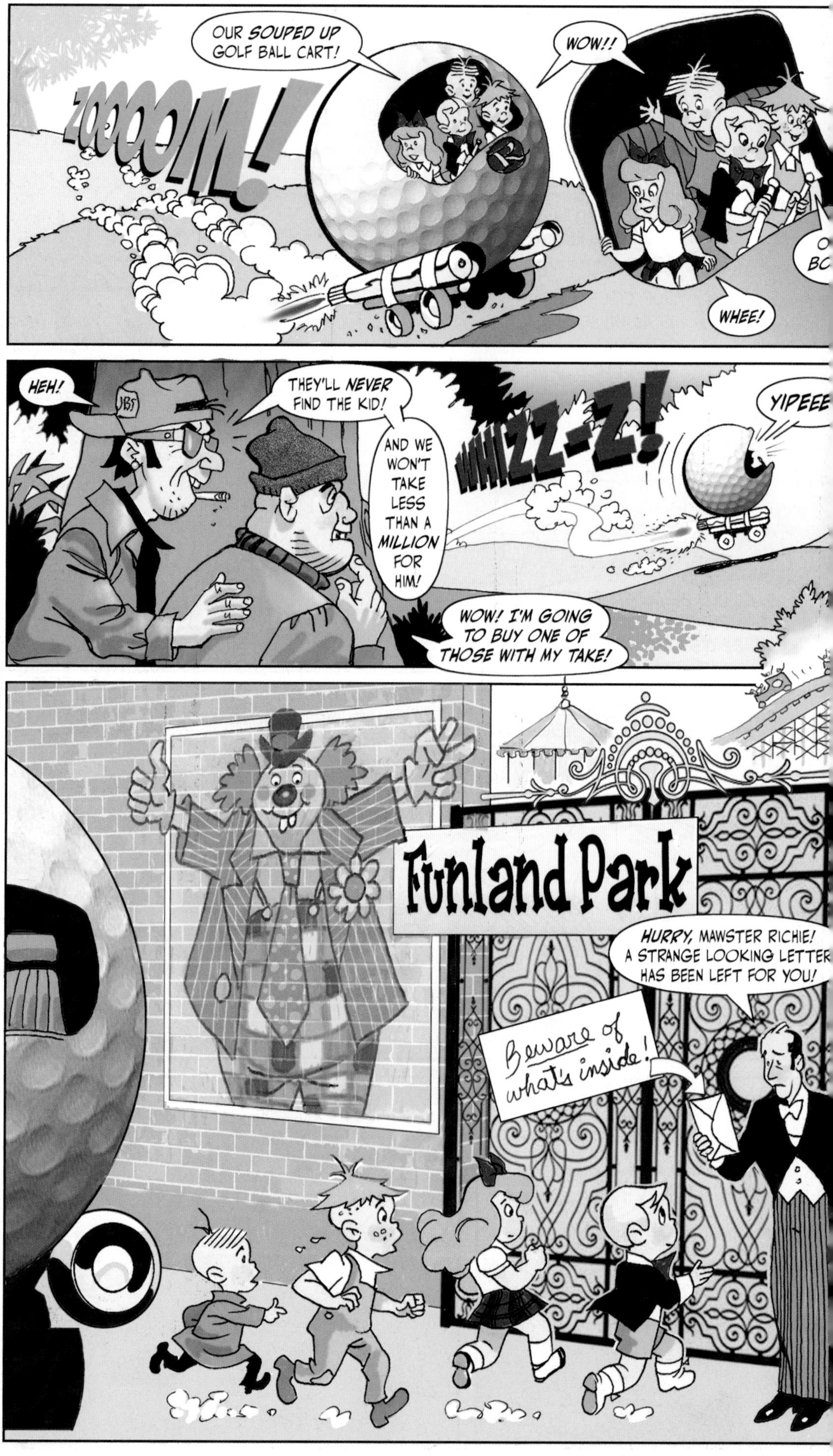
ZOOOOM!
OUR SOUPED UP GOLF BALL CART!
WOW!!
WHEE!
HEH!
THEY'LL NEVER FIND THE KID!
AND WE WON'T TAKE LESS THAN A MILLION FOR HIM!
WHIZZ-Z!
YIPEEE
WOW! I'M GOING TO BUY ONE OF THOSE WITH MY TAKE!
Funland Park
HURRY, MAWSTER RICHIE! A STRANGE LOOKING LETTER HAS BEEN LEFT FOR YOU!
Beware of what's inside!

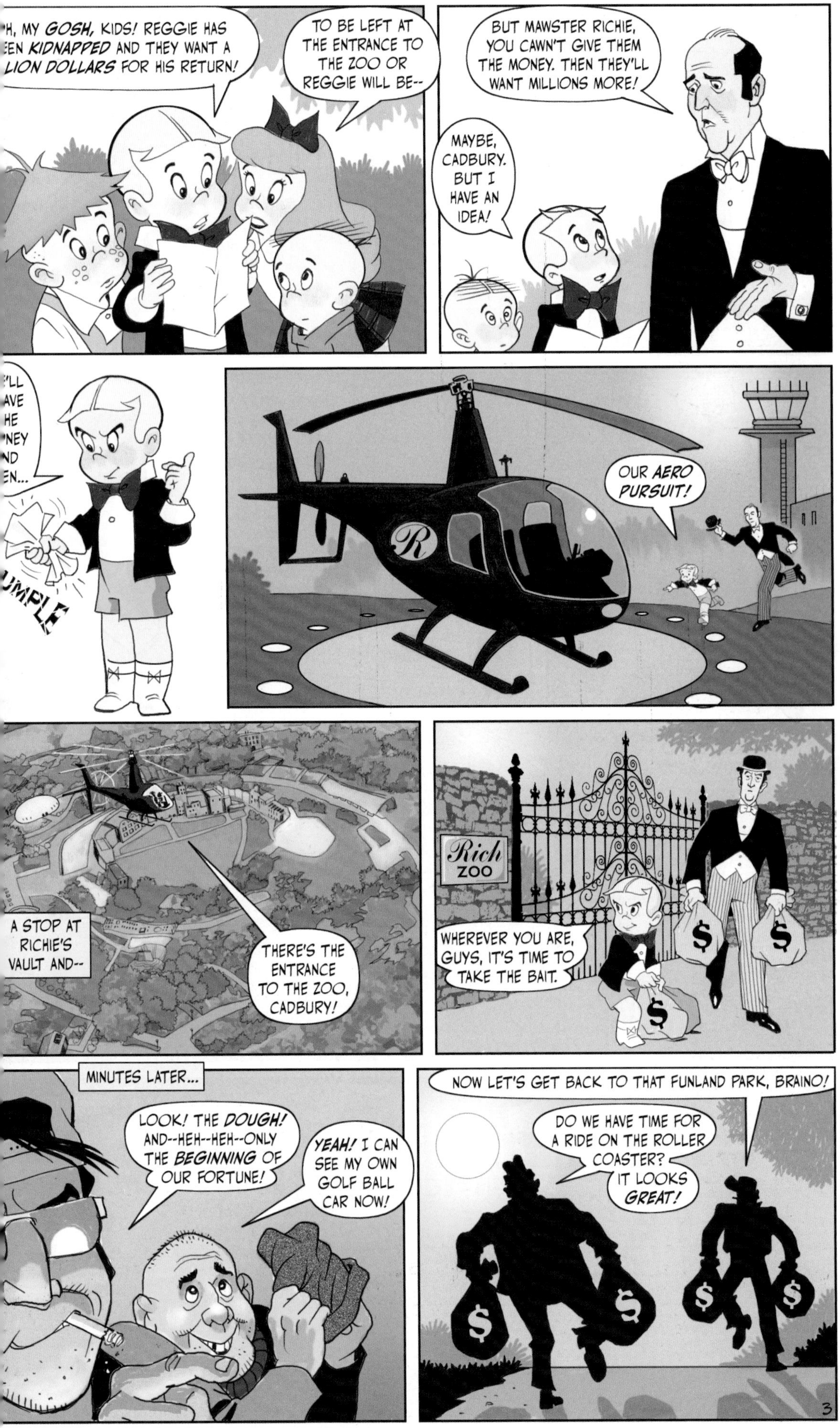

H, MY GOSH, KIDS! REGGIE HAS EEN KIDNAPPED AND THEY WANT A LION DOLLARS FOR HIS RETURN!
TO BE LEFT AT THE ENTRANCE TO THE ZOO OR REGGIE WILL BE--
BUT MAWSTER RICHIE, YOU CAWN'T GIVE THEM THE MONEY. THEN THEY'LL WANT MILLIONS MORE!
MAYBE, CADBURY. BUT I HAVE AN IDEA!
'LL AVE HE NEY ND EN...
UMPLE
OUR AERO PURSUIT!
A STOP AT RICHIE'S VAULT AND--
THERE'S THE ENTRANCE TO THE ZOO, CADBURY!
Rich ZOO
WHEREVER YOU ARE, GUYS, IT'S TIME TO TAKE THE BAIT.
MINUTES LATER...
LOOK! THE DOUGH! AND--HEH--HEH--ONLY THE BEGINNING OF OUR FORTUNE!
YEAH! I CAN SEE MY OWN GOLF BALL CAR NOW!
NOW LET'S GET BACK TO THAT FUNLAND PARK, BRAINO!
DO WE HAVE TIME FOR A RIDE ON THE ROLLER COASTER? IT LOOKS GREAT!

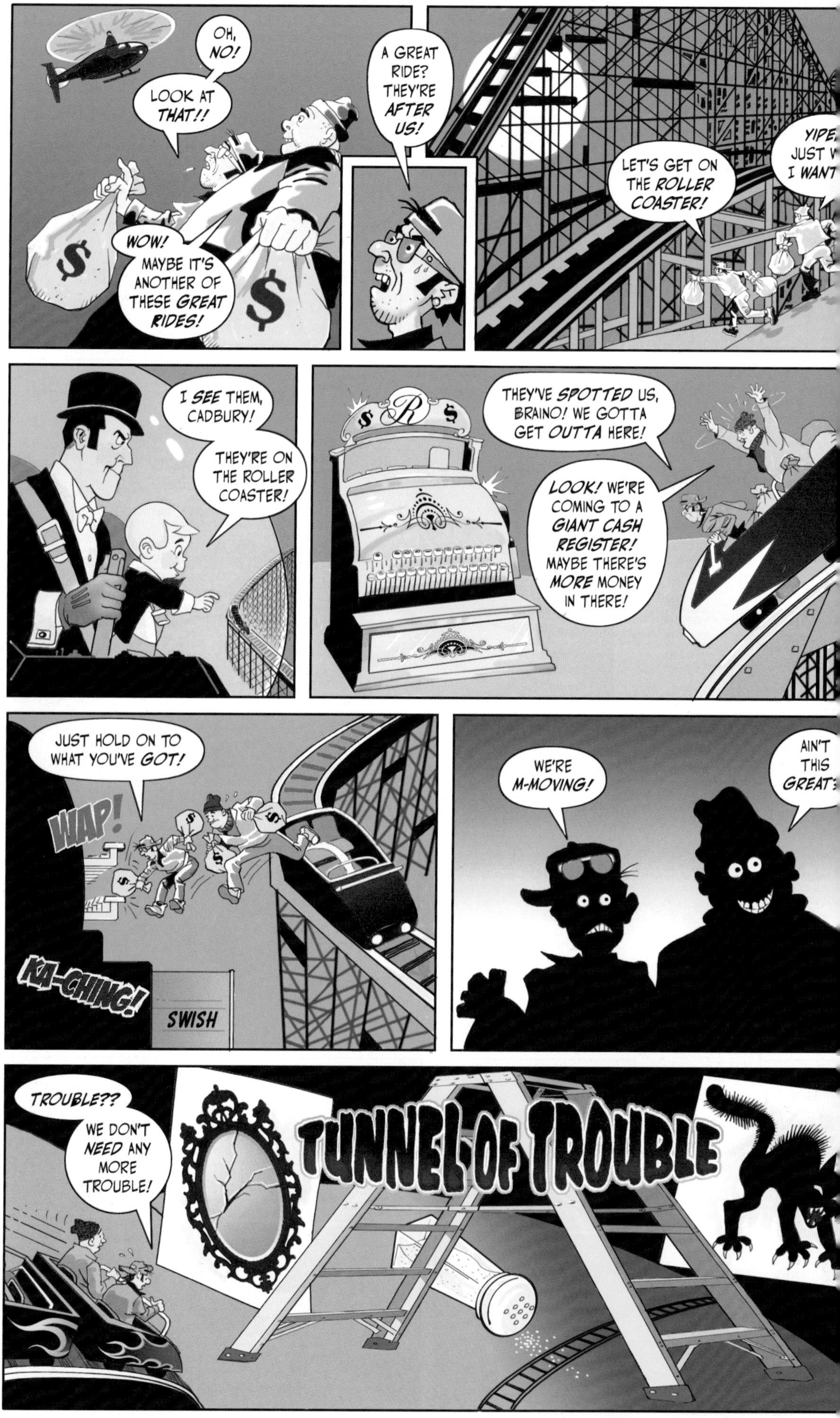
OH, NO!
LOOK AT THAT!!
WOW! MAYBE IT'S ANOTHER OF THESE GREAT RIDES!
A GREAT RIDE? THEY'RE AFTER US!
LET'S GET ON THE ROLLER COASTER!
I SEE THEM, CADBURY!
THEY'RE ON THE ROLLER COASTER!
THEY'VE SPOTTED US, BRAINO! WE GOTTA GET OUTTA HERE!
LOOK! WE'RE COMING TO A GIANT CASH REGISTER! MAYBE THERE'S MORE MONEY IN THERE!
JUST HOLD ON TO WHAT YOU'VE GOT!
WAP!
KA-CHING!
SWISH
WE'RE M-MOVING!
TROUBLE??
WE DON'T NEED ANY MORE TROUBLE!
TUNNEL OF TROUBLE

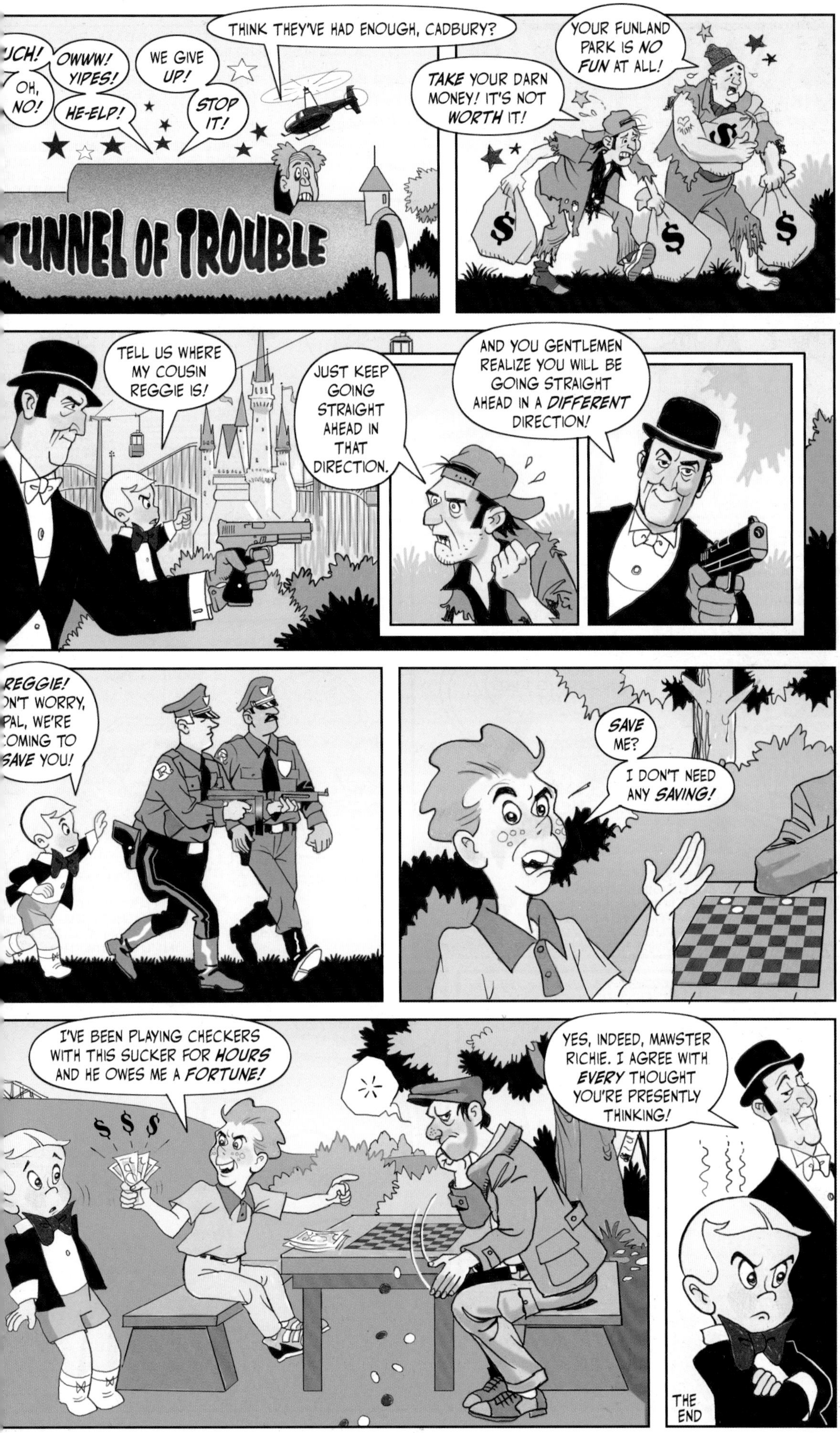

UCH!
OH, NO!
OWWW! YIPES!
HE-ELP!
WE GIVE UP!
STOP IT!
THINK THEY'VE HAD ENOUGH, CADBURY?
TUNNEL OF TROUBLE
YOUR FUNLAND PARK IS NO FUN AT ALL!
TAKE YOUR DARN MONEY! IT'S NOT WORTH IT!
TELL US WHERE MY COUSIN REGGIE IS!
JUST KEEP GOING STRAIGHT AHEAD IN THAT DIRECTION.
AND YOU GENTLEMEN REALIZE YOU WILL BE GOING STRAIGHT AHEAD IN A DIFFERENT DIRECTION!
REGGIE! ON'T WORRY, PAL, WE'RE COMING TO SAVE YOU!
SAVE ME?
I DON'T NEED ANY SAVING!
I'VE BEEN PLAYING CHECKERS WITH THIS SUCKER FOR HOURS AND HE OWES ME A FORTUNE!
YES, INDEED, MAWSTER RICHIE. I AGREE WITH EVERY THOUGHT YOU'RE PRESENTLY THINKING!
THE END

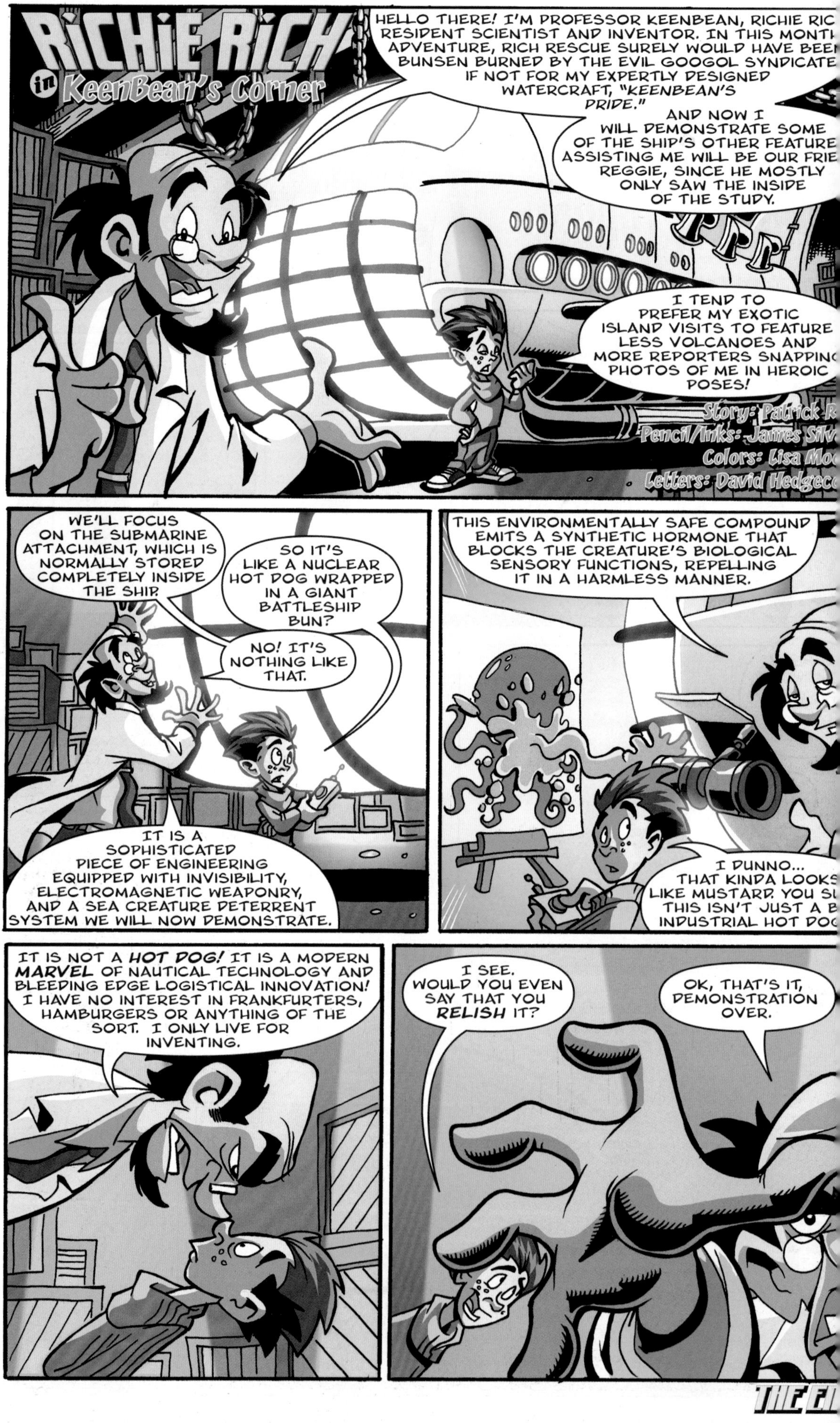
RICHIE RICH
in KeenBean's Corner
HELLO THERE! I'M PROFESSOR KEENBEAN, RICHIE RIC RESIDENT SCIENTIST AND INVENTOR. IN THIS MONTH ADVENTURE, RICH RESCUE SURELY WOULD HAVE BEE BUNSEN BURNED BY THE EVIL GOOGOL SYNDICATE IF NOT FOR MY EXPERTLY DESIGNED WATERCRAFT, "KEENBEAN'S PRIDE."
AND NOW I WILL DEMONSTRATE SOME OF THE SHIP'S OTHER FEATURE ASSISTING ME WILL BE OUR FRIE REGGIE, SINCE HE MOSTLY ONLY SAW THE INSIDE OF THE STUDY.
I TEND TO PREFER MY EXOTIC ISLAND VISITS TO FEATURE LESS VOLCANOES AND MORE REPORTERS SNAPPIN PHOTOS OF ME IN HEROIC POSES!
Story: Patrick R
Pencil/Inks: James Silv
Colors: Lisa Mo
Letters: David Hedgeco
WE'LL FOCUS ON THE SUBMARINE ATTACHMENT, WHICH IS NORMALLY STORED COMPLETELY INSIDE THE SHIP.
SO IT'S LIKE A NUCLEAR HOT DOG WRAPPED IN A GIANT BATTLESHIP BUN?
NO! IT'S NOTHING LIKE THAT.
IT IS A SOPHISTICATED PIECE OF ENGINEERING EQUIPPED WITH INVISIBILITY, ELECTROMAGNETIC WEAPONRY, AND A SEA CREATURE DETERRENT SYSTEM WE WILL NOW DEMONSTRATE.
THIS ENVIRONMENTALLY SAFE COMPOUND EMITS A SYNTHETIC HORMONE THAT BLOCKS THE CREATURE'S BIOLOGICAL SENSORY FUNCTIONS, REPELLING IT IN A HARMLESS MANNER.
I DUNNO... THAT KINDA LOOKS LIKE MUSTARD. YOU S THIS ISN'T JUST A B INDUSTRIAL HOT DO
IT IS NOT A HOT DOG! IT IS A MODERN MARVEL OF NAUTICAL TECHNOLOGY AND BLEEDING EDGE LOGISTICAL INNOVATION! I HAVE NO INTEREST IN FRANKFURTERS, HAMBURGERS OR ANYTHING OF THE SORT. I ONLY LIVE FOR INVENTING.
I SEE. WOULD YOU EVEN SAY THAT YOU RELISH IT?
OK, THAT'S IT, DEMONSTRATION OVER.
THE EN

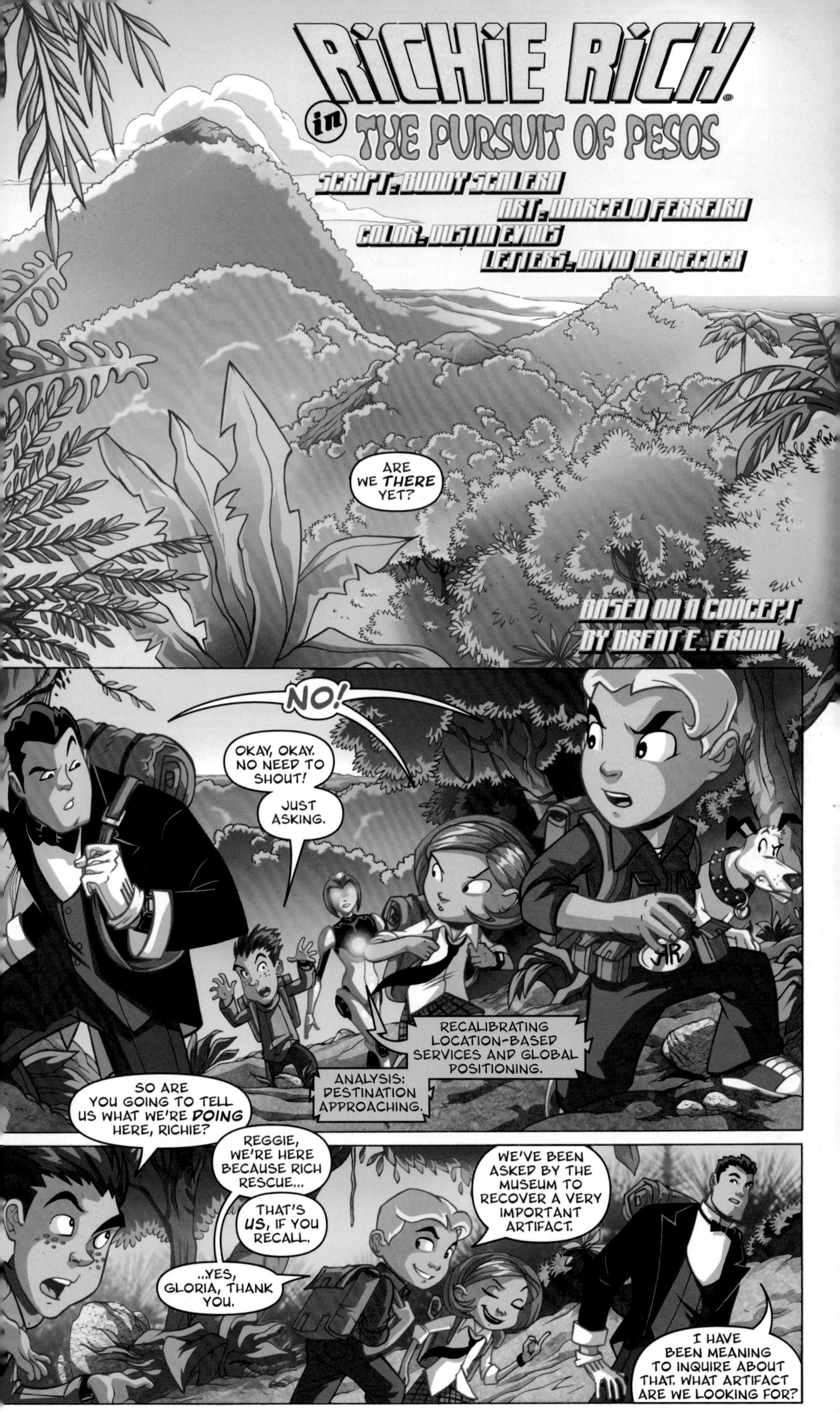
RICHIE RICH®
in THE PURSUIT OF PESOS
SCRIPT: BUDDY SCALERA
ART: MARCELO FERREIRA
COLOR: DUSTIN EVANS
LETTERS: DAVID HEDGECOCK
ARE WE THERE YET?
BASED ON A CONCEPT BY BRENT E. ERWIN
NO!
OKAY, OKAY. NO NEED TO SHOUT!
JUST ASKING.
RECALIBRATING LOCATION-BASED SERVICES AND GLOBAL POSITIONING.
ANALYSIS: DESTINATION APPROACHING.
SO ARE YOU GOING TO TELL US WHAT WE'RE DOING HERE, RICHIE?
REGGIE, WE'RE HERE BECAUSE RICH RESCUE...
THAT'S US, IF YOU RECALL.
...YES, GLORIA, THANK YOU.
WE'VE BEEN ASKED BY THE MUSEUM TO RECOVER A VERY IMPORTANT ARTIFACT.
I HAVE BEEN MEANING TO INQUIRE ABOUT THAT. WHAT ARTIFACT ARE WE LOOKING FOR?

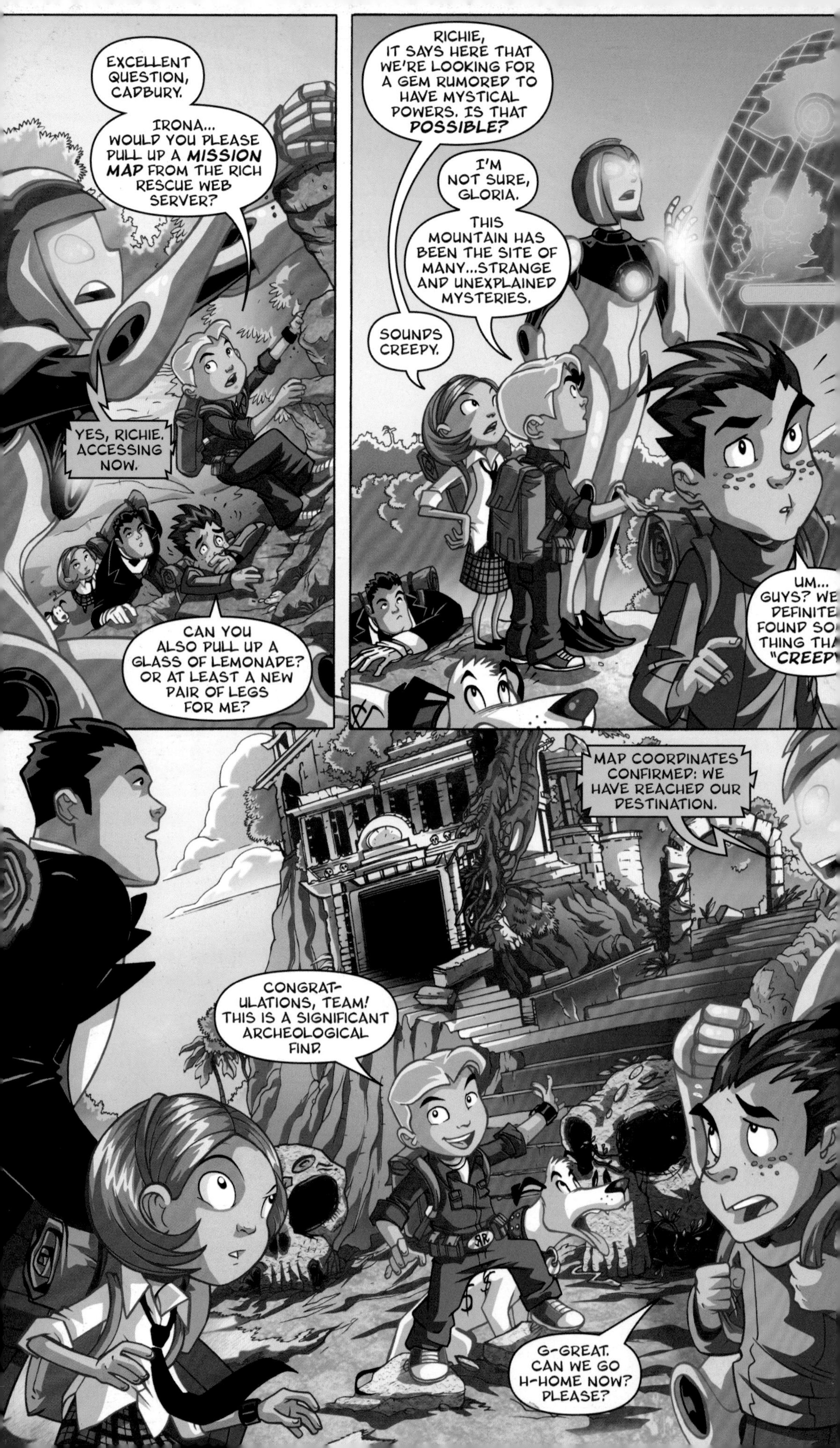
EXCELLENT QUESTION, CADBURY.
IRONA... WOULD YOU PLEASE PULL UP A **MISSION MAP** FROM THE RICH RESCUE WEB SERVER?
YES, RICHIE. ACCESSING NOW.
CAN YOU ALSO PULL UP A GLASS OF LEMONADE? OR AT LEAST A NEW PAIR OF LEGS FOR ME?
RICHIE, IT SAYS HERE THAT WE'RE LOOKING FOR A GEM RUMORED TO HAVE MYSTICAL POWERS. IS THAT **POSSIBLE?**
I'M NOT SURE, GLORIA.
THIS MOUNTAIN HAS BEEN THE SITE OF MANY...STRANGE AND UNEXPLAINED MYSTERIES.
SOUNDS CREEPY.
UM... GUYS? WE DEFINITE FOUND SO THING THA **"CREEP**
MAP COORDINATES CONFIRMED: WE HAVE REACHED OUR DESTINATION.
CONGRAT-ULATIONS, TEAM! THIS IS A SIGNIFICANT ARCHEOLOGICAL FIND.
G-GREAT. CAN WE GO H-HOME NOW? PLEASE?

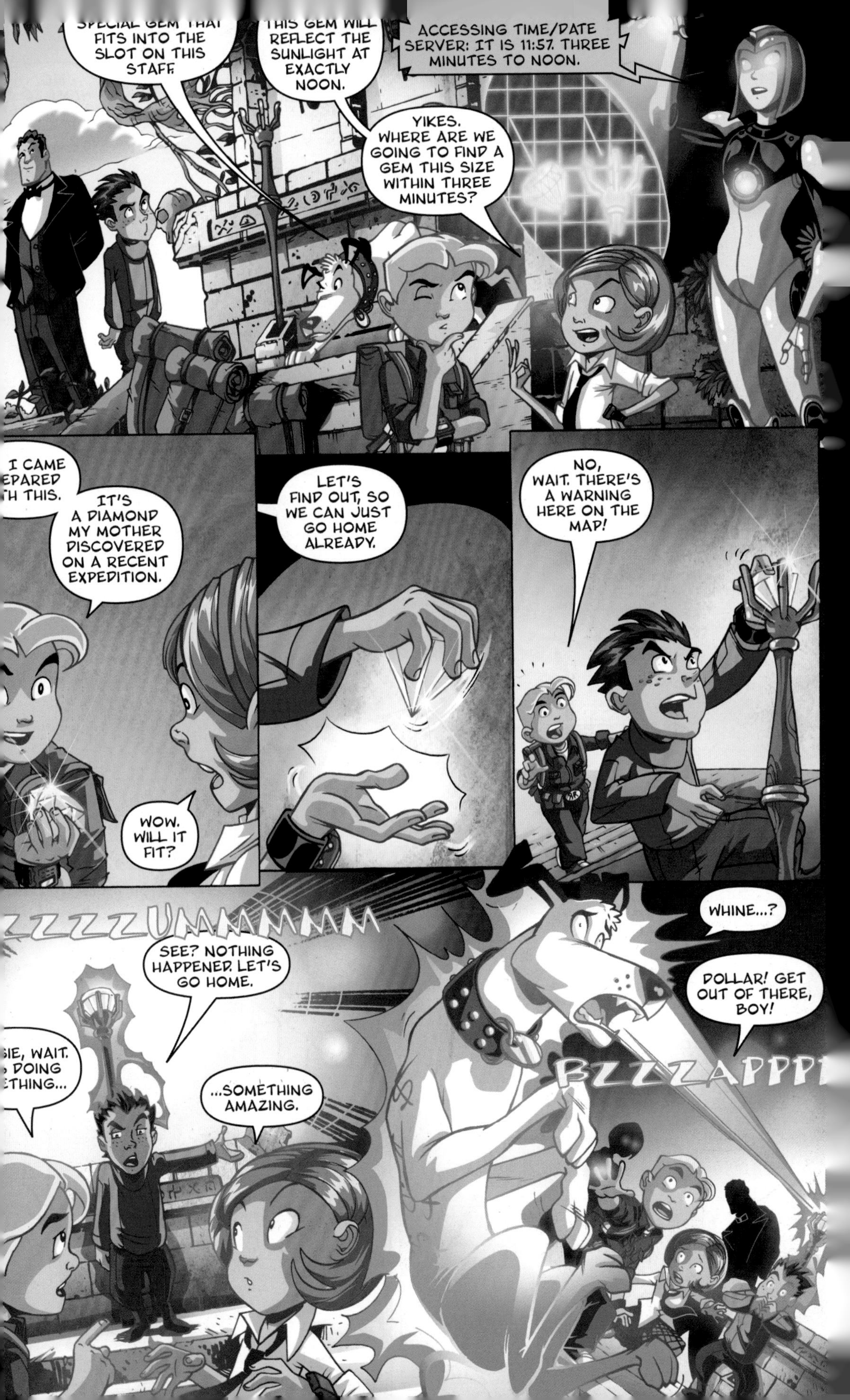
SPECIAL GEM THAT FITS INTO THE SLOT ON THIS STAFF.
THIS GEM WILL REFLECT THE SUNLIGHT AT EXACTLY NOON.
ACCESSING TIME/DATE SERVER: IT IS 11:57. THREE MINUTES TO NOON.
YIKES. WHERE ARE WE GOING TO FIND A GEM THIS SIZE WITHIN THREE MINUTES?
I CAME EPARED TH THIS.
IT'S A DIAMOND MY MOTHER DISCOVERED ON A RECENT EXPEDITION.
WOW. WILL IT FIT?
LET'S FIND OUT, SO WE CAN JUST GO HOME ALREADY.
NO, WAIT. THERE'S A WARNING HERE ON THE MAP!
ZZZZZUMMMMMM
SEE? NOTHING HAPPENED. LET'S GO HOME.
SIE, WAIT. DOING ETHING...
...SOMETHING AMAZING.
WHINE...?
DOLLAR! GET OUT OF THERE, BOY!
BZZZAPPPP

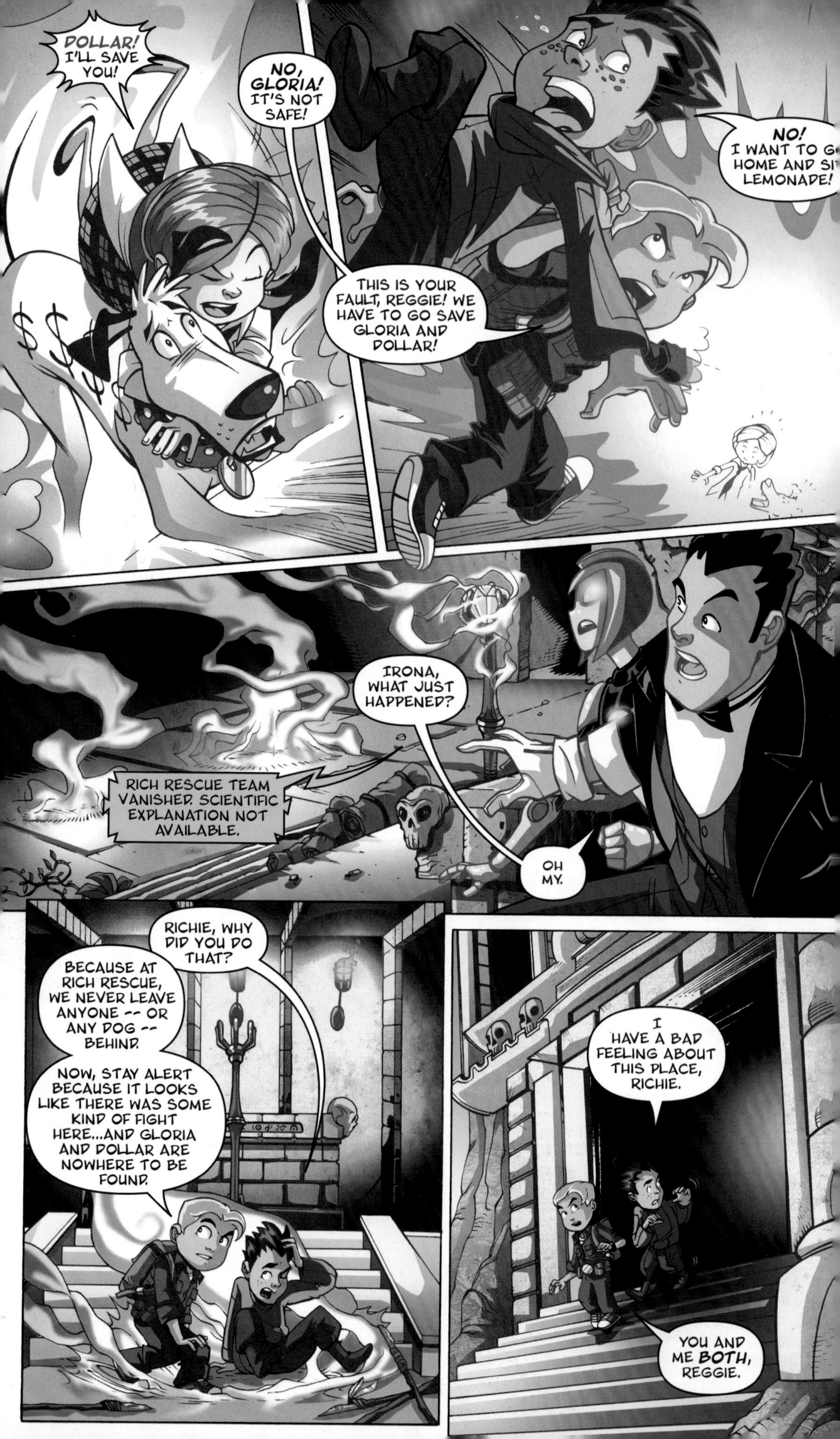
DOLLAR! I'LL SAVE YOU!
NO, GLORIA! IT'S NOT SAFE!
NO! I WANT TO G HOME AND SI LEMONADE!
THIS IS YOUR FAULT, REGGIE! WE HAVE TO GO SAVE GLORIA AND DOLLAR!
IRONA, WHAT JUST HAPPENED?
RICH RESCUE TEAM VANISHED. SCIENTIFIC EXPLANATION NOT AVAILABLE.
OH MY.
RICHIE, WHY DID YOU DO THAT?
BECAUSE AT RICH RESCUE, WE NEVER LEAVE ANYONE -- OR ANY DOG -- BEHIND.
NOW, STAY ALERT BECAUSE IT LOOKS LIKE THERE WAS SOME KIND OF FIGHT HERE...AND GLORIA AND DOLLAR ARE NOWHERE TO BE FOUND.
I HAVE A BAD FEELING ABOUT THIS PLACE, RICHIE.
YOU AND ME BOTH, REGGIE.

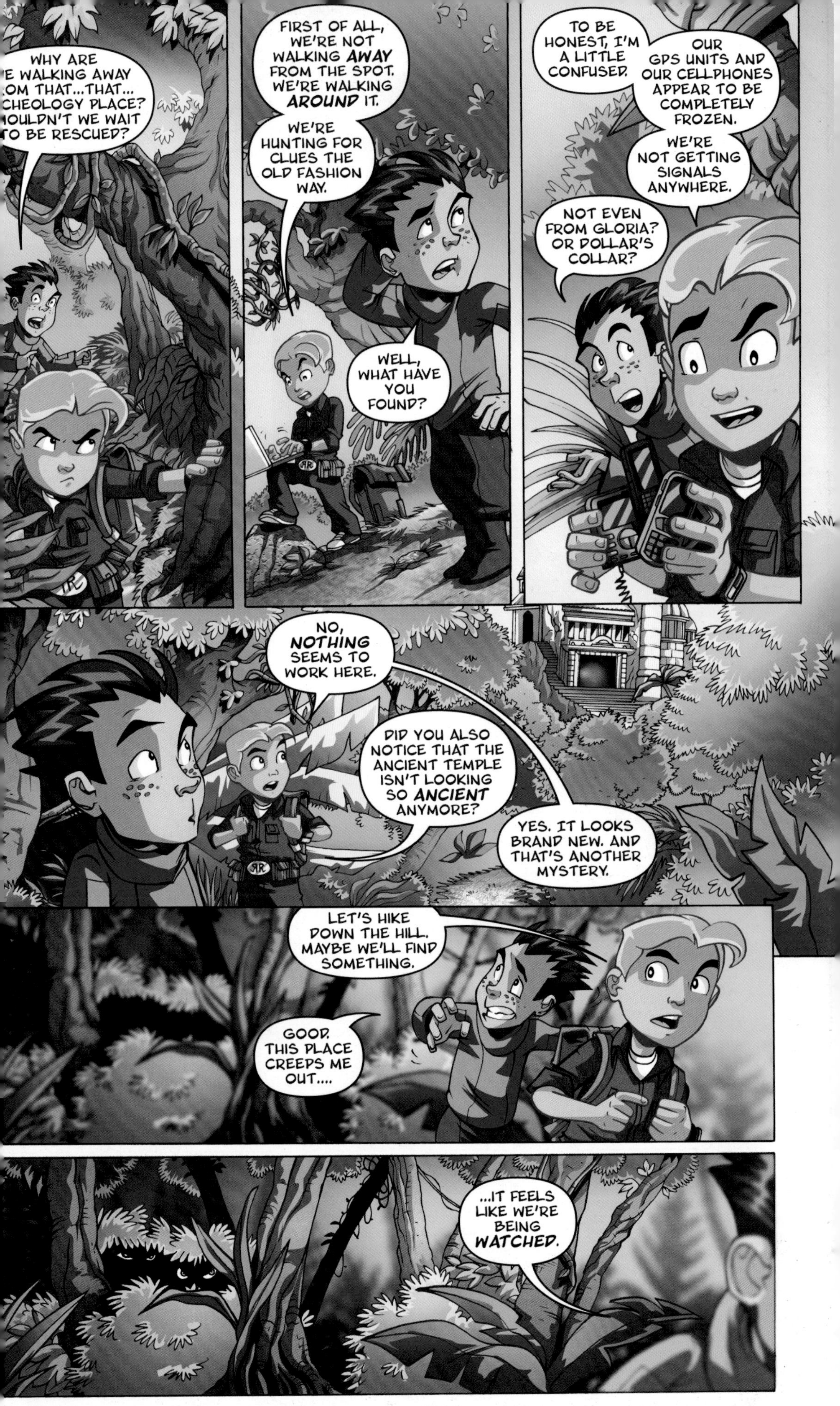
WHY ARE
E WALKING AWAY
OM THAT...THAT...
CHEOLOGY PLACE?
OULDN'T WE WAIT
TO BE RESCUED?
FIRST OF ALL, WE'RE NOT WALKING AWAY FROM THE SPOT. WE'RE WALKING AROUND IT.
WE'RE HUNTING FOR CLUES THE OLD FASHION WAY.
WELL, WHAT HAVE YOU FOUND?
TO BE HONEST, I'M A LITTLE CONFUSED.
OUR GPS UNITS AND OUR CELLPHONES APPEAR TO BE COMPLETELY FROZEN.
WE'RE NOT GETTING SIGNALS ANYWHERE.
NOT EVEN FROM GLORIA? OR DOLLAR'S COLLAR?
NO, NOTHING SEEMS TO WORK HERE.
DID YOU ALSO NOTICE THAT THE ANCIENT TEMPLE ISN'T LOOKING SO ANCIENT ANYMORE?
YES. IT LOOKS BRAND NEW. AND THAT'S ANOTHER MYSTERY.
LET'S HIKE DOWN THE HILL. MAYBE WE'LL FIND SOMETHING.
GOOD. THIS PLACE CREEPS ME OUT....
...IT FEELS LIKE WE'RE BEING WATCHED.

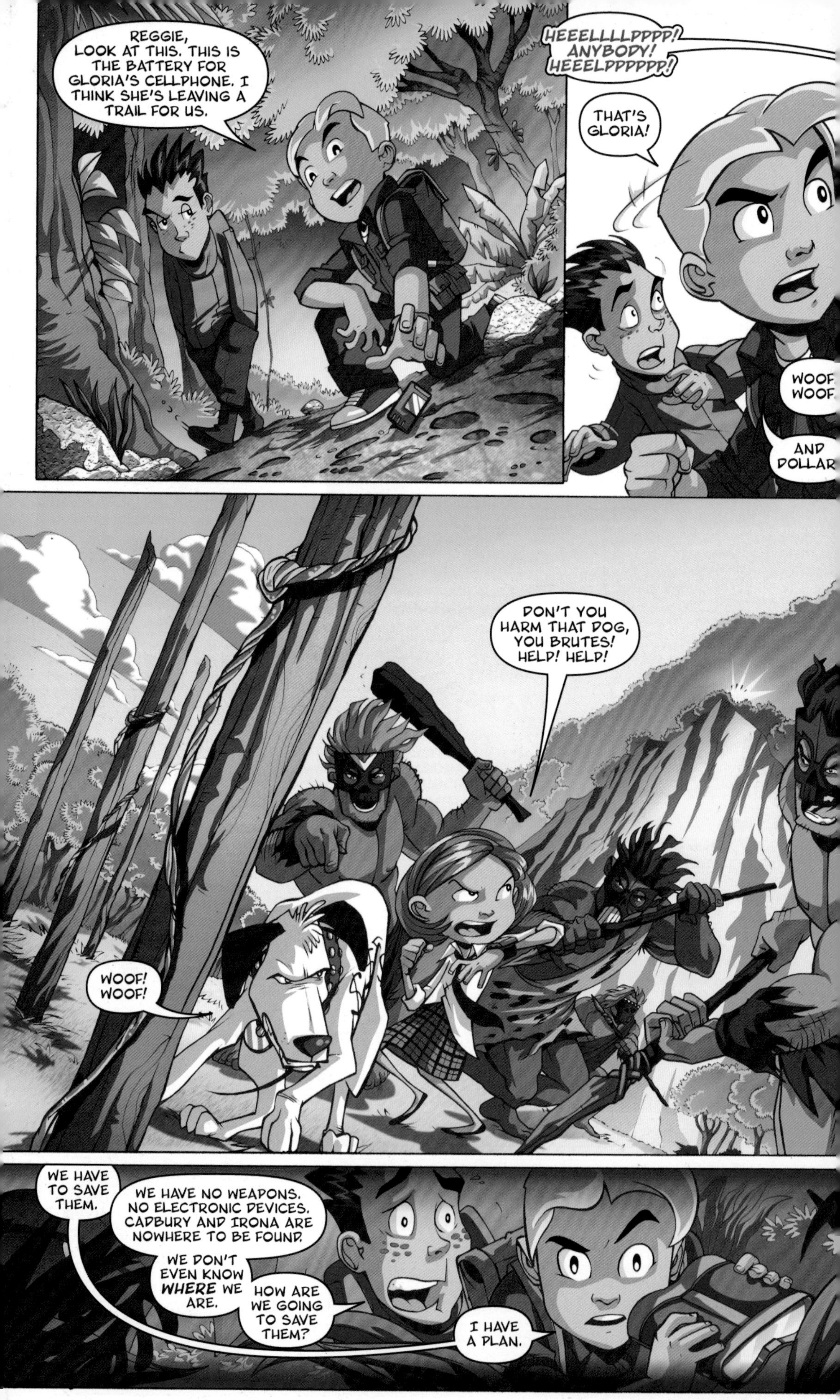
REGGIE, LOOK AT THIS. THIS IS THE BATTERY FOR GLORIA'S CELLPHONE. I THINK SHE'S LEAVING A TRAIL FOR US.
HEEELLLLPPPP! ANYBODY! HEEELPPPPPP!
THAT'S GLORIA!
WOOF WOOF
AND DOLLAR
DON'T YOU HARM THAT DOG, YOU BRUTES! HELP! HELP!
WOOF! WOOF!
WE HAVE TO SAVE THEM.
WE HAVE NO WEAPONS. NO ELECTRONIC DEVICES. CADBURY AND IRONA ARE NOWHERE TO BE FOUND.
WE DON'T EVEN KNOW **WHERE** WE ARE.
HOW ARE WE GOING TO SAVE THEM?
I HAVE A PLAN.

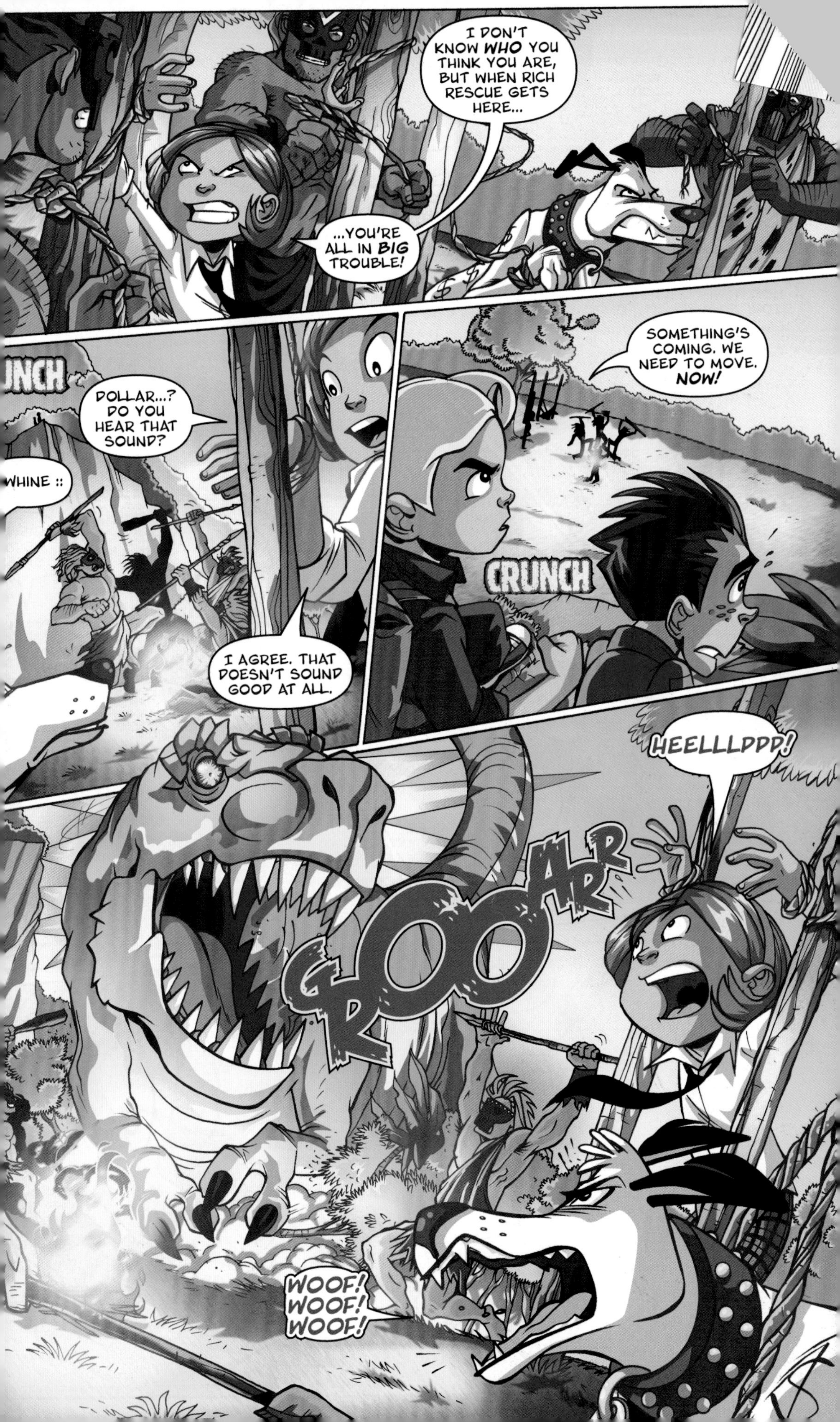
I DON'T KNOW WHO YOU THINK YOU ARE, BUT WHEN RICH RESCUE GETS HERE...
...YOU'RE ALL IN BIG TROUBLE!
UNCH
DOLLAR...? DO YOU HEAR THAT SOUND?
WHINE ::
I AGREE. THAT DOESN'T SOUND GOOD AT ALL.
SOMETHING'S COMING. WE NEED TO MOVE. NOW!
CRUNCH
HEELLLPPP!
GROOARR
WOOF! WOOF! WOOF!

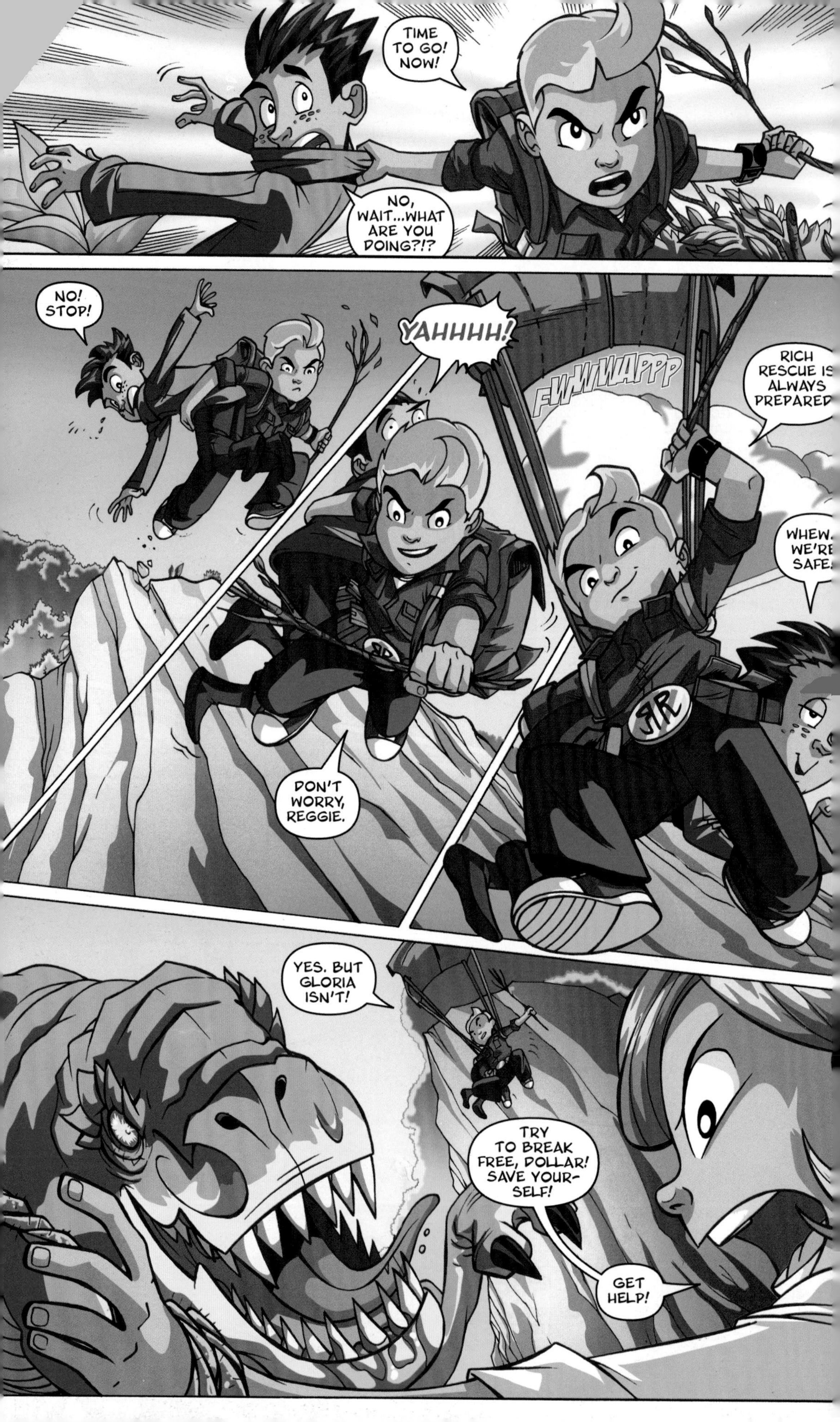
TIME TO GO! NOW!
NO, WAIT...WHAT ARE YOU DOING?!?
NO! STOP!
YAHHHH!
FWWWAPPP
RICH RESCUE IS ALWAYS PREPARED
DON'T WORRY, REGGIE.
WHEW... WE'RE SAFE.
YES. BUT GLORIA ISN'T!
TRY TO BREAK FREE, DOLLAR! SAVE YOUR-SELF!
GET HELP!

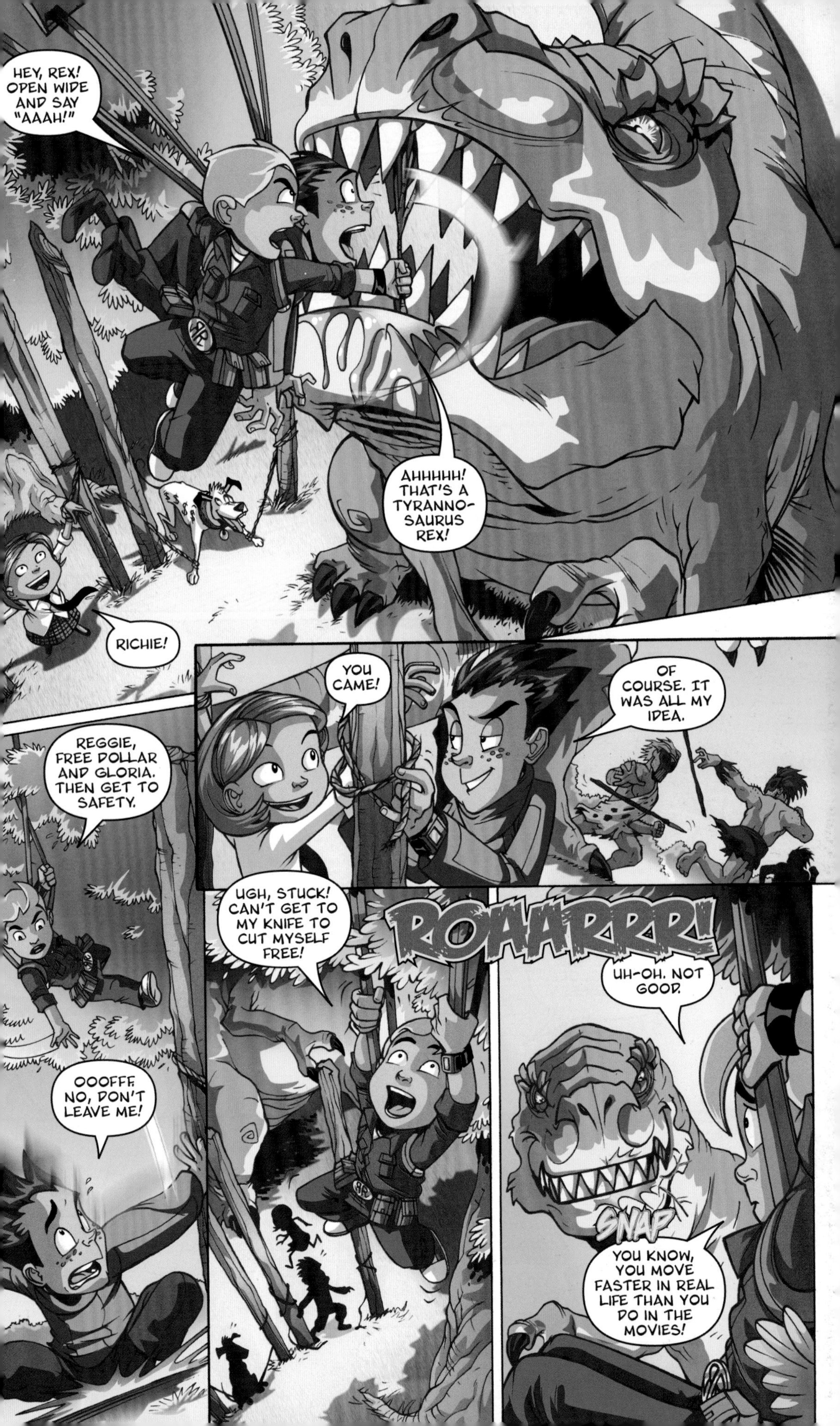
HEY, REX! OPEN WIDE AND SAY "AAAH!"
AHHHHH! THAT'S A TYRANNO-SAURUS REX!
RICHIE!
YOU CAME!
OF COURSE. IT WAS ALL MY IDEA.
REGGIE, FREE DOLLAR AND GLORIA. THEN GET TO SAFETY.
OOOFF. NO, DON'T LEAVE ME!
UGH, STUCK! CAN'T GET TO MY KNIFE TO CUT MYSELF FREE!
ROAARRR!
UH-OH. NOT GOOD.
SNAP
YOU KNOW, YOU MOVE FASTER IN REAL LIFE THAN YOU DO IN THE MOVIES!

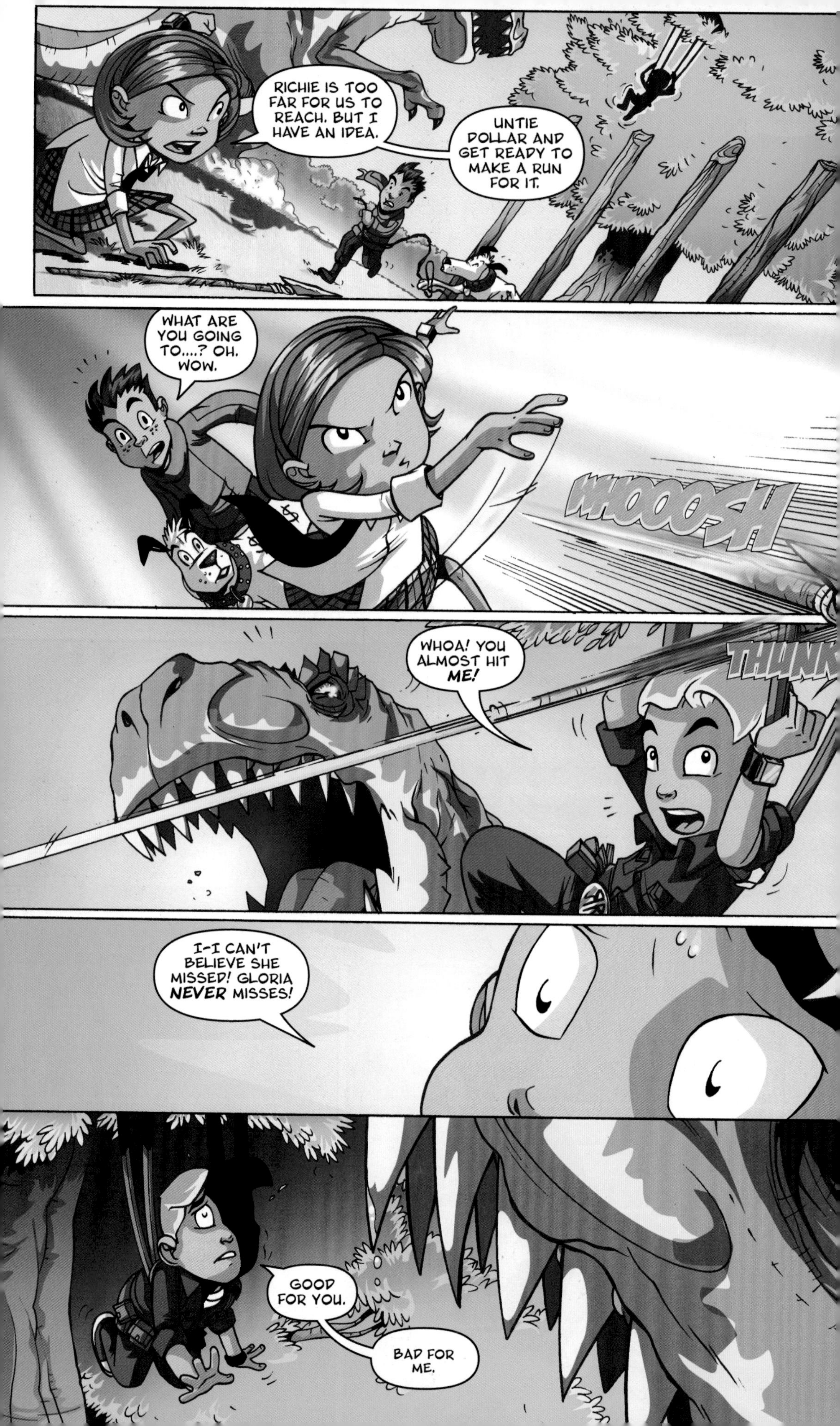
RICHIE IS TOO FAR FOR US TO REACH. BUT I HAVE AN IDEA.
UNTIE DOLLAR AND GET READY TO MAKE A RUN FOR IT.
WHAT ARE YOU GOING TO....? OH. WOW.
WHOOOSH
THUNK
WHOA! YOU ALMOST HIT ME!
I-I CAN'T BELIEVE SHE MISSED! GLORIA NEVER MISSES!
GOOD FOR YOU.
BAD FOR ME.

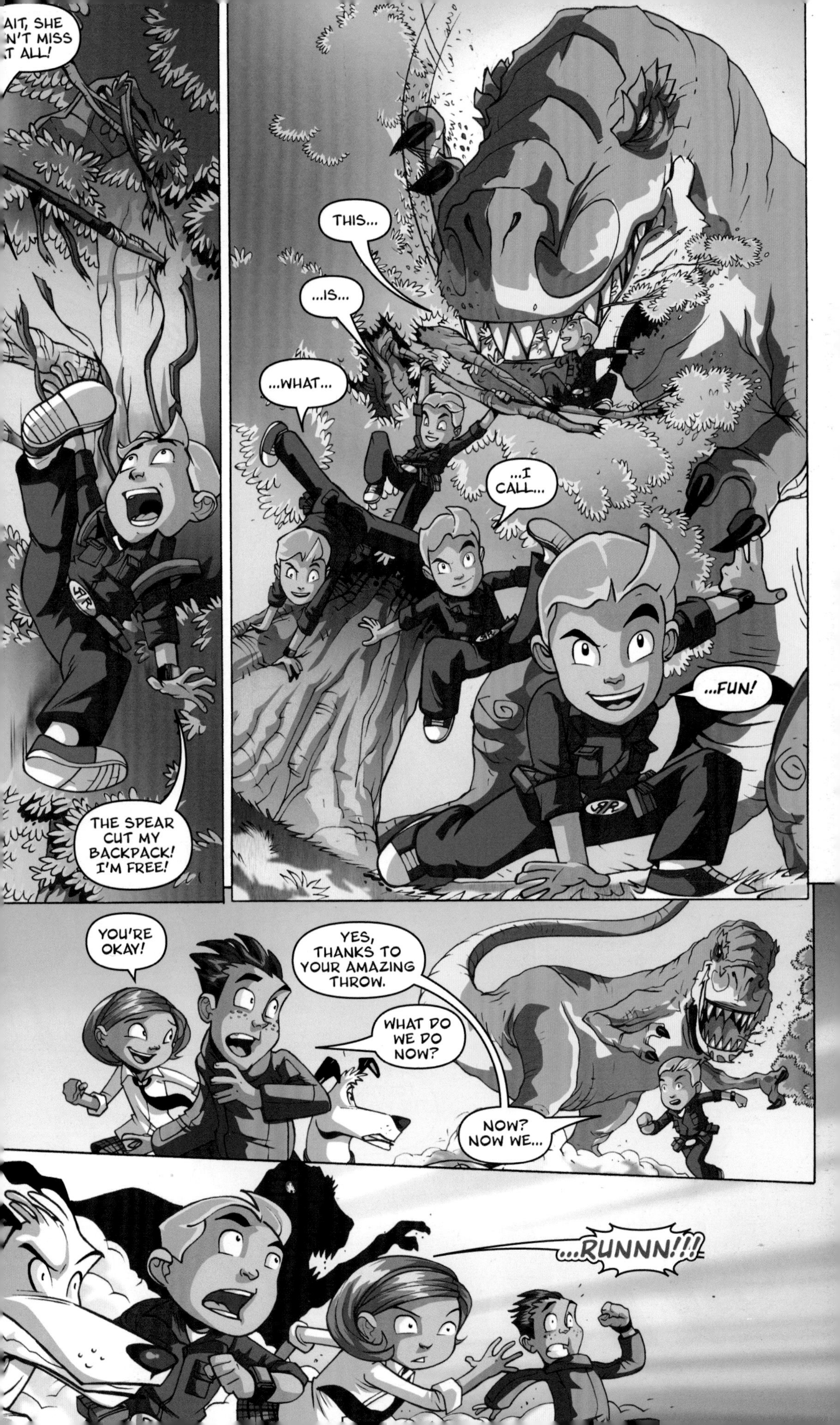

AIT, SHE
N'T MISS
T ALL!
THE SPEAR CUT MY BACKPACK! I'M FREE!
THIS...
...IS...
...WHAT...
...I CALL...
...FUN!
YOU'RE OKAY!
YES, THANKS TO YOUR AMAZING THROW.
WHAT DO WE DO NOW?
NOW? NOW WE...
...RUNNN!!!

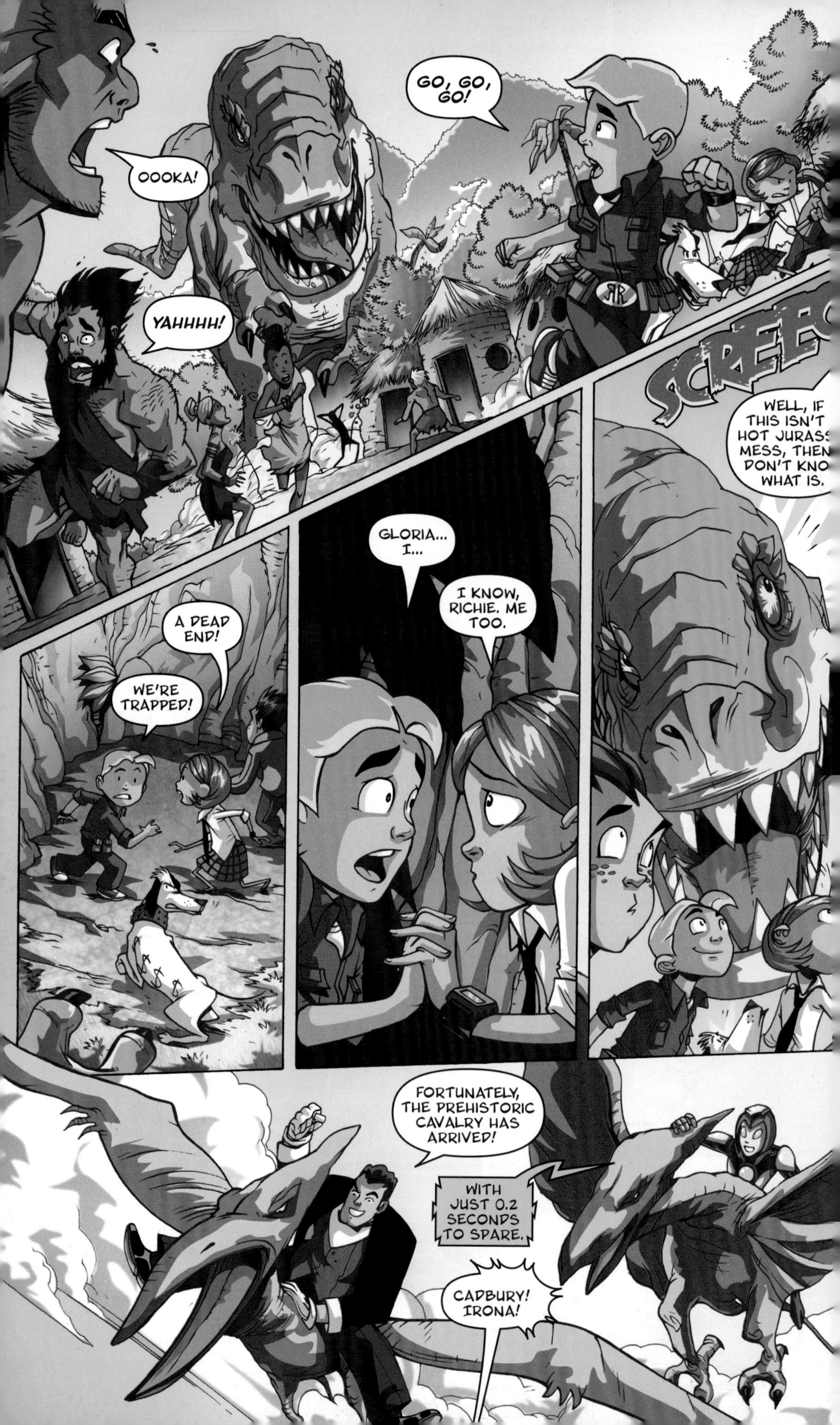
OOOKA!
GO, GO, GO!
YAHHHH!
A DEAD END!
WE'RE TRAPPED!
GLORIA... I...
I KNOW, RICHIE. ME TOO.
WELL, IF THIS ISN'T HOT JURASS MESS, THEN DON'T KNO WHAT IS.
FORTUNATELY, THE PREHISTORIC CAVALRY HAS ARRIVED!
WITH JUST 0.2 SECONDS TO SPARE.
CADBURY! IRONA!

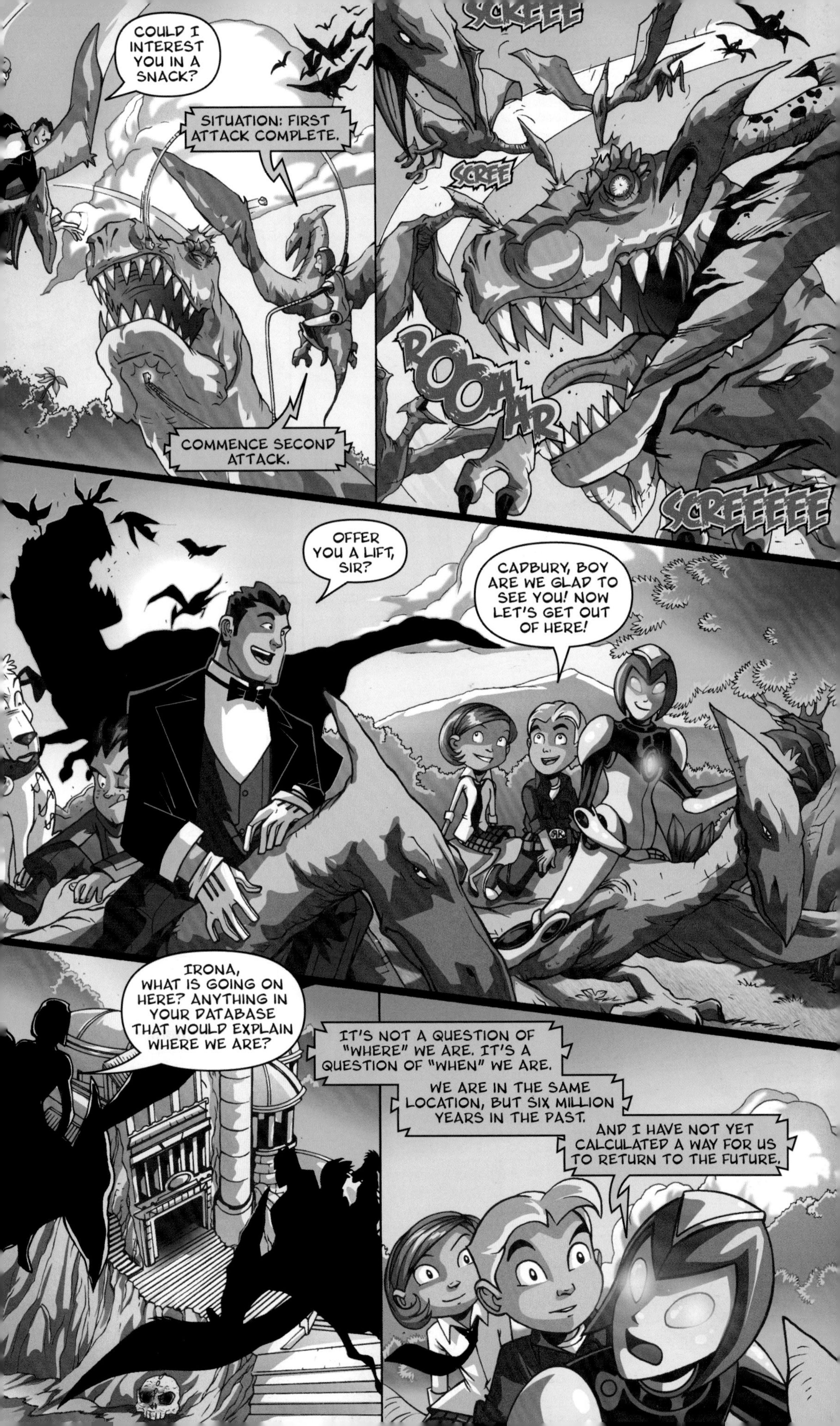
COULD I INTEREST YOU IN A SNACK?
SITUATION: FIRST ATTACK COMPLETE.
COMMENCE SECOND ATTACK.
SCREEE
SCREE
ROOOAAR
SCREEEEE
OFFER YOU A LIFT, SIR?
CADBURY, BOY ARE WE GLAD TO SEE YOU! NOW LET'S GET OUT OF HERE!
IRONA, WHAT IS GOING ON HERE? ANYTHING IN YOUR DATABASE THAT WOULD EXPLAIN WHERE WE ARE?
IT'S NOT A QUESTION OF "WHERE" WE ARE. IT'S A QUESTION OF "WHEN" WE ARE.
WE ARE IN THE SAME LOCATION, BUT SIX MILLION YEARS IN THE PAST.
AND I HAVE NOT YET CALCULATED A WAY FOR US TO RETURN TO THE FUTURE.

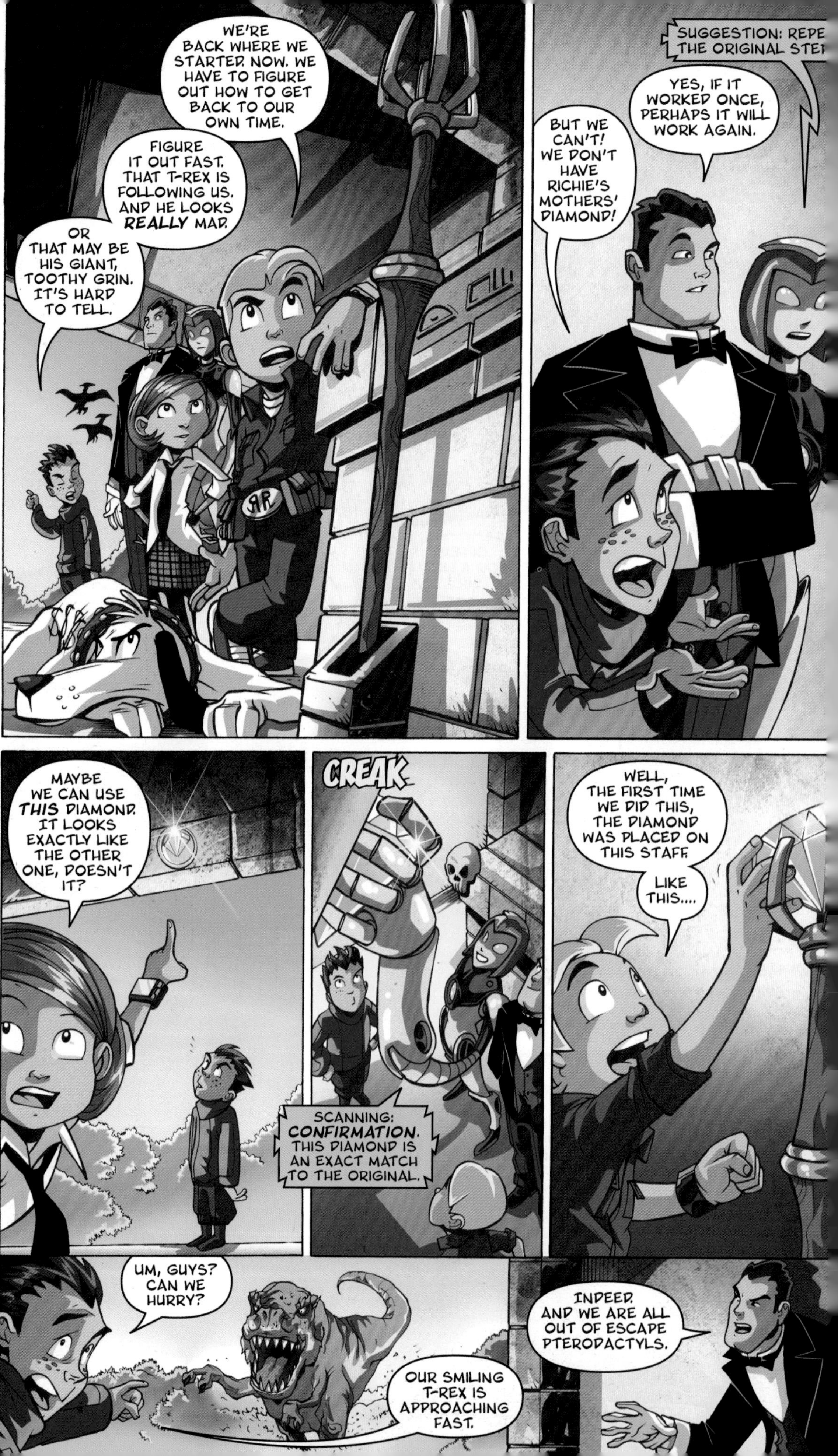

WE'RE BACK WHERE WE STARTED. NOW. WE HAVE TO FIGURE OUT HOW TO GET BACK TO OUR OWN TIME.
FIGURE IT OUT FAST. THAT T-REX IS FOLLOWING US. AND HE LOOKS REALLY MAD.
OR THAT MAY BE HIS GIANT, TOOTHY GRIN. IT'S HARD TO TELL.
SUGGESTION: REPE THE ORIGINAL STE
YES, IF IT WORKED ONCE, PERHAPS IT WILL WORK AGAIN.
BUT WE CAN'T! WE DON'T HAVE RICHIE'S MOTHERS' DIAMOND!
MAYBE WE CAN USE THIS DIAMOND. IT LOOKS EXACTLY LIKE THE OTHER ONE, DOESN'T IT?
CREAK
SCANNING: CONFIRMATION. THIS DIAMOND IS AN EXACT MATCH TO THE ORIGINAL.
WELL, THE FIRST TIME WE DID THIS, THE DIAMOND WAS PLACED ON THIS STAFF.
LIKE THIS....
UM, GUYS? CAN WE HURRY?
OUR SMILING T-REX IS APPROACHING FAST.
INDEED. AND WE ARE ALL OUT OF ESCAPE PTERODACTYLS.

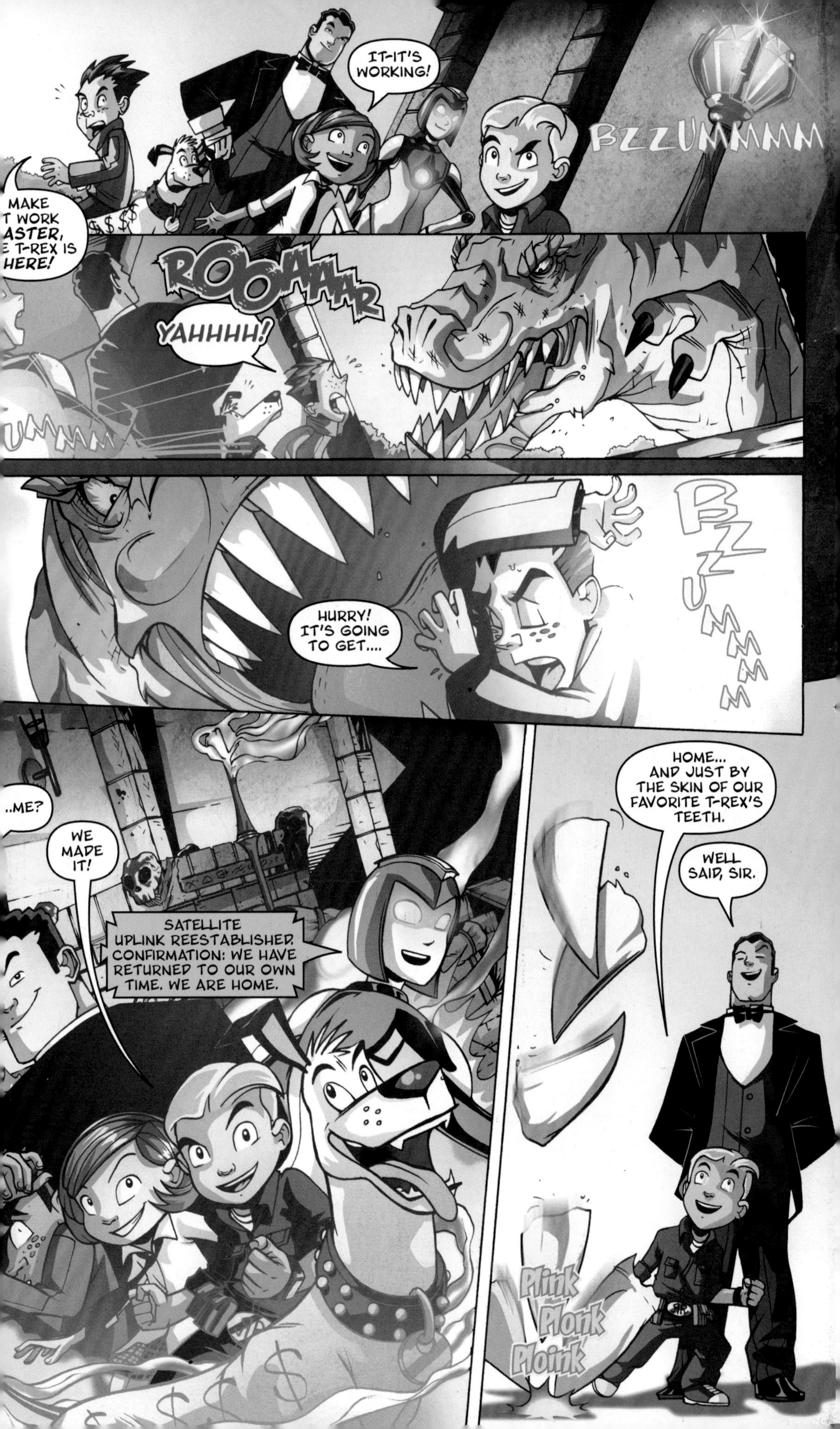

IT-IT'S WORKING!
BZZUMMMM
MAKE
T WORK
ASTER,
E T-REX IS
HERE!
ROOAAAR
YAHHHH!
UMMMM
BZZUMMMMM
HURRY! IT'S GOING TO GET....
..ME?
WE MADE IT!
SATELLITE UPLINK REESTABLISHED. CONFIRMATION: WE HAVE RETURNED TO OUR OWN TIME. WE ARE HOME.
HOME... AND JUST BY THE SKIN OF OUR FAVORITE T-REX'S TEETH.
WELL SAID, SIR.
Plink
Plonk
Ploink

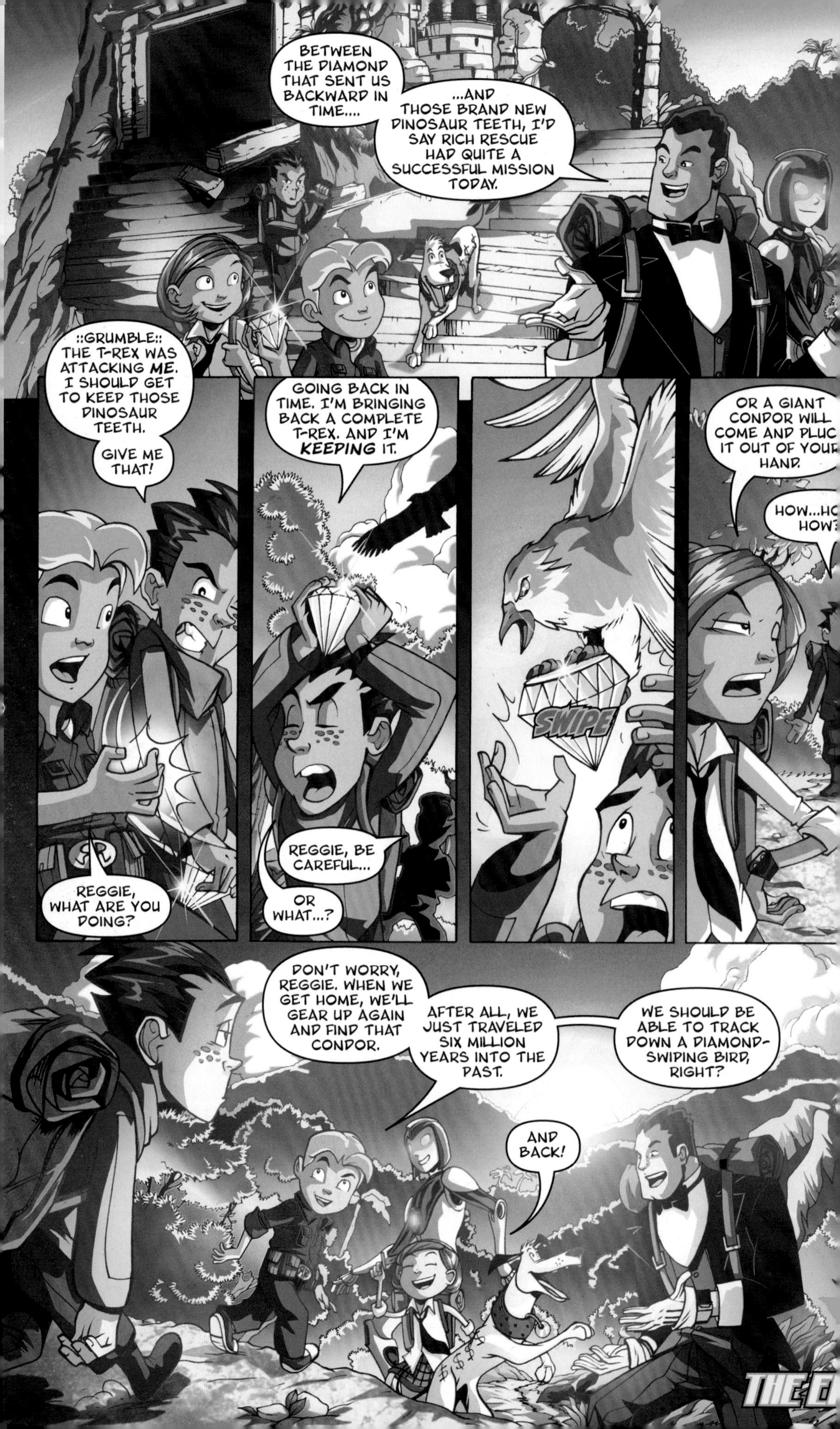
BETWEEN THE DIAMOND THAT SENT US BACKWARD IN TIME....
...AND THOSE BRAND NEW DINOSAUR TEETH, I'D SAY RICH RESCUE HAD QUITE A SUCCESSFUL MISSION TODAY.
::GRUMBLE:: THE T-REX WAS ATTACKING ME. I SHOULD GET TO KEEP THOSE DINOSAUR TEETH.
GIVE ME THAT!
REGGIE, WHAT ARE YOU DOING?
GOING BACK IN TIME. I'M BRINGING BACK A COMPLETE T-REX. AND I'M KEEPING IT.
REGGIE, BE CAREFUL...
OR WHAT...?
SWIPE
OR A GIANT CONDOR WILL COME AND PLUC IT OUT OF YOUR HAND.
HOW...HO HOW?
DON'T WORRY, REGGIE. WHEN WE GET HOME, WE'LL GEAR UP AGAIN AND FIND THAT CONDOR.
AFTER ALL, WE JUST TRAVELED SIX MILLION YEARS INTO THE PAST.
WE SHOULD BE ABLE TO TRACK DOWN A DIAMOND-SWIPING BIRD, RIGHT?
AND BACK!
THE E

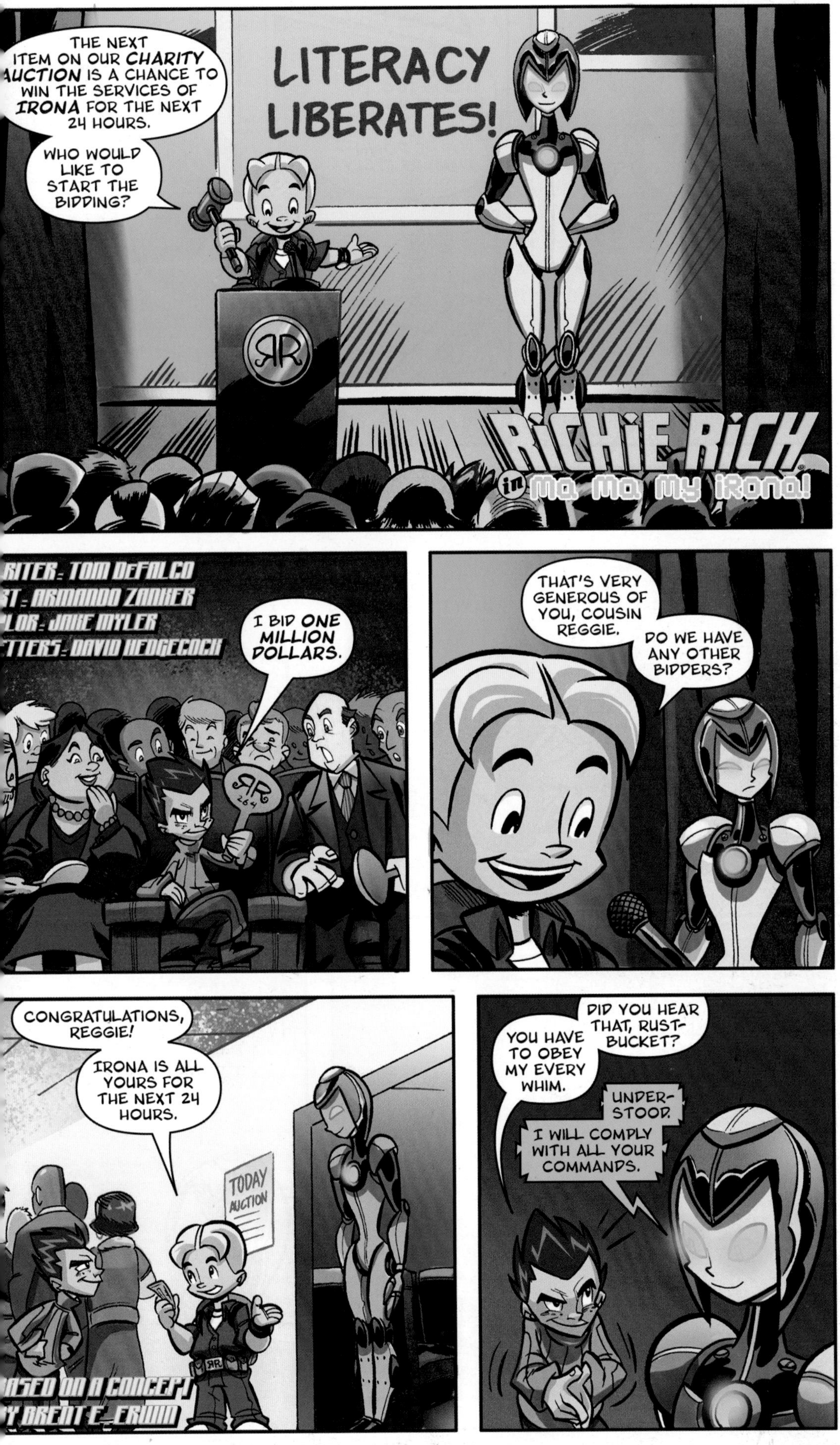

THE NEXT ITEM ON OUR CHARITY AUCTION IS A CHANCE TO WIN THE SERVICES OF IRONA FOR THE NEXT 24 HOURS.
WHO WOULD LIKE TO START THE BIDDING?
LITERACY LIBERATES!
RICHIE RICH
in Ma, Ma, My iRona!
RITER: TOM DEFALCO
ST: ARMANDO ZANKER
LOR: JAKE MYLER
TTERS: DAVID HEDGECOCK
I BID ONE MILLION DOLLARS.
264
THAT'S VERY GENEROUS OF YOU, COUSIN REGGIE.
DO WE HAVE ANY OTHER BIDDERS?
CONGRATULATIONS, REGGIE!
IRONA IS ALL YOURS FOR THE NEXT 24 HOURS.
TODAY AUCTION
ASED ON A CONCEPT
Y BRENT E. ERWIN
DID YOU HEAR THAT, RUST-BUCKET?
YOU HAVE TO OBEY MY EVERY WHIM.
UNDER-STOOD.
I WILL COMPLY WITH ALL YOUR COMMANDS.

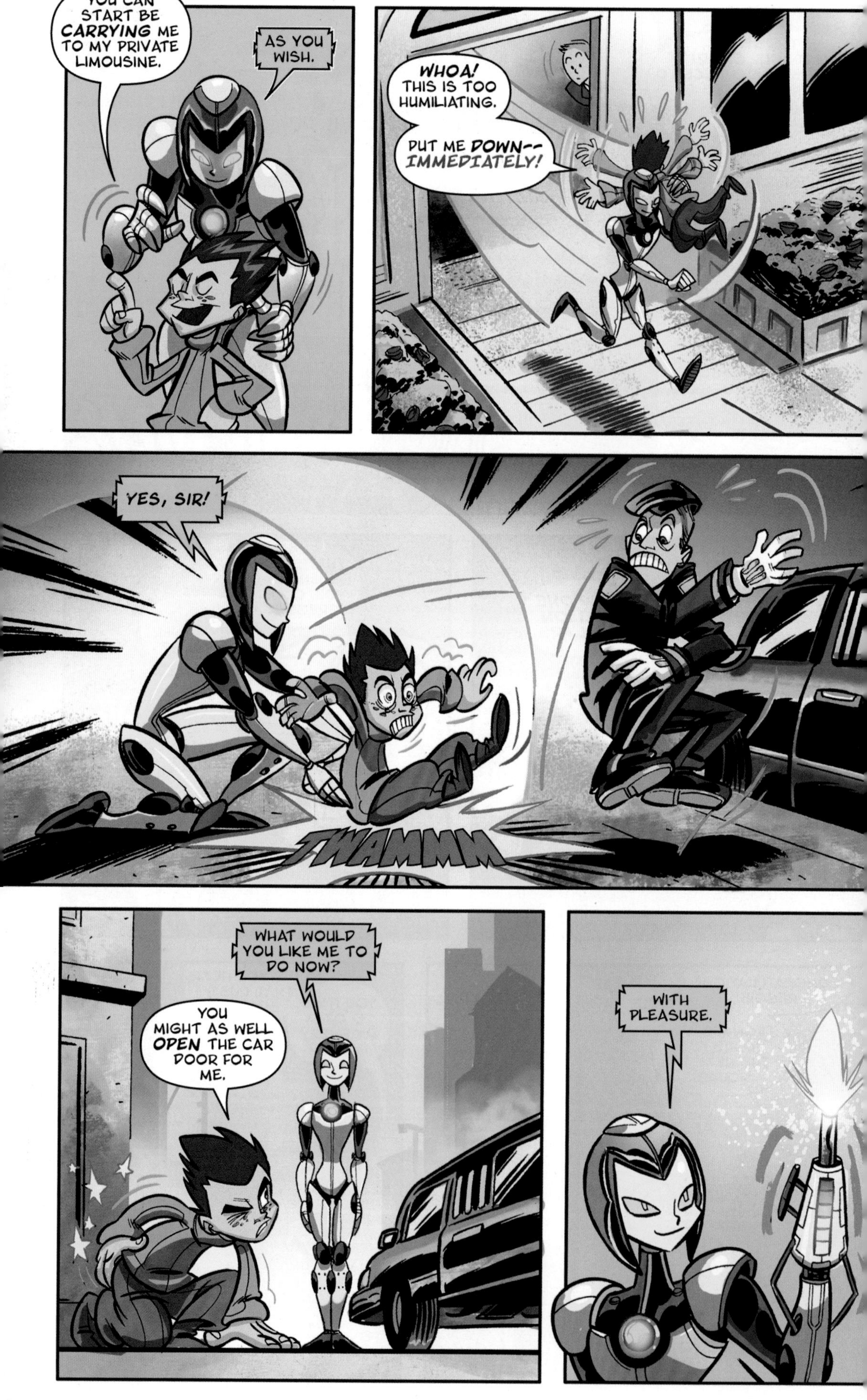

YOU CAN START BE CARRYING ME TO MY PRIVATE LIMOUSINE.
AS YOU WISH.
WHOA! THIS IS TOO HUMILIATING.
PUT ME DOWN-- IMMEDIATELY!
YES, SIR!
TWAMMM
WHAT WOULD YOU LIKE ME TO DO NOW?
YOU MIGHT AS WELL OPEN THE CAR DOOR FOR ME.
WITH PLEASURE.

SKWAAAK

Y-YOU'VE **RUINED** MY BEAUTIFUL LIMOUSINE.

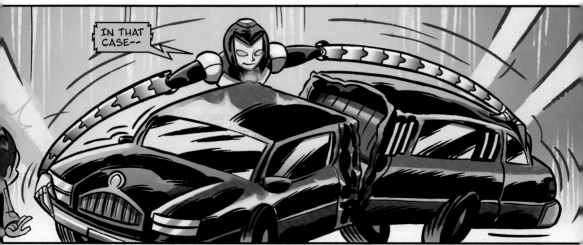

IN THAT CASE--

cRUNCH

--WE SHOULD GET IT OFF THE STREET--

--AND DISCARD IT WITH THE REST OF THE TRASH.

HOW AM I SUPPOSED TO GET HOME NOW?

I COULD **FLY** YOU THERE.

OKAY, BUT I WANT YOU TO BE VERY **CAREFUL.**

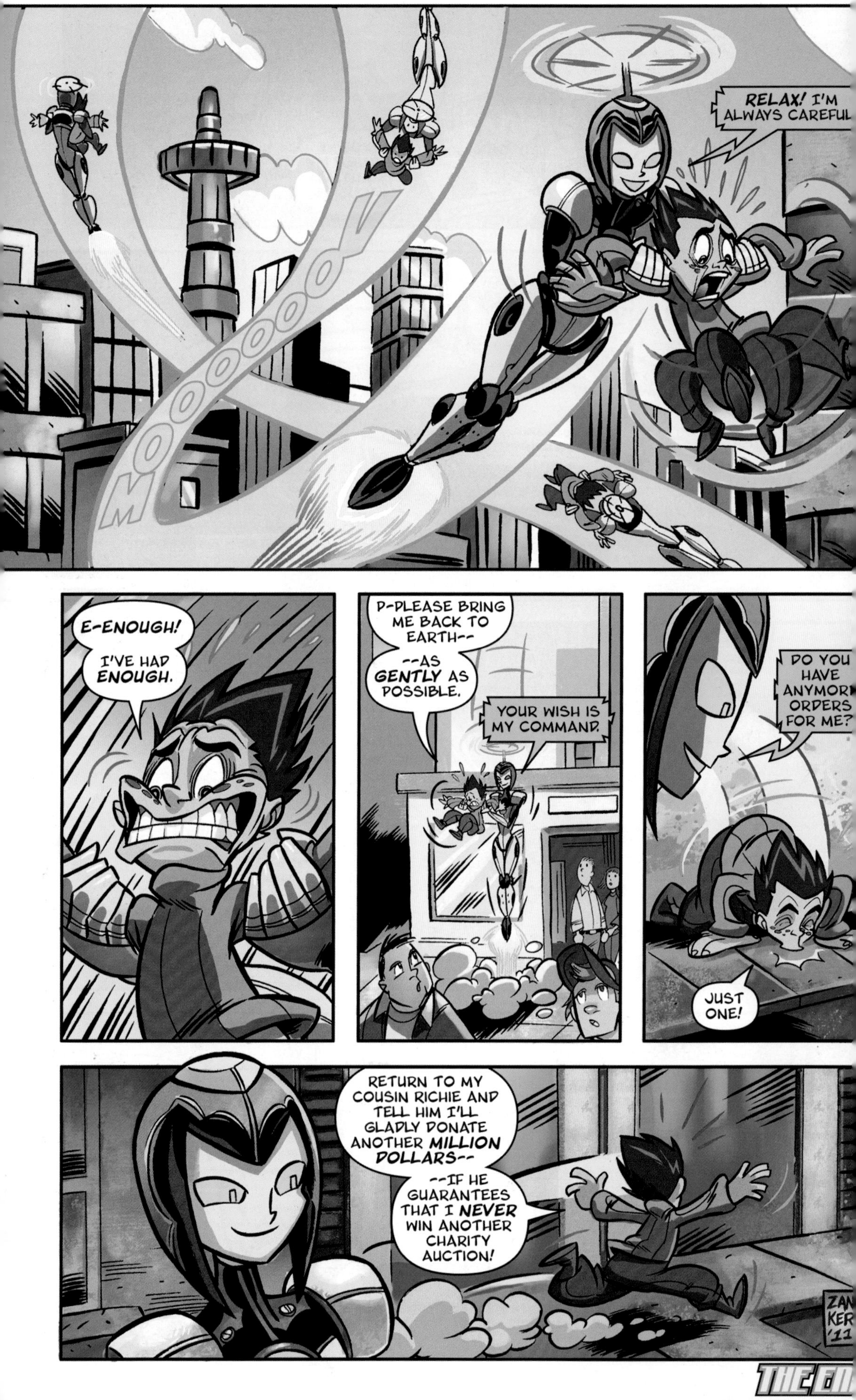
RELAX! I'M ALWAYS CAREFUL
MOOOOOOV
E-ENOUGH!
I'VE HAD ENOUGH.
P-PLEASE BRING ME BACK TO EARTH--
--AS GENTLY AS POSSIBLE.
YOUR WISH IS MY COMMAND.
DO YOU HAVE ANYMOR ORDERS FOR ME?
JUST ONE!
RETURN TO MY COUSIN RICHIE AND TELL HIM I'LL GLADLY DONATE ANOTHER MILLION DOLLARS--
--IF HE GUARANTEES THAT I NEVER WIN ANOTHER CHARITY AUCTION!
ZANKER '11
THE EN

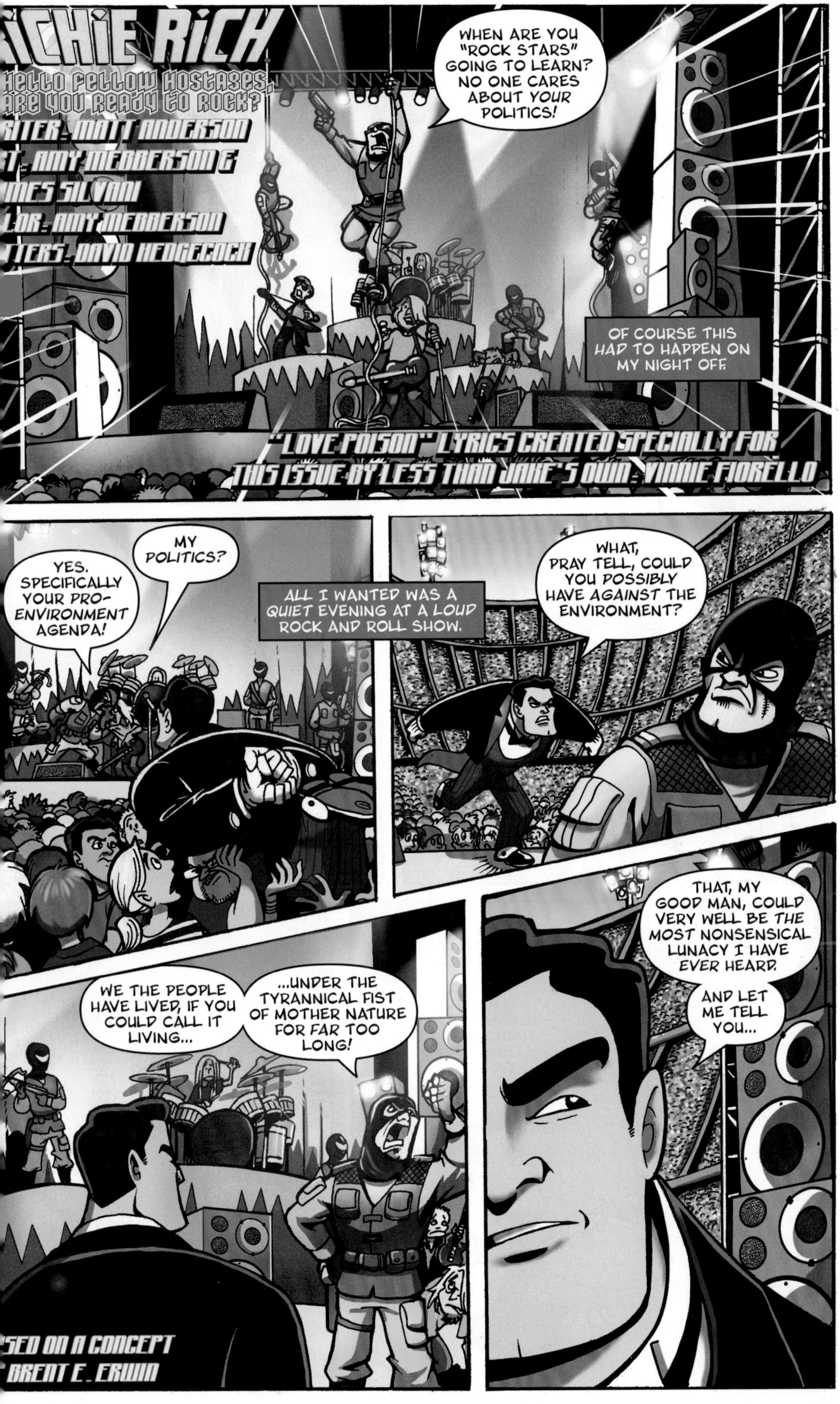
ICHIE RICH
HELLO FELLOW HOSTAGES, ARE YOU READY TO ROCK?
RITER - MATT ANDERSON
T - AMY MEBBERSON &
MES SILVANI
LOR - AMY MEBBERSON
TTERS - DAVID HEDGECOCK
WHEN ARE YOU "ROCK STARS" GOING TO LEARN? NO ONE CARES ABOUT YOUR POLITICS!
OF COURSE THIS HAD TO HAPPEN ON MY NIGHT OFF.
"LOVE POISON" LYRICS CREATED SPECIALLY FOR THIS ISSUE BY LESS THAN JAKE'S OWN - VINNIE FIORELLO
MY POLITICS?
YES. SPECIFICALLY YOUR PRO-ENVIRONMENT AGENDA!
ALL I WANTED WAS A QUIET EVENING AT A LOUD ROCK AND ROLL SHOW.
WHAT, PRAY TELL, COULD YOU POSSIBLY HAVE AGAINST THE ENVIRONMENT?
WE THE PEOPLE HAVE LIVED, IF YOU COULD CALL IT LIVING...
...UNDER THE TYRANNICAL FIST OF MOTHER NATURE FOR FAR TOO LONG!
SED ON A CONCEPT
BRENT E. ERWIN
THAT, MY GOOD MAN, COULD VERY WELL BE THE MOST NONSENSICAL LUNACY I HAVE EVER HEARD.
AND LET ME TELL YOU...

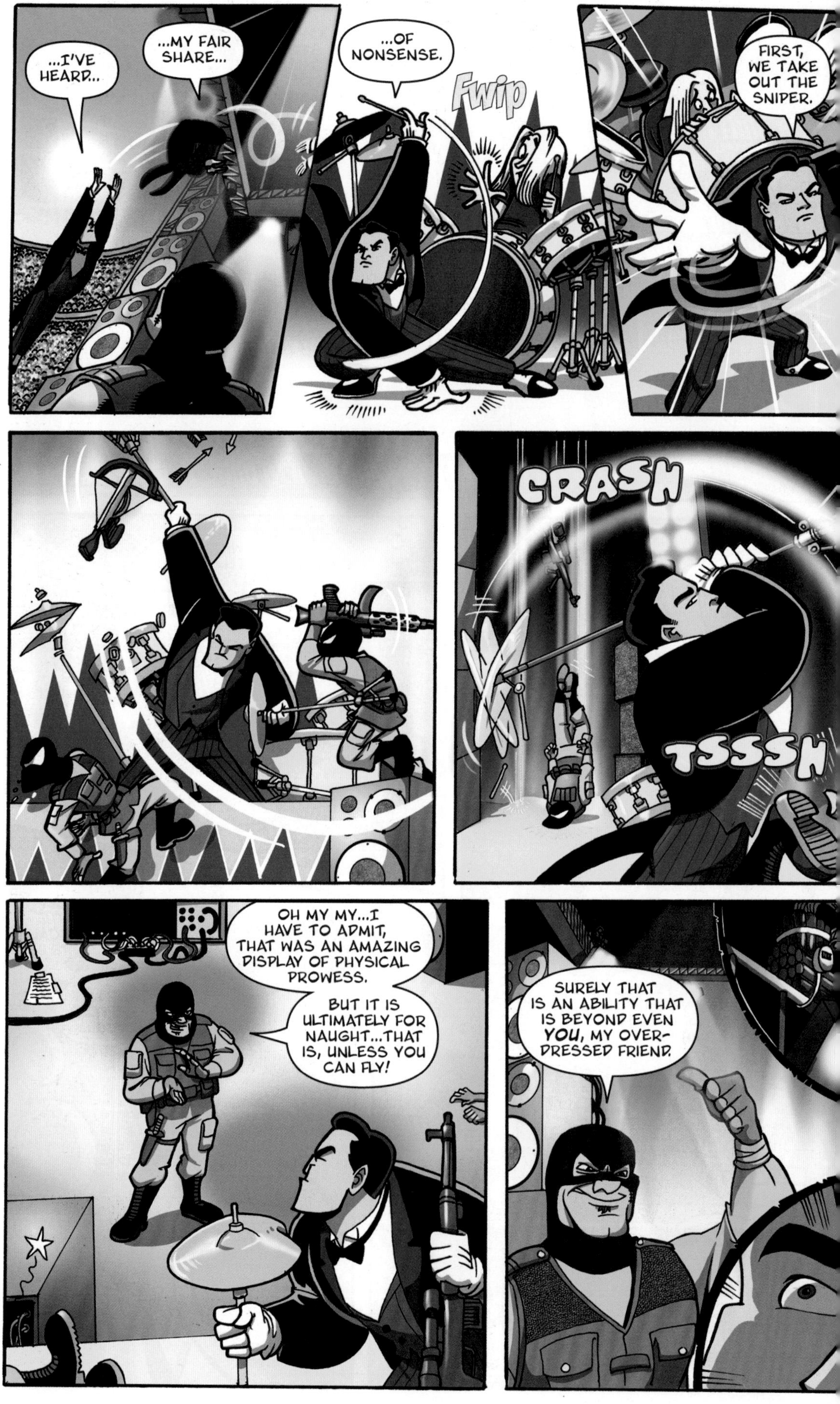
...I'VE HEARD...
...MY FAIR SHARE...
...OF NONSENSE.
Fwip
FIRST, WE TAKE OUT THE SNIPER.
CRASH
TSSSH
OH MY MY...I HAVE TO ADMIT, THAT WAS AN AMAZING DISPLAY OF PHYSICAL PROWESS.
BUT IT IS ULTIMATELY FOR NAUGHT...THAT IS, UNLESS YOU CAN FLY!
SURELY THAT IS AN ABILITY THAT IS BEYOND EVEN YOU, MY OVER-DRESSED FRIEND.

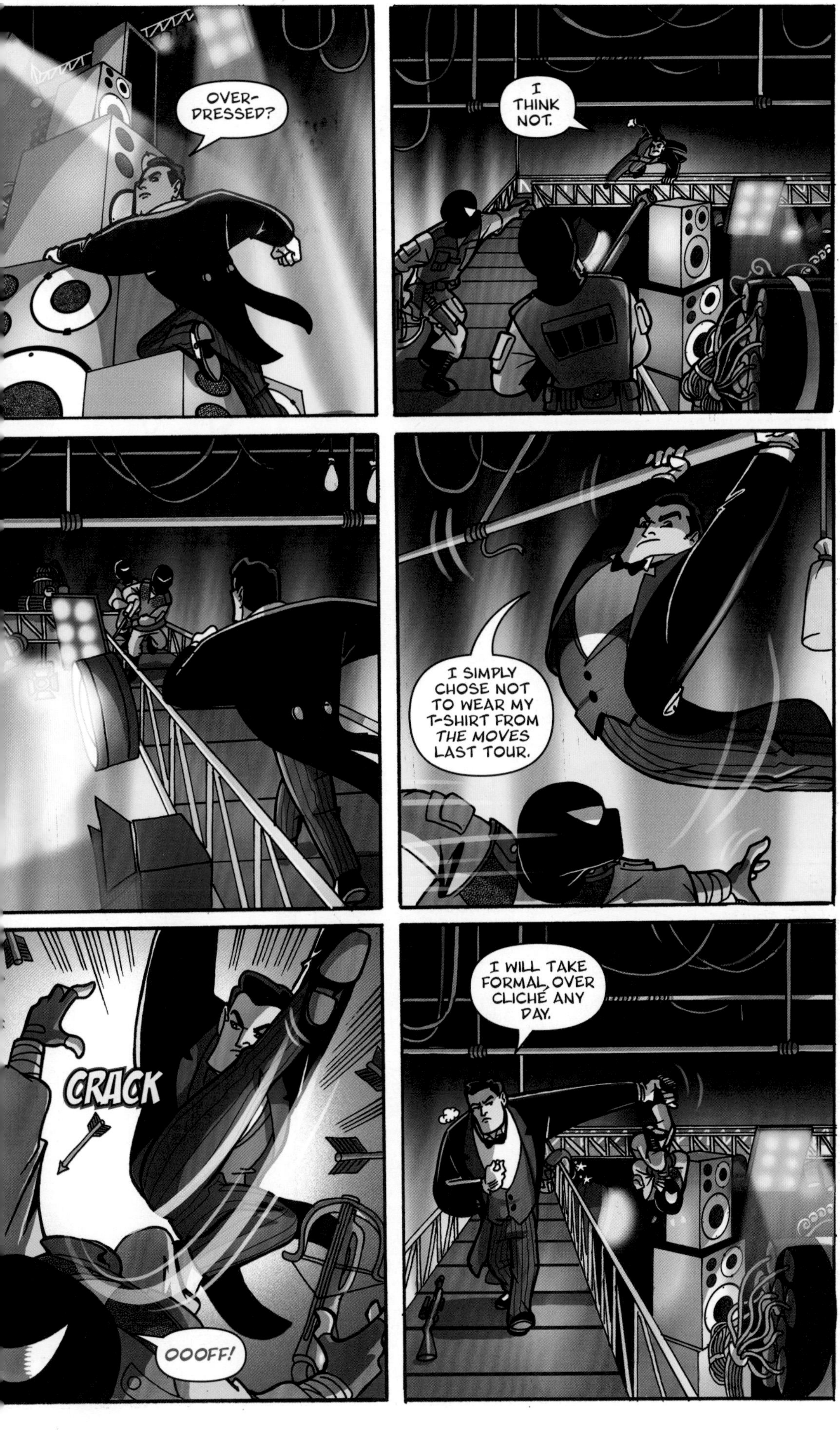
OVER-DRESSED?
I THINK NOT.
I SIMPLY CHOSE NOT TO WEAR MY T-SHIRT FROM THE MOVES LAST TOUR.
CRACK
OOOFF!
I WILL TAKE FORMAL OVER CLICHÉ ANY DAY.

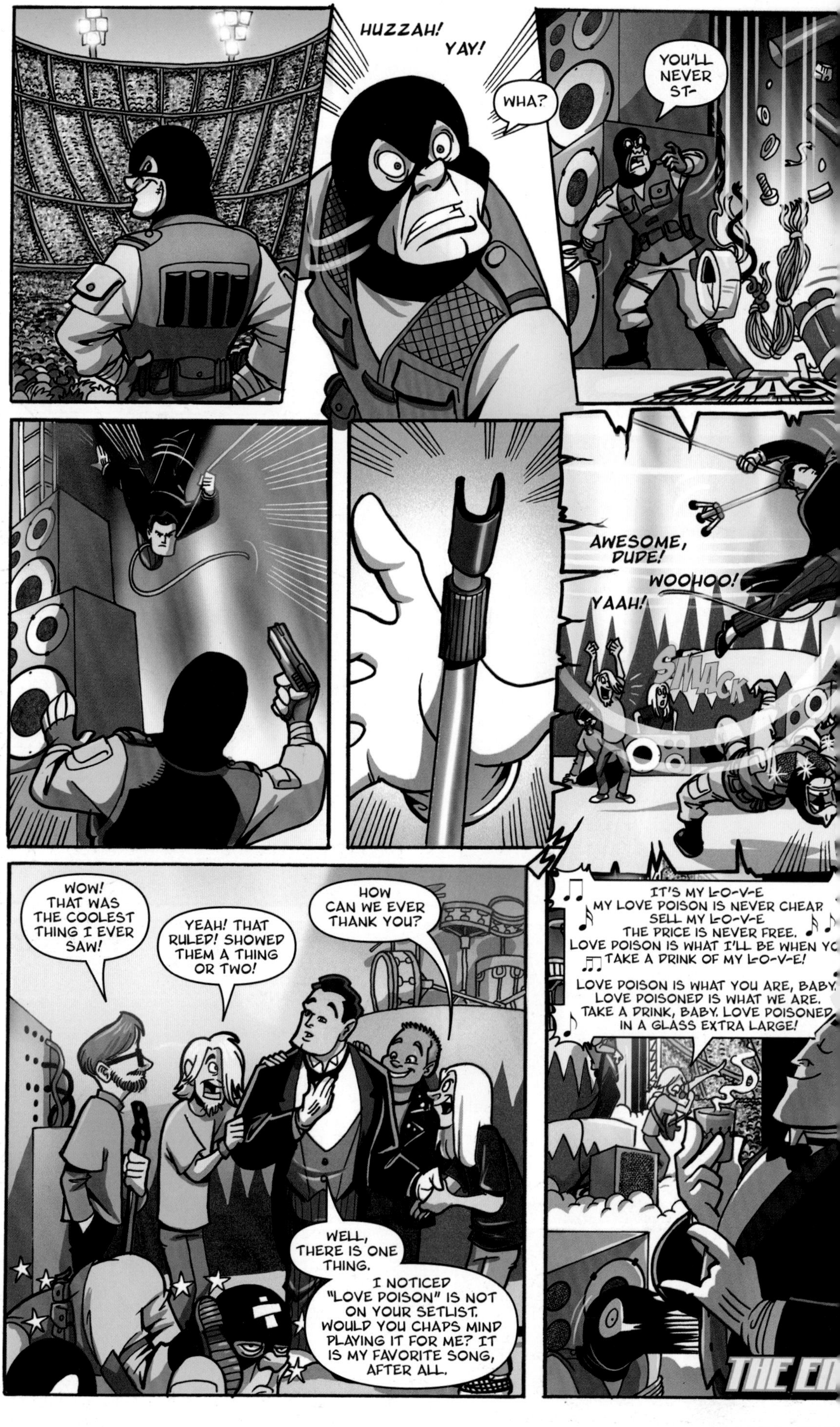
HUZZAH!
YAY!
WHA?
YOU'LL NEVER ST-
SMASH
AWESOME, DUDE!
WOOHOO!
YAAH!
SMACK
WOW! THAT WAS THE COOLEST THING I EVER SAW!
YEAH! THAT RULED! SHOWED THEM A THING OR TWO!
HOW CAN WE EVER THANK YOU?
WELL, THERE IS ONE THING.
I NOTICED "LOVE POISON" IS NOT ON YOUR SETLIST. WOULD YOU CHAPS MIND PLAYING IT FOR ME? IT IS MY FAVORITE SONG, AFTER ALL.
IT'S MY L-O-V-E
MY LOVE POISON IS NEVER CHEAP.
SELL MY L-O-V-E
THE PRICE IS NEVER FREE.
LOVE POISON IS WHAT I'LL BE WHEN YO
TAKE A DRINK OF MY L-O-V-E!
LOVE POISON IS WHAT YOU ARE, BABY.
LOVE POISONED IS WHAT WE ARE.
TAKE A DRINK, BABY. LOVE POISONED
IN A GLASS EXTRA LARGE!
THE EN

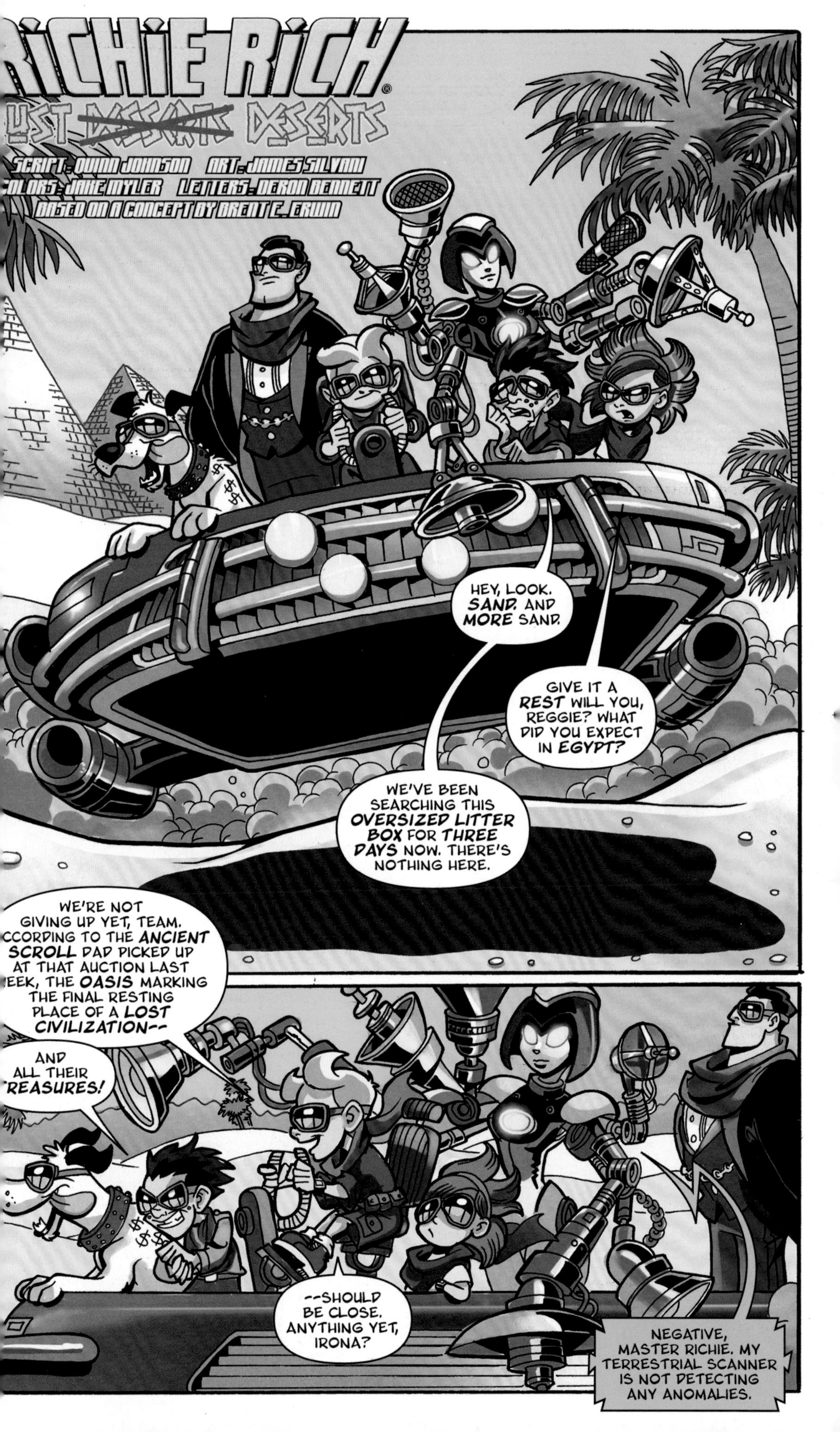

RICHIE RICH®
UST ~~DESSERTS~~ DESERTS
SCRIPT: QUINN JOHNSON ART: JAMES SILVANI
OLORS: JAKE MYLER LETTERS: DERON BENNETT
BASED ON A CONCEPT BY BRENT E. ERWIN
HEY, LOOK. SAND. AND MORE SAND.
GIVE IT A REST WILL YOU, REGGIE? WHAT DID YOU EXPECT IN EGYPT?
WE'VE BEEN SEARCHING THIS OVERSIZED LITTER BOX FOR THREE DAYS NOW. THERE'S NOTHING HERE.
WE'RE NOT GIVING UP YET, TEAM. CCORDING TO THE ANCIENT SCROLL DAD PICKED UP AT THAT AUCTION LAST EEK, THE OASIS MARKING THE FINAL RESTING PLACE OF A LOST CIVILIZATION--
AND ALL THEIR REASURES!
--SHOULD BE CLOSE. ANYTHING YET, IRONA?
NEGATIVE, MASTER RICHIE. MY TERRESTRIAL SCANNER IS NOT DETECTING ANY ANOMALIES.

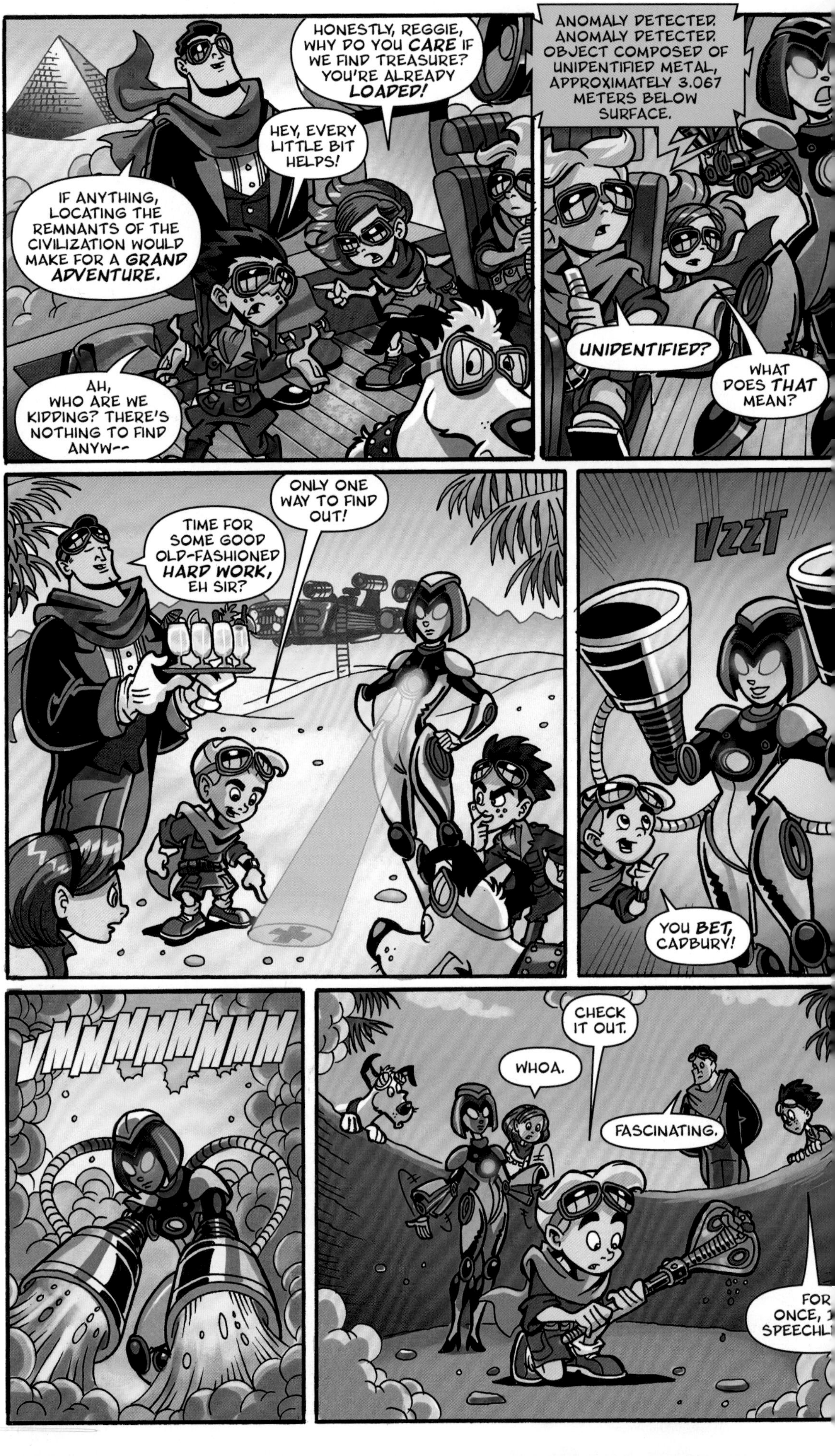
HONESTLY, REGGIE, WHY DO YOU CARE IF WE FIND TREASURE? YOU'RE ALREADY LOADED!
HEY, EVERY LITTLE BIT HELPS!
IF ANYTHING, LOCATING THE REMNANTS OF THE CIVILIZATION WOULD MAKE FOR A GRAND ADVENTURE.
AH, WHO ARE WE KIDDING? THERE'S NOTHING TO FIND ANYW--
ANOMALY DETECTED. ANOMALY DETECTED. OBJECT COMPOSED OF UNIDENTIFIED METAL, APPROXIMATELY 3.067 METERS BELOW SURFACE.
UNIDENTIFIED?
WHAT DOES THAT MEAN?
TIME FOR SOME GOOD OLD-FASHIONED HARD WORK, EH SIR?
ONLY ONE WAY TO FIND OUT!
VZZT
YOU BET, CADBURY!
VMMMMMMMMM
CHECK IT OUT.
WHOA.
FASCINATING.

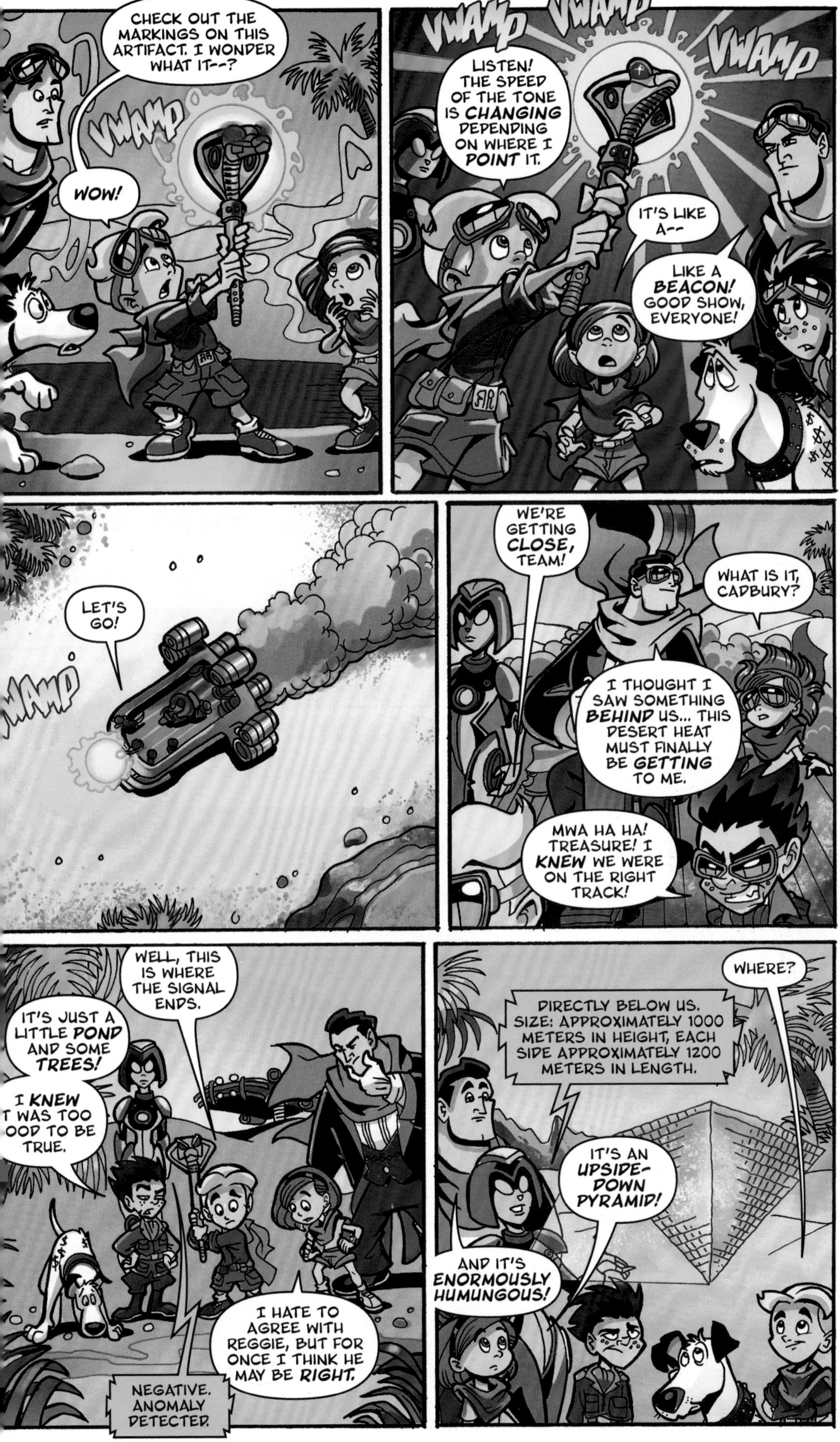

CHECK OUT THE MARKINGS ON THIS ARTIFACT. I WONDER WHAT IT--?
VWAMP
WOW!
VWAMP VWAMP VWAMP
LISTEN! THE SPEED OF THE TONE IS CHANGING DEPENDING ON WHERE I POINT IT.
IT'S LIKE A--
LIKE A BEACON! GOOD SHOW, EVERYONE!
LET'S GO!
VWAMP
WE'RE GETTING CLOSE, TEAM!
WHAT IS IT, CADBURY?
I THOUGHT I SAW SOMETHING BEHIND US... THIS DESERT HEAT MUST FINALLY BE GETTING TO ME.
MWA HA HA! TREASURE! I KNEW WE WERE ON THE RIGHT TRACK!
WELL, THIS IS WHERE THE SIGNAL ENDS.
IT'S JUST A LITTLE POND AND SOME TREES!
I KNEW T WAS TOO OOD TO BE TRUE.
I HATE TO AGREE WITH REGGIE, BUT FOR ONCE I THINK HE MAY BE RIGHT.
NEGATIVE. ANOMALY DETECTED.
WHERE?
DIRECTLY BELOW US. SIZE: APPROXIMATELY 1000 METERS IN HEIGHT, EACH SIDE APPROXIMATELY 1200 METERS IN LENGTH.
IT'S AN UPSIDE-DOWN PYRAMID!
AND IT'S ENORMOUSLY HUMUNGOUS!

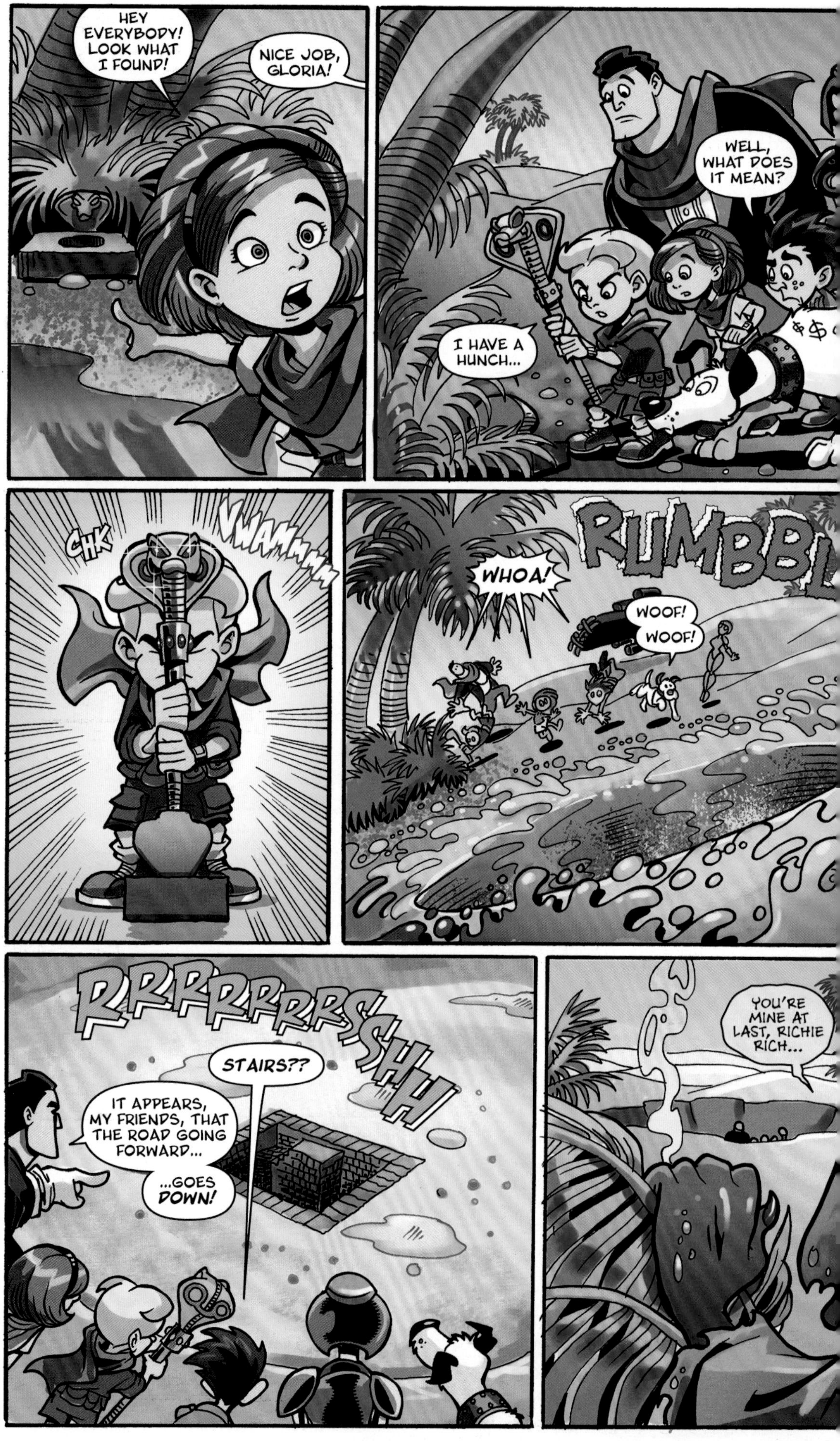
HEY EVERYBODY! LOOK WHAT I FOUND!
NICE JOB, GLORIA!
WELL, WHAT DOES IT MEAN?
I HAVE A HUNCH...
CHK
VWAMMMM
RUMBBL
WHOA!
WOOF! WOOF!
RRRRRRRSHH
STAIRS??
IT APPEARS, MY FRIENDS, THAT THE ROAD GOING FORWARD...
...GOES DOWN!
YOU'RE MINE AT LAST, RICHIE RICH...

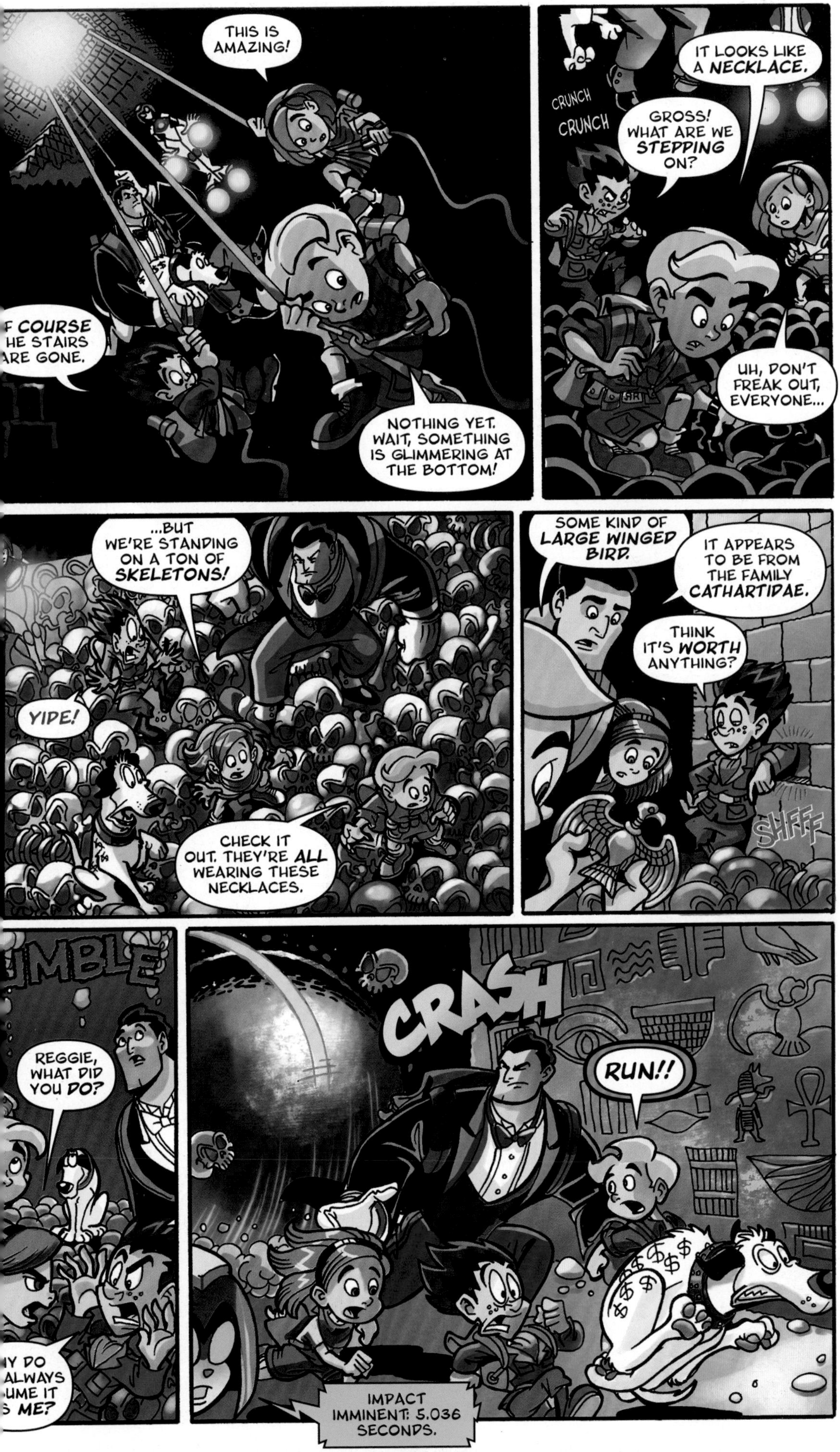
THIS IS AMAZING!
F COURSE HE STAIRS ARE GONE.
NOTHING YET. WAIT, SOMETHING IS GLIMMERING AT THE BOTTOM!
CRUNCH
CRUNCH
IT LOOKS LIKE A NECKLACE.
GROSS! WHAT ARE WE STEPPING ON?
UH, DON'T FREAK OUT, EVERYONE...
...BUT WE'RE STANDING ON A TON OF SKELETONS!
YIPE!
CHECK IT OUT. THEY'RE ALL WEARING THESE NECKLACES.
SOME KIND OF LARGE WINGED BIRD.
IT APPEARS TO BE FROM THE FAMILY CATHARTIDAE.
THINK IT'S WORTH ANYTHING?
SHFFF
UMBLE
REGGIE, WHAT DID YOU DO?
Y DO ALWAYS UME IT S ME?
CRASH
RUN!!
IMPACT IMMINENT: 5.036 SECONDS.

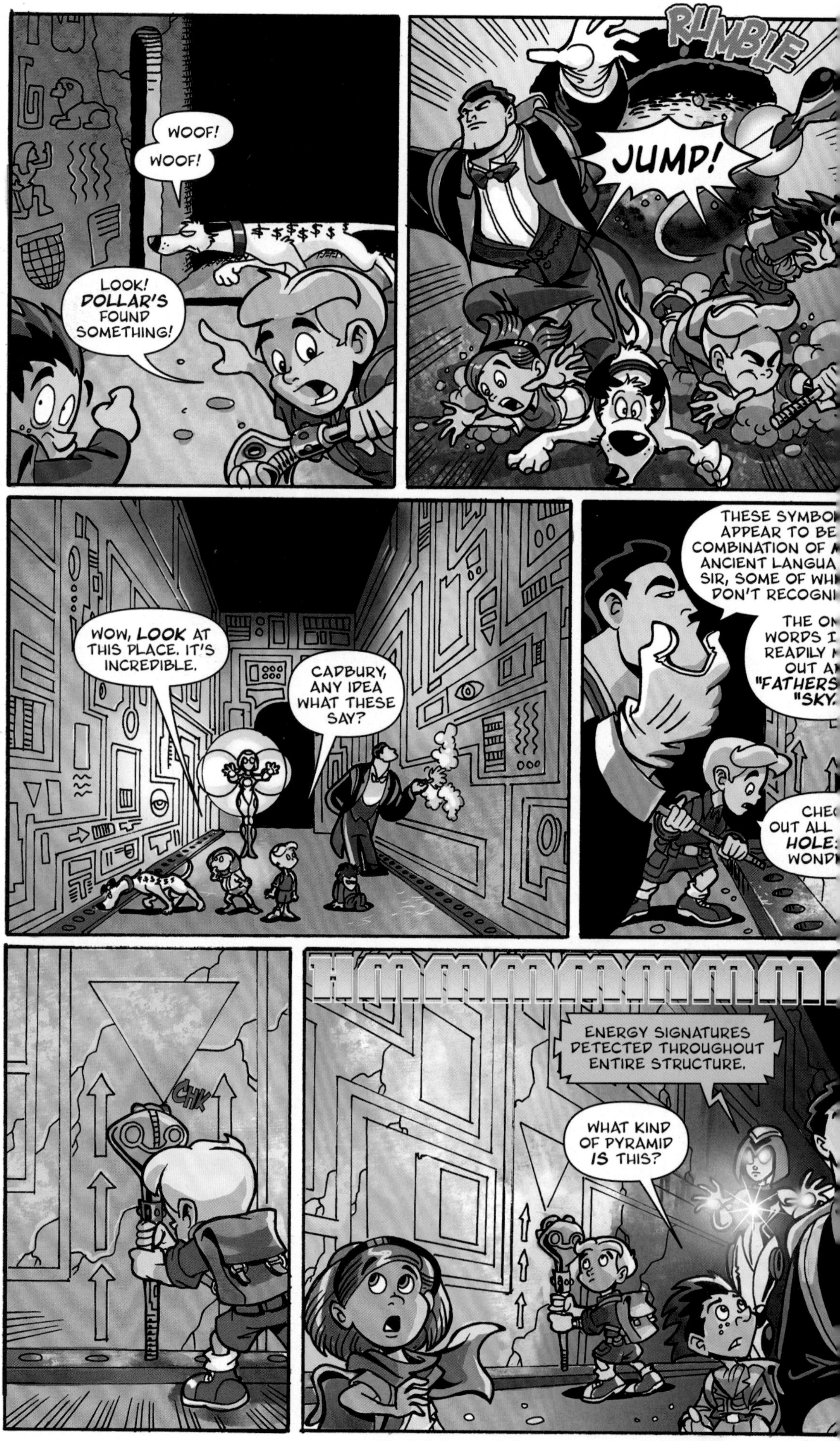

WOOF!
WOOF!
LOOK! **DOLLAR'S** FOUND SOMETHING!
RUMBLE
JUMP!
WOW, **LOOK** AT THIS PLACE. IT'S INCREDIBLE.
CADBURY, ANY IDEA WHAT THESE SAY?
THESE SYMBO APPEAR TO BE COMBINATION OF ANCIENT LANGUA SIR, SOME OF WHI DON'T RECOGNI
THE ON WORDS I READILY M OUT A **"FATHERS "SKY.**
CHE OUT ALL **HOLE** WOND
CHK
ENERGY SIGNATURES DETECTED THROUGHOUT ENTIRE STRUCTURE.
WHAT KIND OF PYRAMID **IS** THIS?

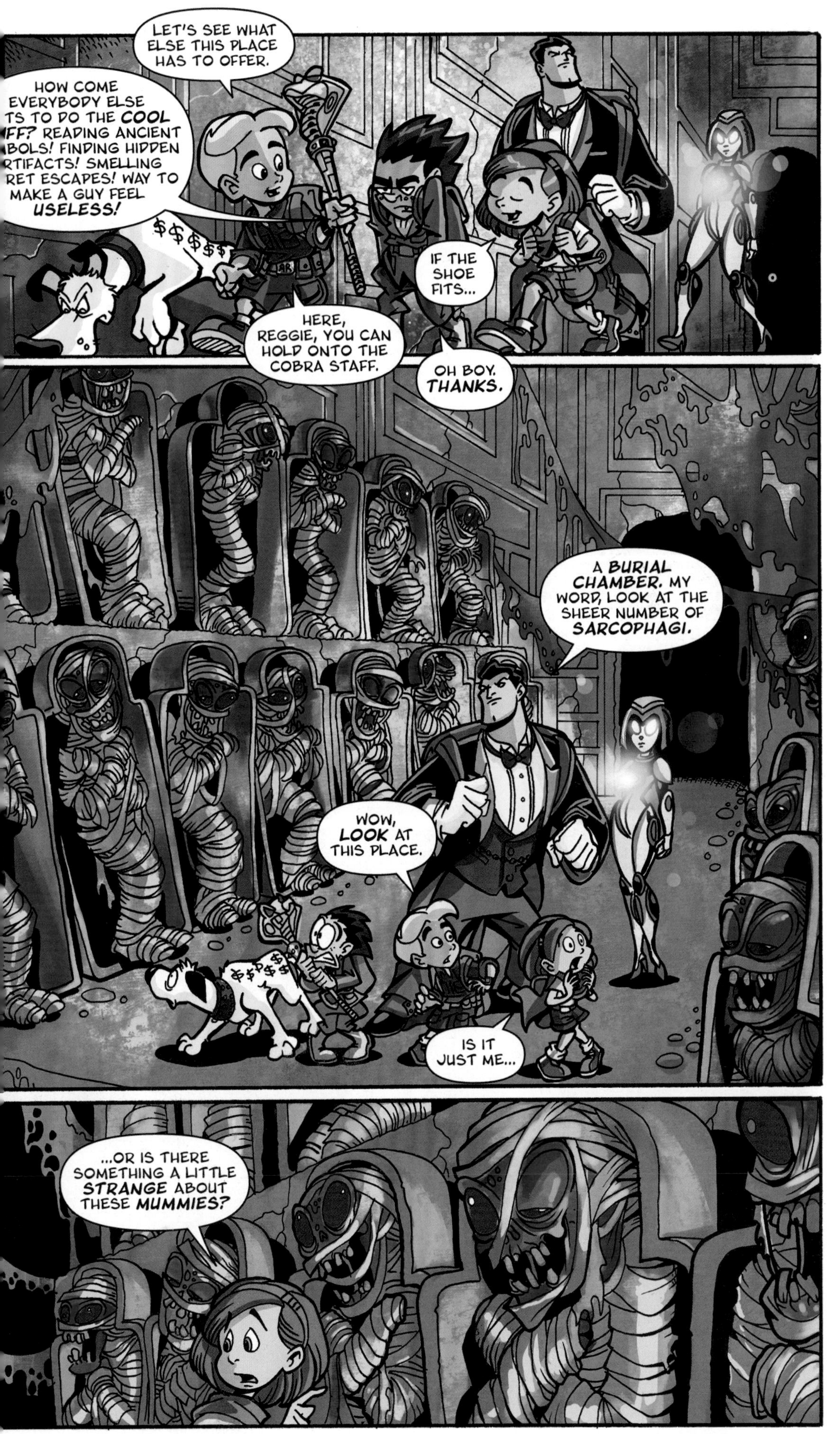

LET'S SEE WHAT ELSE THIS PLACE HAS TO OFFER.
HOW COME EVERYBODY ELSE TS TO DO THE COOL FF? READING ANCIENT BOLS! FINDING HIDDEN RTIFACTS! SMELLING RET ESCAPES! WAY TO MAKE A GUY FEEL USELESS!
IF THE SHOE FITS...
HERE, REGGIE, YOU CAN HOLD ONTO THE COBRA STAFF.
OH BOY. THANKS.
A BURIAL CHAMBER. MY WORD, LOOK AT THE SHEER NUMBER OF SARCOPHAGI.
WOW, LOOK AT THIS PLACE.
IS IT JUST ME...
...OR IS THERE SOMETHING A LITTLE STRANGE ABOUT THESE MUMMIES?

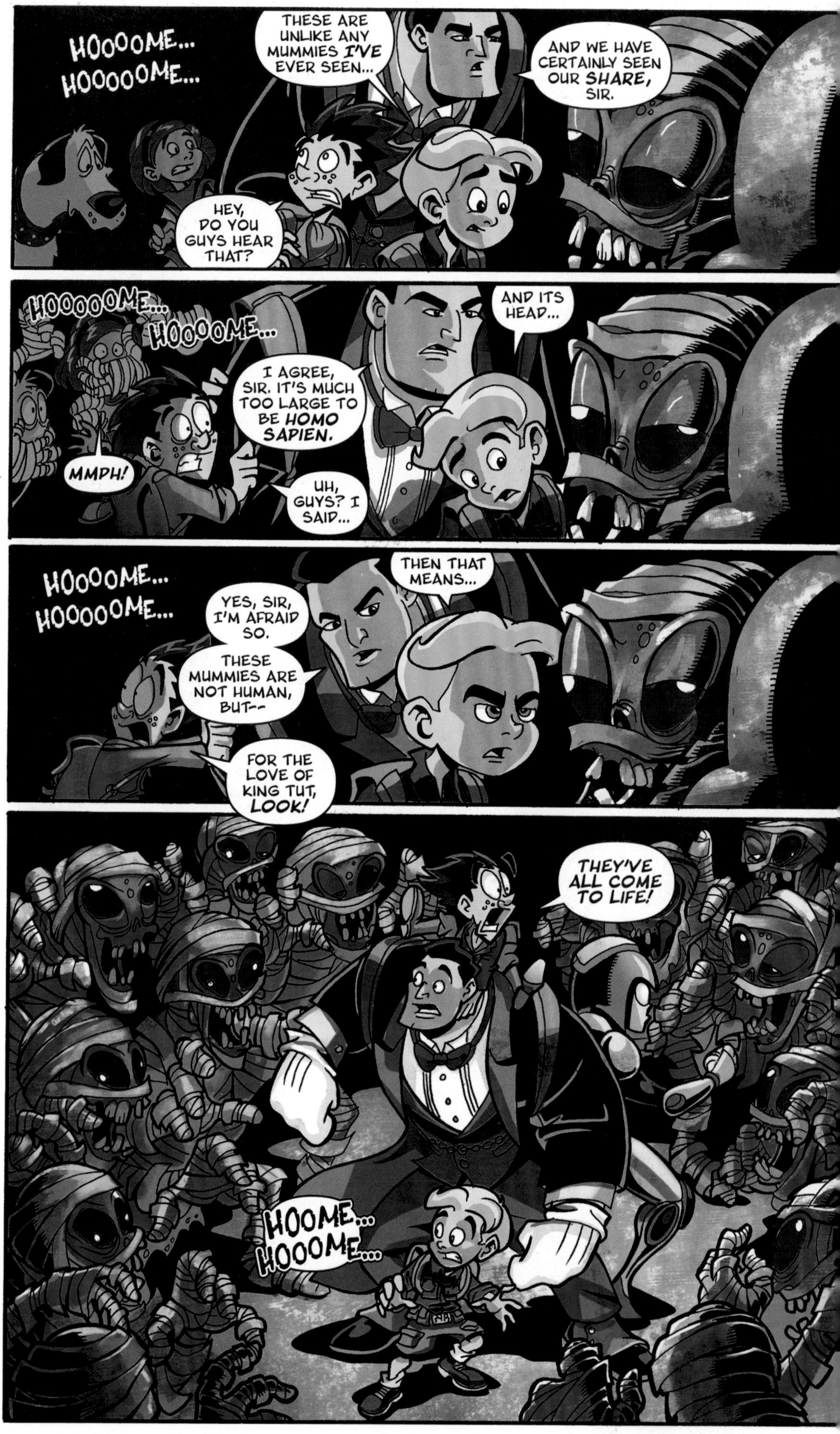
HOOOOME...
HOOOOOME...
THESE ARE UNLIKE ANY MUMMIES I'VE EVER SEEN...
AND WE HAVE CERTAINLY SEEN OUR SHARE, SIR.
HEY, DO YOU GUYS HEAR THAT?
HOOOOOME...
HOOOOME...
AND ITS HEAD...
I AGREE, SIR. IT'S MUCH TOO LARGE TO BE HOMO SAPIEN.
MMPH!
UH, GUYS? I SAID...
HOOOOME...
HOOOOOME...
THEN THAT MEANS...
YES, SIR, I'M AFRAID SO.
THESE MUMMIES ARE NOT HUMAN, BUT--
FOR THE LOVE OF KING TUT, LOOK!
THEY'VE ALL COME TO LIFE!
HOOME...
HOOOME...

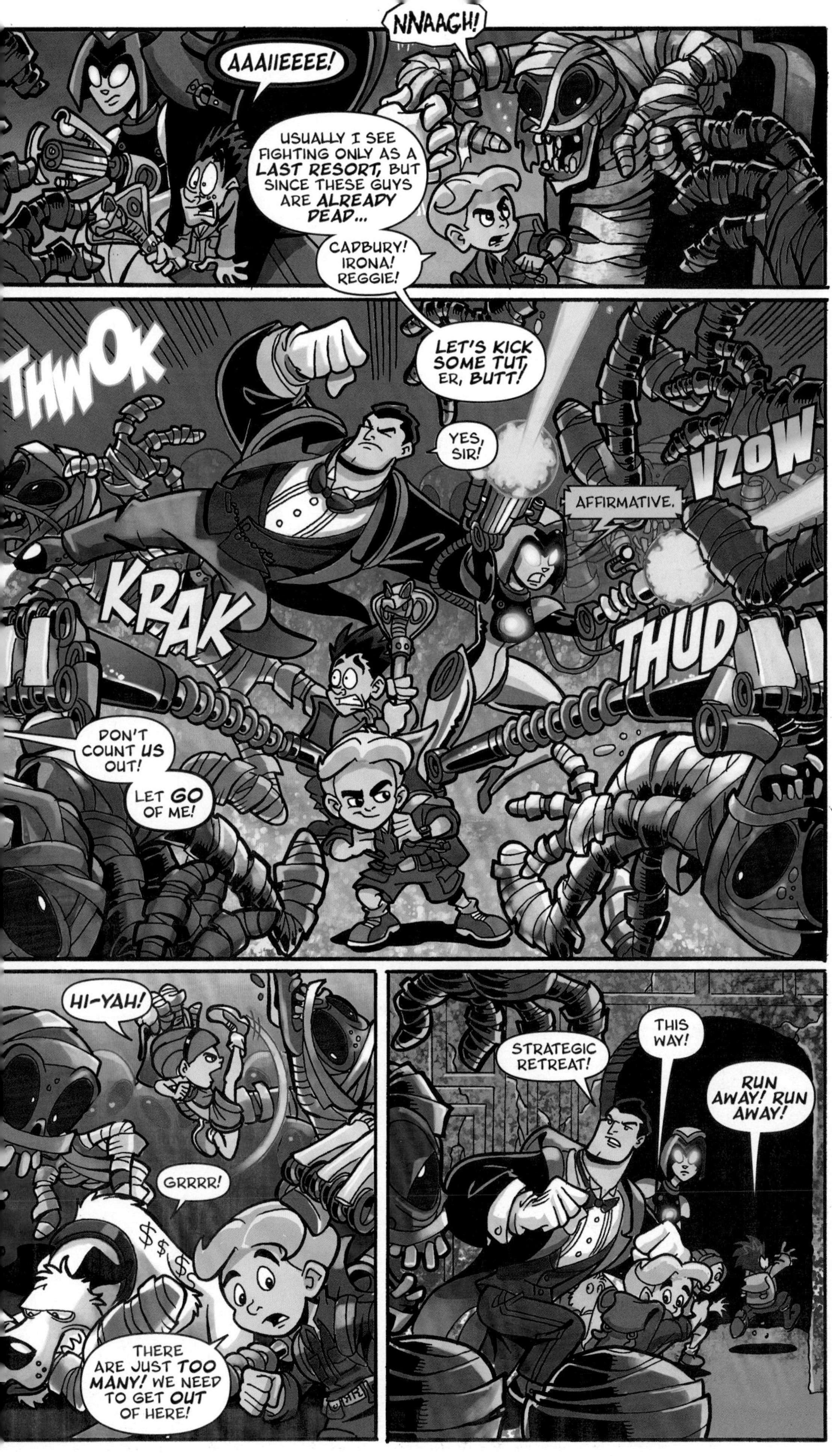
NNAAGH!
AAAIIEEEE!
USUALLY I SEE FIGHTING ONLY AS A LAST RESORT, BUT SINCE THESE GUYS ARE ALREADY DEAD...
CADBURY! IRONA! REGGIE!
LET'S KICK SOME TUT, ER, BUTT!
THWOK
YES, SIR!
VZOW
AFFIRMATIVE.
KRAK
THUD
DON'T COUNT US OUT!
LET GO OF ME!
HI-YAH!
GRRRR!
THERE ARE JUST TOO MANY! WE NEED TO GET OUT OF HERE!
STRATEGIC RETREAT!
THIS WAY!
RUN AWAY! RUN AWAY!

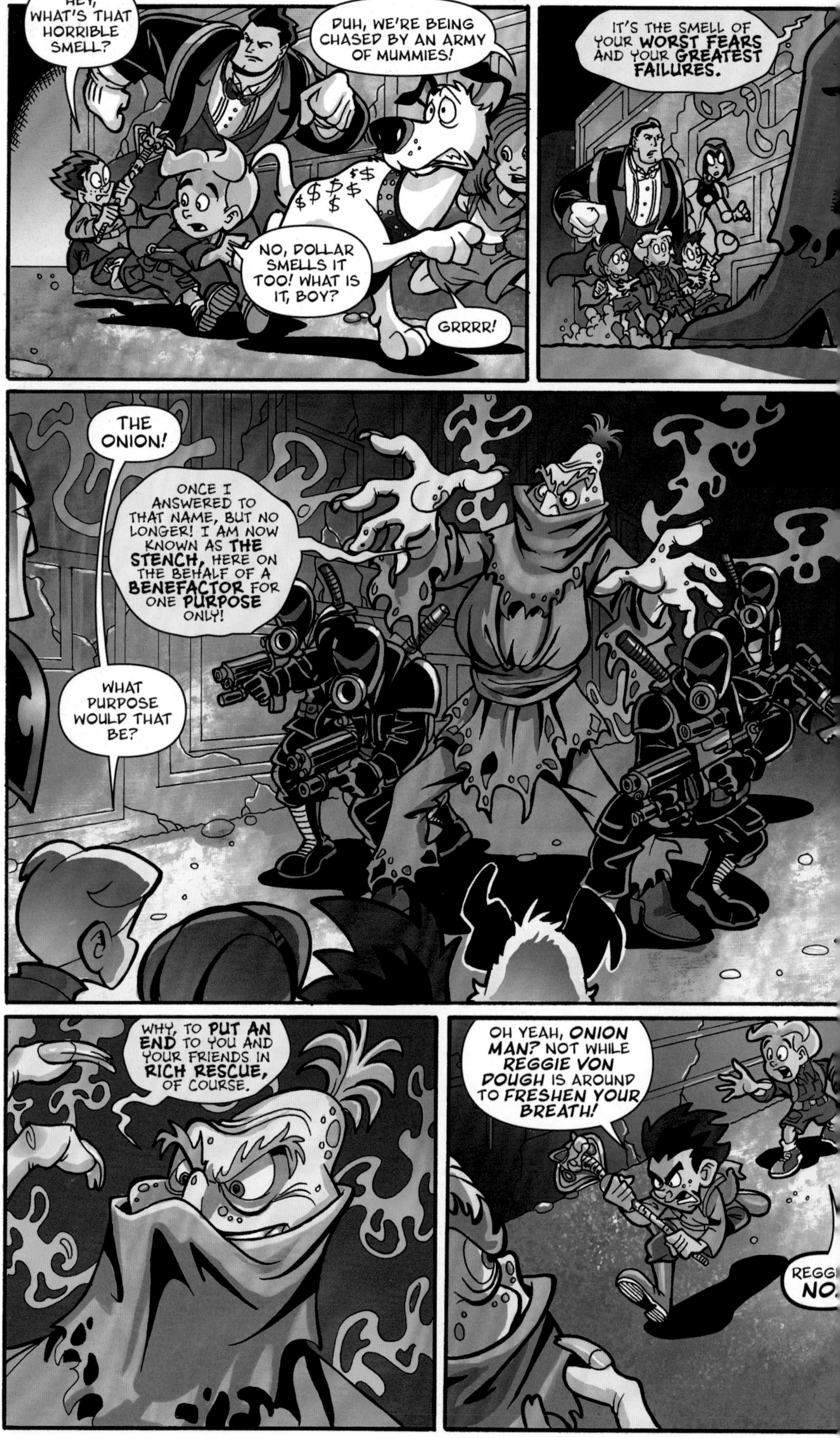
HEY, WHAT'S THAT HORRIBLE SMELL?
DUH, WE'RE BEING CHASED BY AN ARMY OF MUMMIES!
NO, DOLLAR SMELLS IT TOO! WHAT IS IT, BOY?
GRRRR!
IT'S THE SMELL OF YOUR WORST FEARS AND YOUR GREATEST FAILURES.
THE ONION!
ONCE I ANSWERED TO THAT NAME, BUT NO LONGER! I AM NOW KNOWN AS THE STENCH, HERE ON THE BEHALF OF A BENEFACTOR FOR ONE PURPOSE ONLY!
WHAT PURPOSE WOULD THAT BE?
WHY, TO PUT AN END TO YOU AND YOUR FRIENDS IN RICH RESCUE, OF COURSE.
OH YEAH, ONION MAN? NOT WHILE REGGIE VON DOUGH IS AROUND TO FRESHEN YOUR BREATH!

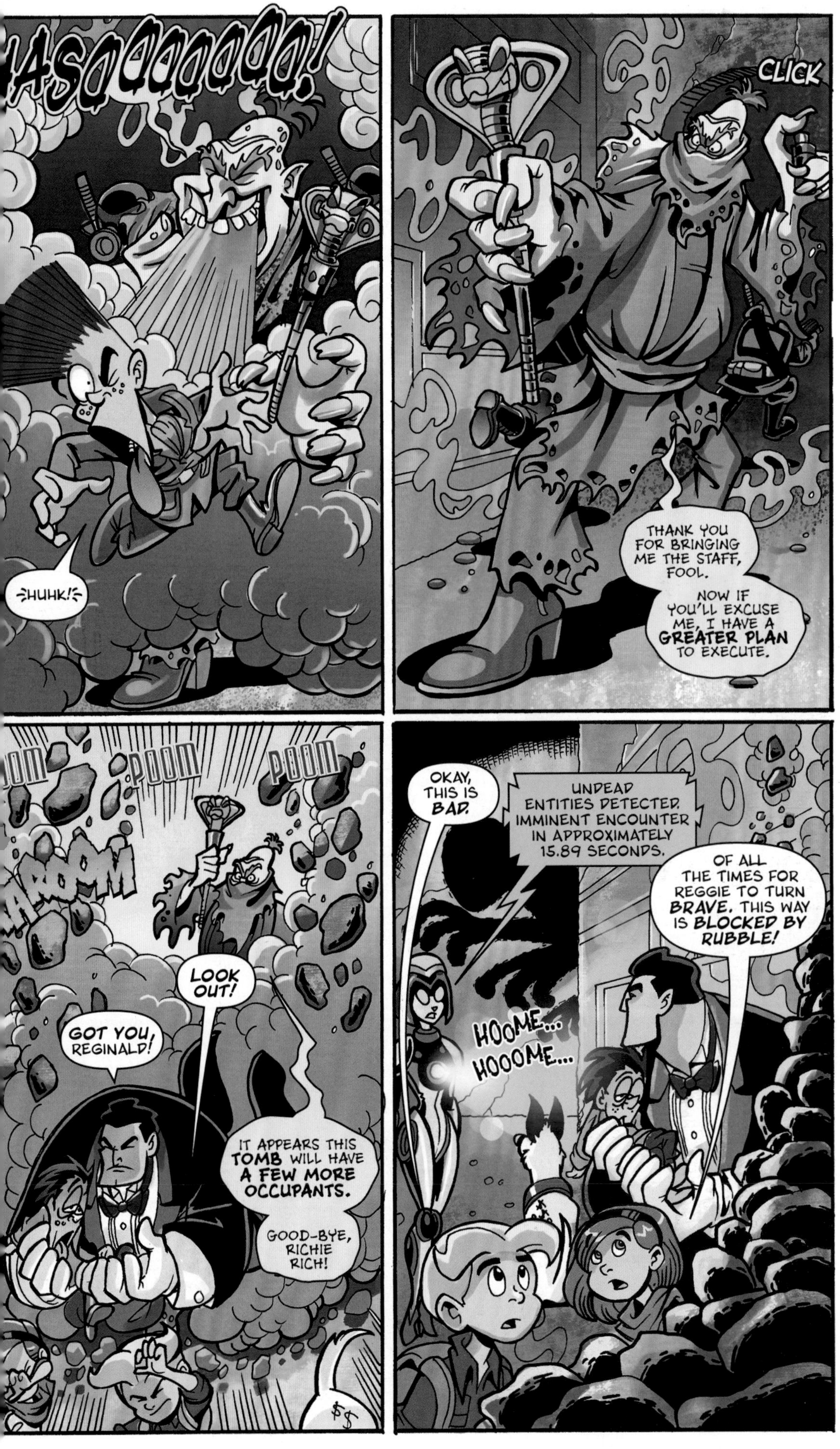
HUHK!
CLICK
THANK YOU FOR BRINGING ME THE STAFF, FOOL.
NOW IF YOU'LL EXCUSE ME, I HAVE A **GREATER PLAN** TO EXECUTE.
POOM
POOM
LOOK OUT!
GOT YOU, REGINALD!
IT APPEARS THIS **TOMB** WILL HAVE **A FEW MORE OCCUPANTS.**
GOOD-BYE, RICHIE RICH!
OKAY, THIS IS **BAD.**
UNDEAD ENTITIES DETECTED. IMMINENT ENCOUNTER IN APPROXIMATELY 15.89 SECONDS.
OF ALL THE TIMES FOR REGGIE TO TURN **BRAVE.** THIS WAY IS **BLOCKED BY RUBBLE!**
HOOME... HOOOME...

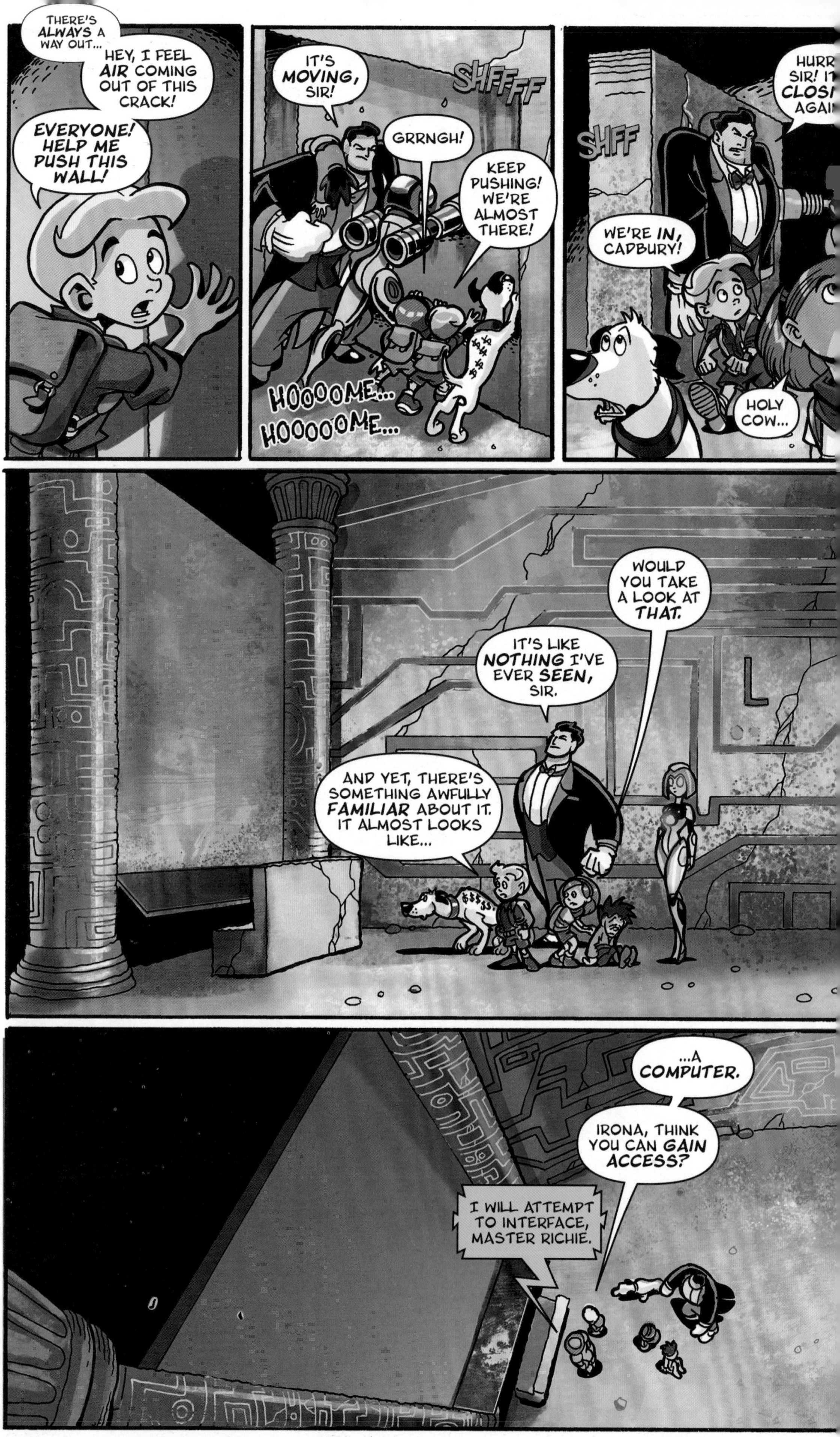

THERE'S ALWAYS A WAY OUT...
HEY, I FEEL AIR COMING OUT OF THIS CRACK!
EVERYONE! HELP ME PUSH THIS WALL!
IT'S MOVING, SIR!
SHFFFF
GRRNGH!
KEEP PUSHING! WE'RE ALMOST THERE!
HOOOOME...
HOOOOOME...
SHFF
HURR SIR! IT CLOSI AGAI
WE'RE IN, CADBURY!
HOLY COW...
WOULD YOU TAKE A LOOK AT THAT.
IT'S LIKE NOTHING I'VE EVER SEEN, SIR.
AND YET, THERE'S SOMETHING AWFULLY FAMILIAR ABOUT IT. IT ALMOST LOOKS LIKE...
...A COMPUTER.
IRONA, THINK YOU CAN GAIN ACCESS?
I WILL ATTEMPT TO INTERFACE, MASTER RICHIE.

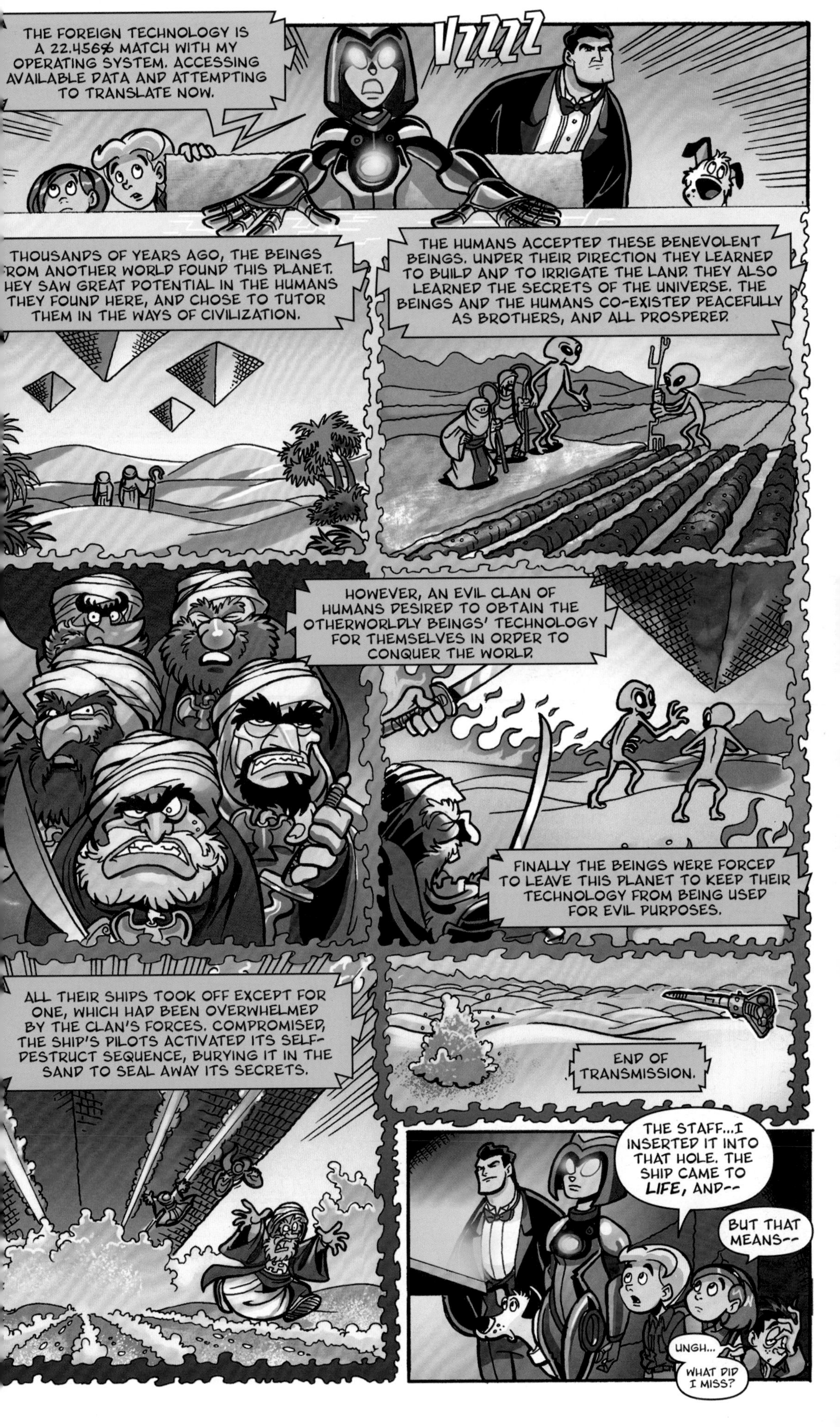
THE FOREIGN TECHNOLOGY IS A 22.456% MATCH WITH MY OPERATING SYSTEM. ACCESSING AVAILABLE DATA AND ATTEMPTING TO TRANSLATE NOW.
VZZZZ
THOUSANDS OF YEARS AGO, THE BEINGS FROM ANOTHER WORLD FOUND THIS PLANET. THEY SAW GREAT POTENTIAL IN THE HUMANS THEY FOUND HERE, AND CHOSE TO TUTOR THEM IN THE WAYS OF CIVILIZATION.
THE HUMANS ACCEPTED THESE BENEVOLENT BEINGS. UNDER THEIR DIRECTION THEY LEARNED TO BUILD AND TO IRRIGATE THE LAND. THEY ALSO LEARNED THE SECRETS OF THE UNIVERSE. THE BEINGS AND THE HUMANS CO-EXISTED PEACEFULLY AS BROTHERS, AND ALL PROSPERED.
HOWEVER, AN EVIL CLAN OF HUMANS DESIRED TO OBTAIN THE OTHERWORLDLY BEINGS' TECHNOLOGY FOR THEMSELVES IN ORDER TO CONQUER THE WORLD.
FINALLY THE BEINGS WERE FORCED TO LEAVE THIS PLANET TO KEEP THEIR TECHNOLOGY FROM BEING USED FOR EVIL PURPOSES.
ALL THEIR SHIPS TOOK OFF EXCEPT FOR ONE, WHICH HAD BEEN OVERWHELMED BY THE CLAN'S FORCES. COMPROMISED, THE SHIP'S PILOTS ACTIVATED ITS SELF-DESTRUCT SEQUENCE, BURYING IT IN THE SAND TO SEAL AWAY ITS SECRETS.
END OF TRANSMISSION.
THE STAFF...I INSERTED IT INTO THAT HOLE. THE SHIP CAME TO LIFE, AND--
BUT THAT MEANS--
UNGH...
WHAT DID I MISS?

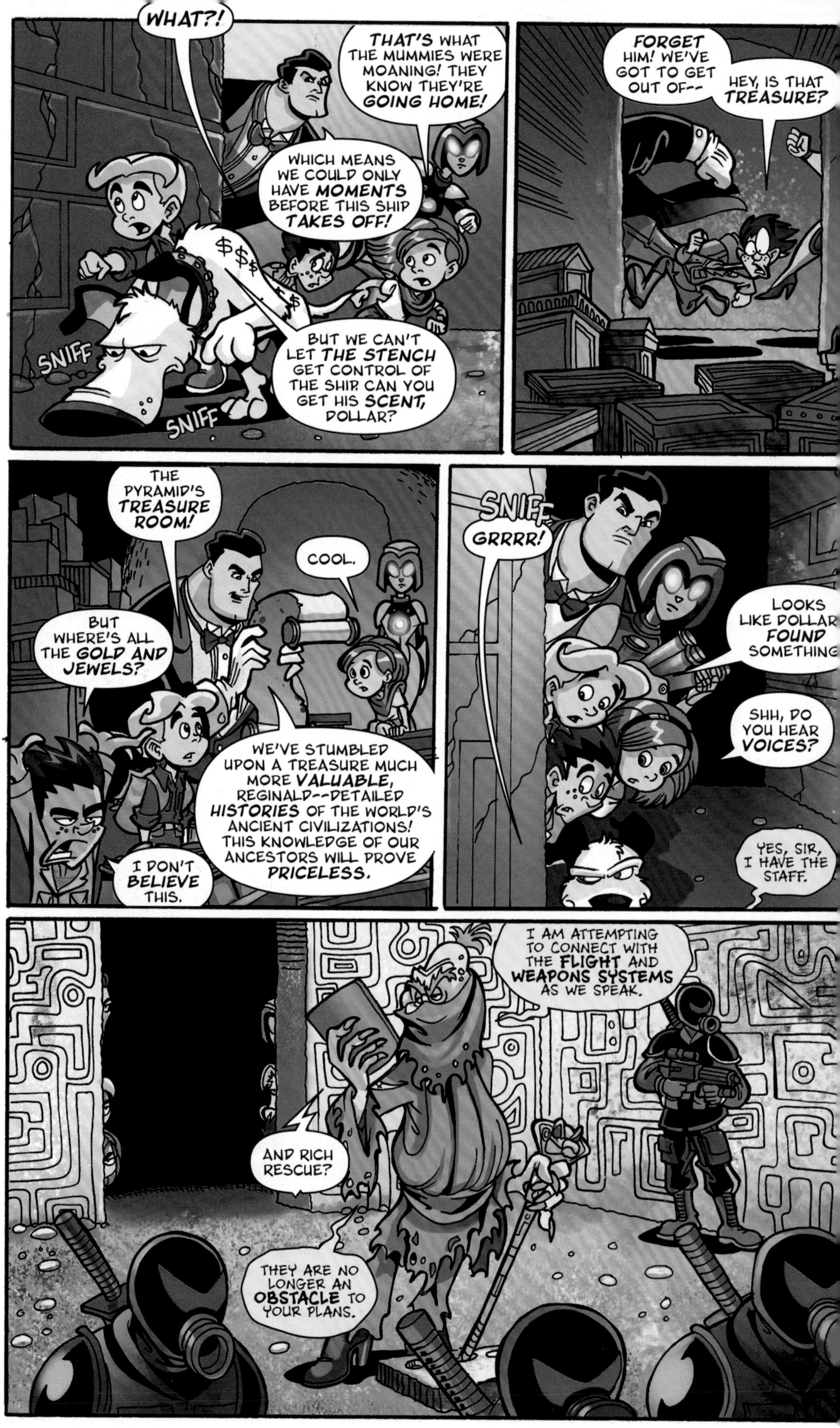
WHAT?!
THAT'S WHAT THE MUMMIES WERE MOANING! THEY KNOW THEY'RE GOING HOME!
WHICH MEANS WE COULD ONLY HAVE MOMENTS BEFORE THIS SHIP TAKES OFF!
SNIFF
SNIFF
BUT WE CAN'T LET THE STENCH GET CONTROL OF THE SHIP. CAN YOU GET HIS SCENT, DOLLAR?
FORGET HIM! WE'VE GOT TO GET OUT OF--
HEY, IS THAT TREASURE?
THE PYRAMID'S TREASURE ROOM!
COOL.
BUT WHERE'S ALL THE GOLD AND JEWELS?
WE'VE STUMBLED UPON A TREASURE MUCH MORE VALUABLE, REGINALD--DETAILED HISTORIES OF THE WORLD'S ANCIENT CIVILIZATIONS! THIS KNOWLEDGE OF OUR ANCESTORS WILL PROVE PRICELESS.
I DON'T BELIEVE THIS.
SNIFF
GRRRR!
LOOKS LIKE DOLLAR FOUND SOMETHING
SHH, DO YOU HEAR VOICES?
YES, SIR, I HAVE THE STAFF.
I AM ATTEMPTING TO CONNECT WITH THE FLIGHT AND WEAPONS SYSTEMS AS WE SPEAK.
AND RICH RESCUE?
THEY ARE NO LONGER AN OBSTACLE TO YOUR PLANS.

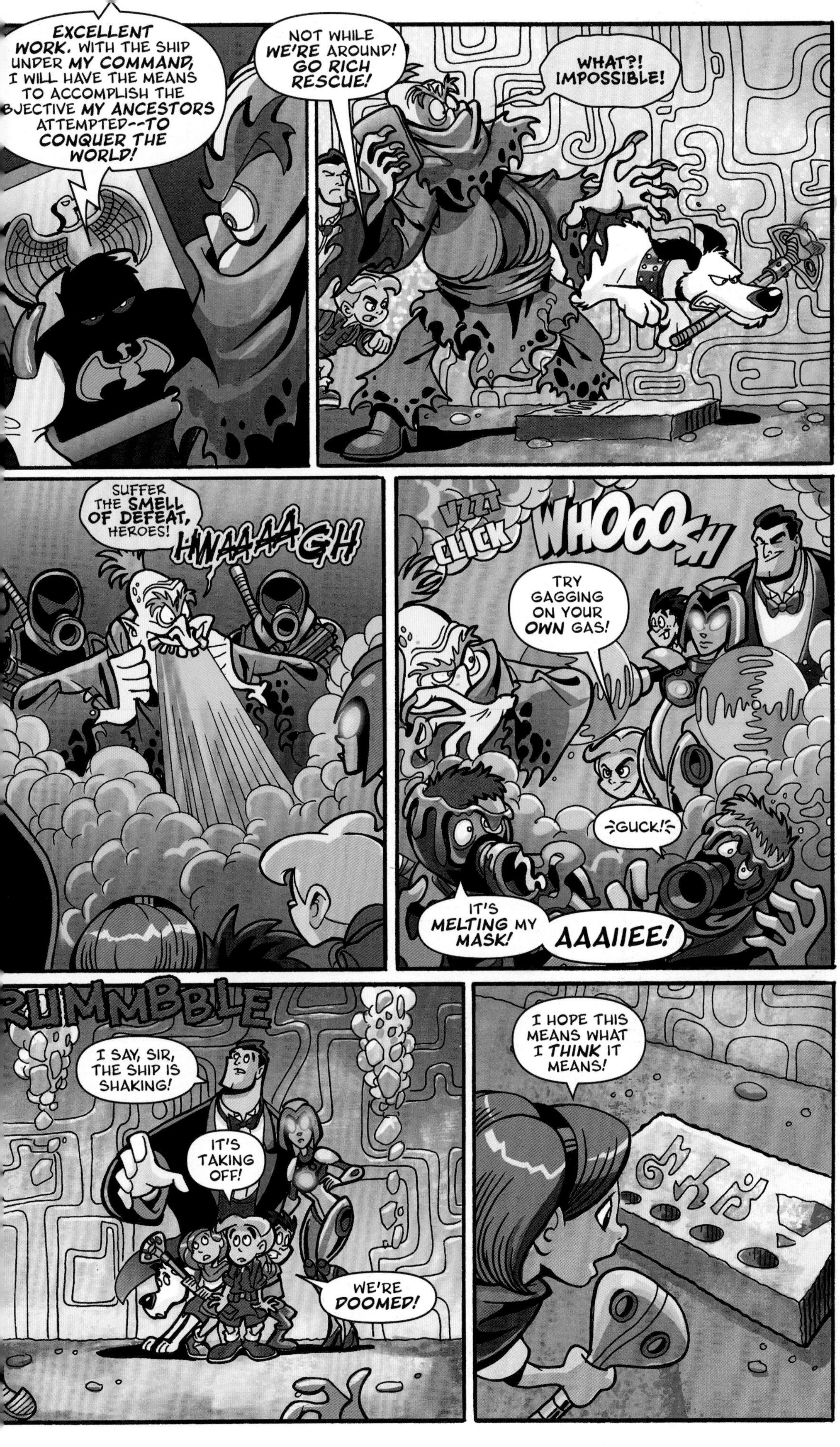
EXCELLENT WORK. WITH THE SHIP UNDER MY COMMAND, I WILL HAVE THE MEANS TO ACCOMPLISH THE BJECTIVE MY ANCESTORS ATTEMPTED--TO CONQUER THE WORLD!
NOT WHILE WE'RE AROUND! GO RICH RESCUE!
WHAT?! IMPOSSIBLE!
SUFFER THE SMELL OF DEFEAT, HEROES!
HWAAAAGH
VZZT
CLICK
WHOOOOSH
TRY GAGGING ON YOUR OWN GAS!
GUCK!
IT'S MELTING MY MASK!
AAAIIEE!
RUMMBBLE
I SAY, SIR, THE SHIP IS SHAKING!
IT'S TAKING OFF!
WE'RE DOOMED!
I HOPE THIS MEANS WHAT I THINK IT MEANS!

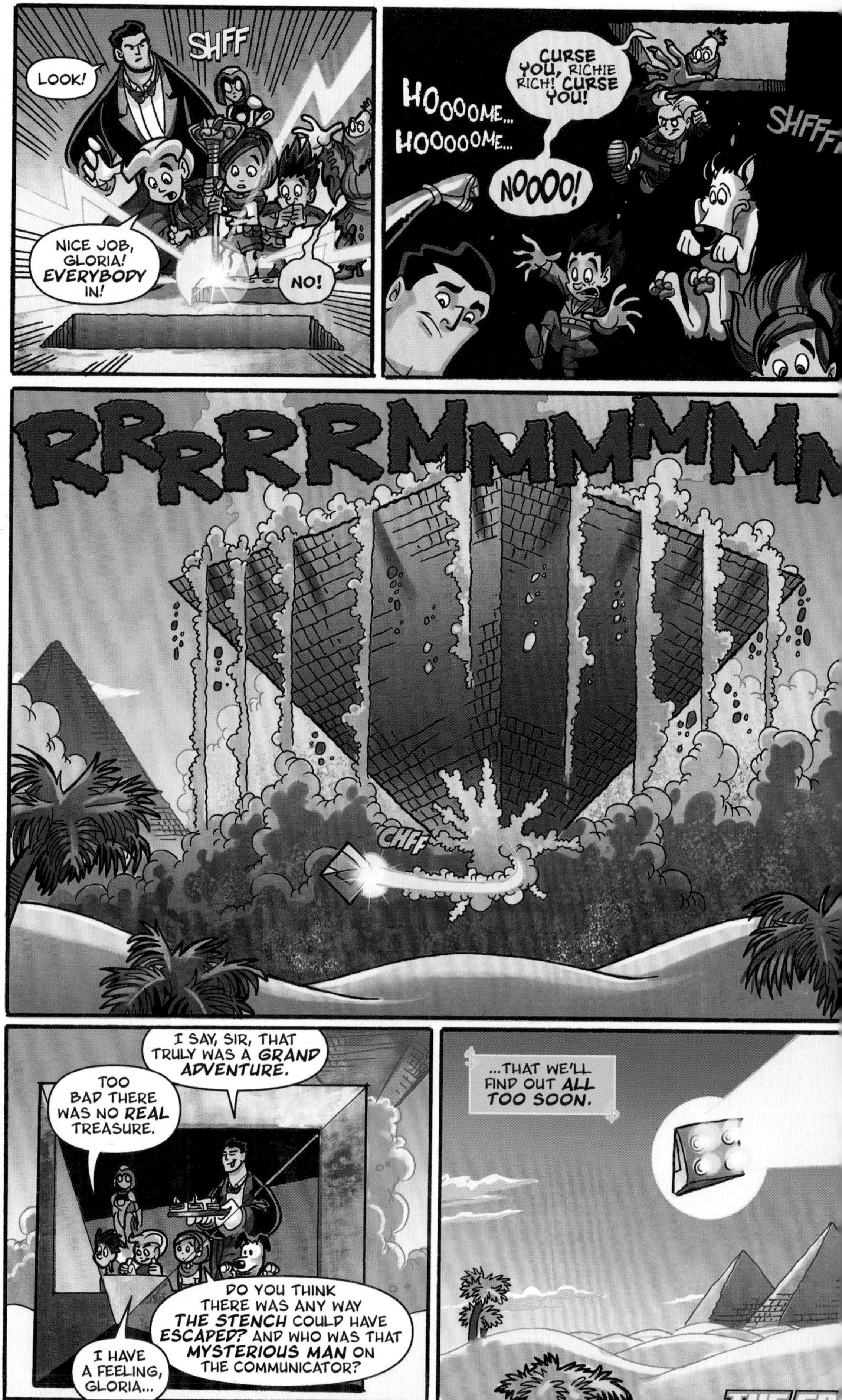

SHFF
LOOK!
NICE JOB, GLORIA! EVERYBODY IN!
NO!
HOOOOME... HOOOOOME...
CURSE YOU, RICHIE RICH! CURSE YOU!
NOOOO!
SHFFF
RRRRRMMMMMM
CHFF
I SAY, SIR, THAT TRULY WAS A GRAND ADVENTURE.
TOO BAD THERE WAS NO REAL TREASURE.
DO YOU THINK THERE WAS ANY WAY THE STENCH COULD HAVE ESCAPED? AND WHO WAS THAT MYSTERIOUS MAN ON THE COMMUNICATOR?
I HAVE A FEELING, GLORIA...
...THAT WE'LL FIND OUT ALL TOO SOON.

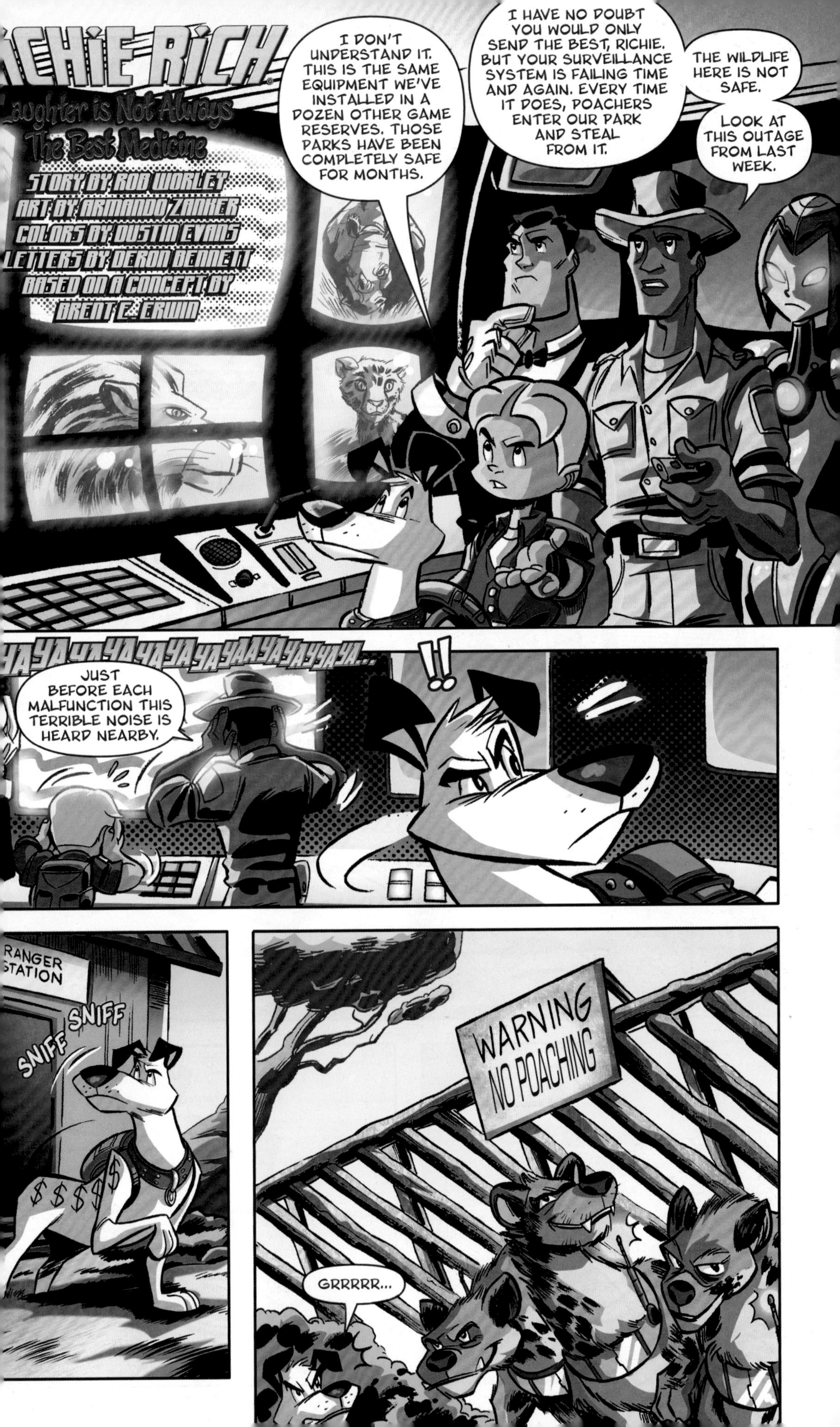
CHIE RICH
Laughter is Not Always The Best Medicine
STORY BY ROB WORLEY
ART BY ARMANDO ZANKER
COLORS BY DUSTIN EVANS
LETTERS BY DERON BENNETT
BASED ON A CONCEPT BY
BRENT E. ERWIN
I DON'T UNDERSTAND IT. THIS IS THE SAME EQUIPMENT WE'VE INSTALLED IN A DOZEN OTHER GAME RESERVES. THOSE PARKS HAVE BEEN COMPLETELY SAFE FOR MONTHS.
I HAVE NO DOUBT YOU WOULD ONLY SEND THE BEST, RICHIE. BUT YOUR SURVEILLANCE SYSTEM IS FAILING TIME AND AGAIN. EVERY TIME IT DOES, POACHERS ENTER OUR PARK AND STEAL FROM IT.
THE WILDLIFE HERE IS NOT SAFE.
LOOK AT THIS OUTAGE FROM LAST WEEK.
JUST BEFORE EACH MALFUNCTION THIS TERRIBLE NOISE IS HEARD NEARBY.
!!
RANGER STATION
SNIFF SNIFF
WARNING NO POACHING
GRRRRR...

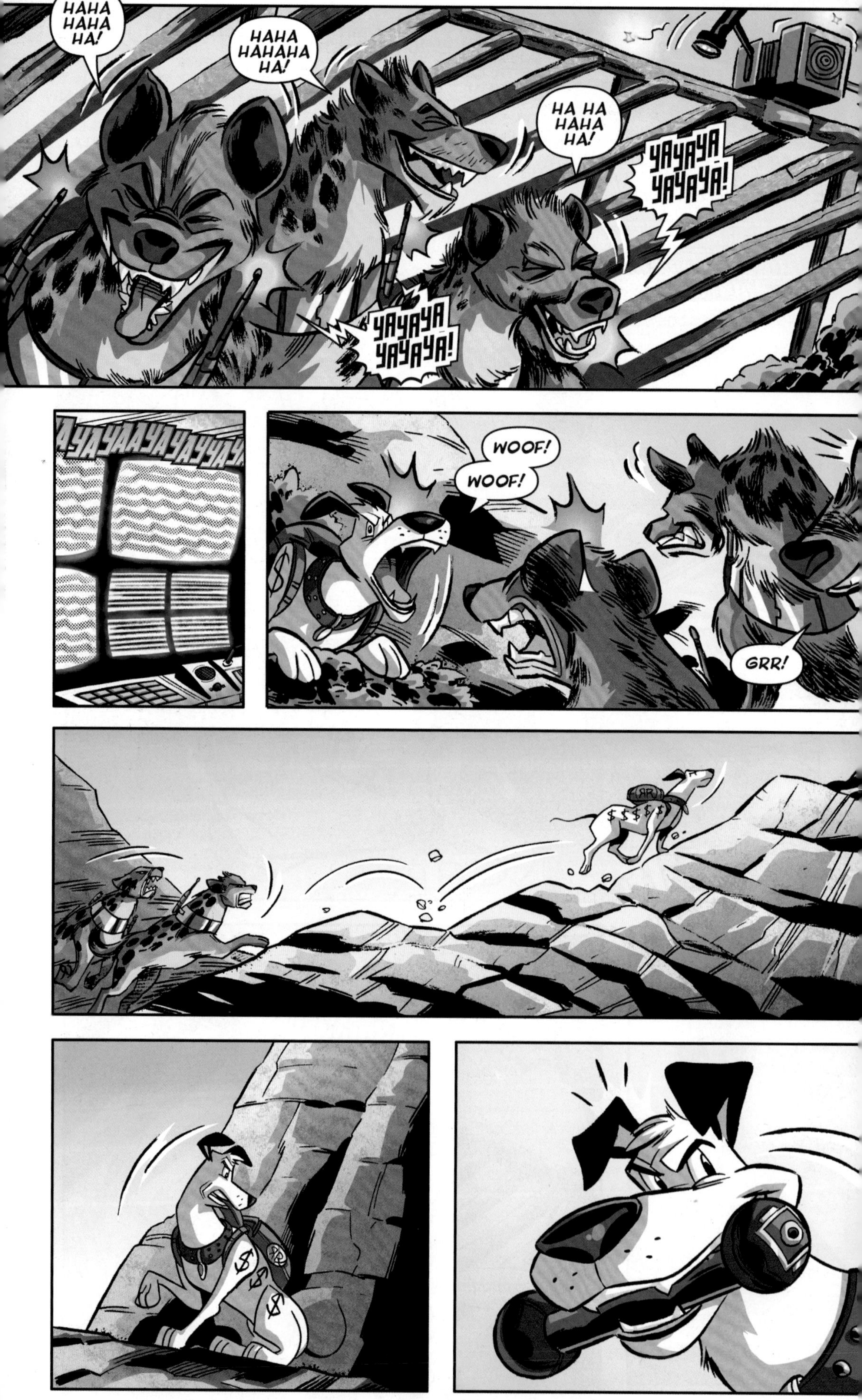
HAHA HAHAHA HA!
HAHA HAHAHA HA!
HA HA HAHA HA!
YAYAYA YAYAYA!
YAYAYA YAYAYA!
YAYAAYAYAYYAYA
WOOF!
WOOF!
GRR!

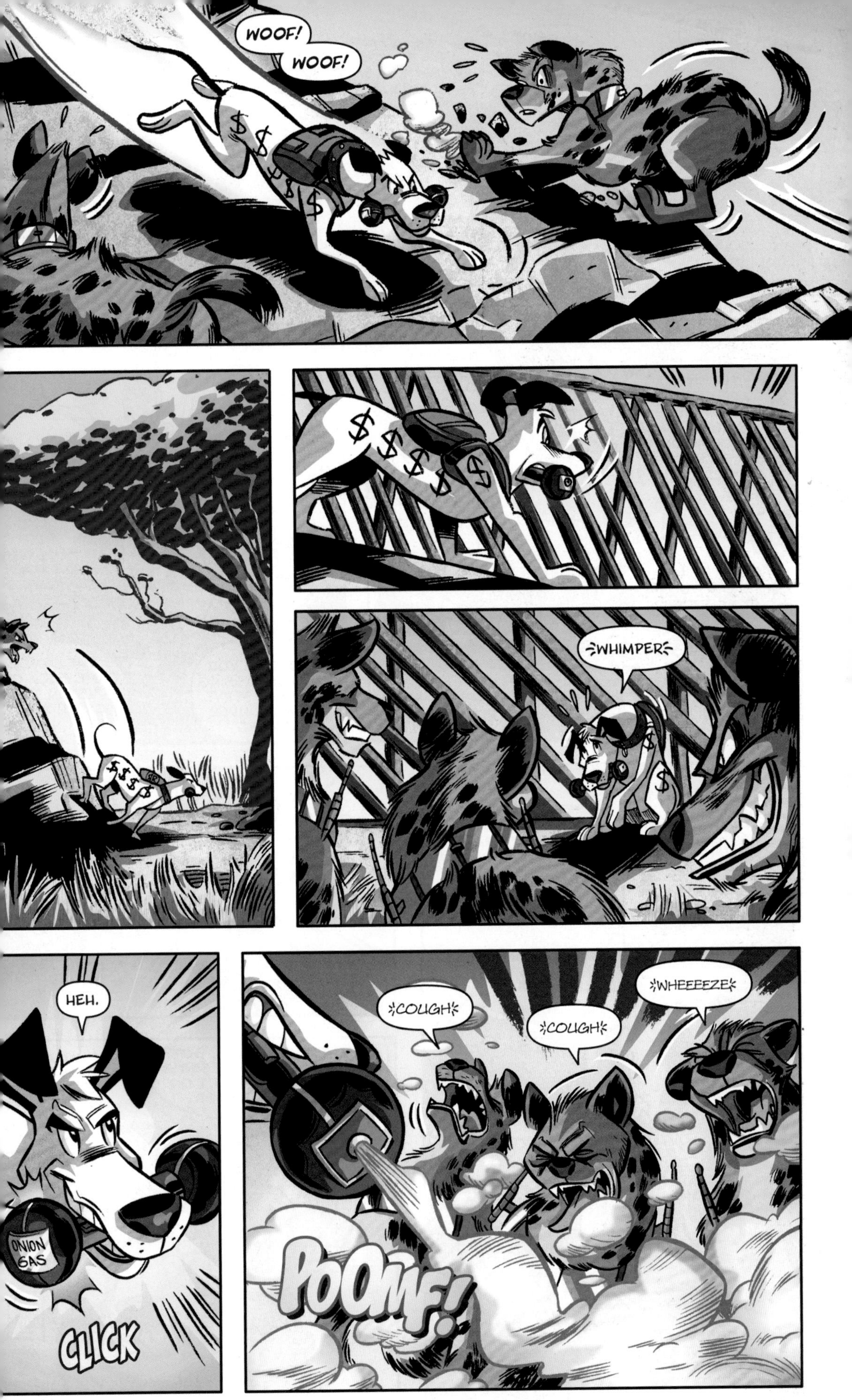
WOOF!
WOOF!
WHIMPER
HEH.
ONION GAS
CLICK
COUGH
COUGH
WHEEEEZE
POOMF!

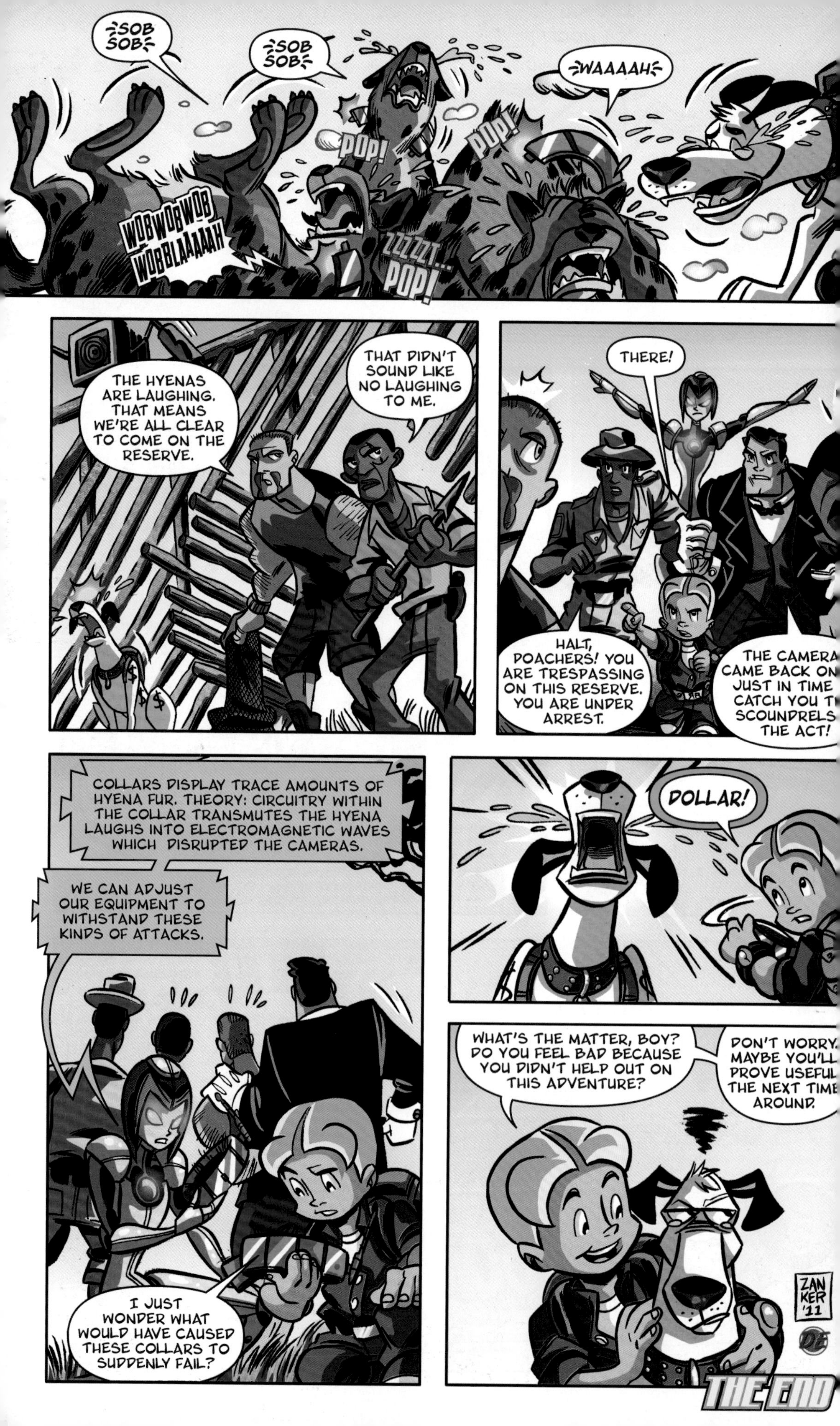
SOB SOB
SOB SOB
WAAAAH
POP!
POP!
WOBWOBWOB WOBBLAAAAAH
ZZZZZT... POP!
THE HYENAS ARE LAUGHING. THAT MEANS WE'RE ALL CLEAR TO COME ON THE RESERVE.
THAT DIDN'T SOUND LIKE NO LAUGHING TO ME.
THERE!
HALT, POACHERS! YOU ARE TRESPASSING ON THIS RESERVE. YOU ARE UNDER ARREST.
THE CAMERA CAME BACK ON JUST IN TIME CATCH YOU T SCOUNDRELS THE ACT!
COLLARS DISPLAY TRACE AMOUNTS OF HYENA FUR. THEORY: CIRCUITRY WITHIN THE COLLAR TRANSMUTES THE HYENA LAUGHS INTO ELECTROMAGNETIC WAVES WHICH DISRUPTED THE CAMERAS.
WE CAN ADJUST OUR EQUIPMENT TO WITHSTAND THESE KINDS OF ATTACKS.
I JUST WONDER WHAT WOULD HAVE CAUSED THESE COLLARS TO SUDDENLY FAIL?
DOLLAR!
WHAT'S THE MATTER, BOY? DO YOU FEEL BAD BECAUSE YOU DIDN'T HELP OUT ON THIS ADVENTURE?
DON'T WORRY. MAYBE YOU'LL PROVE USEFUL THE NEXT TIME AROUND.
ZANKER '11
THE END

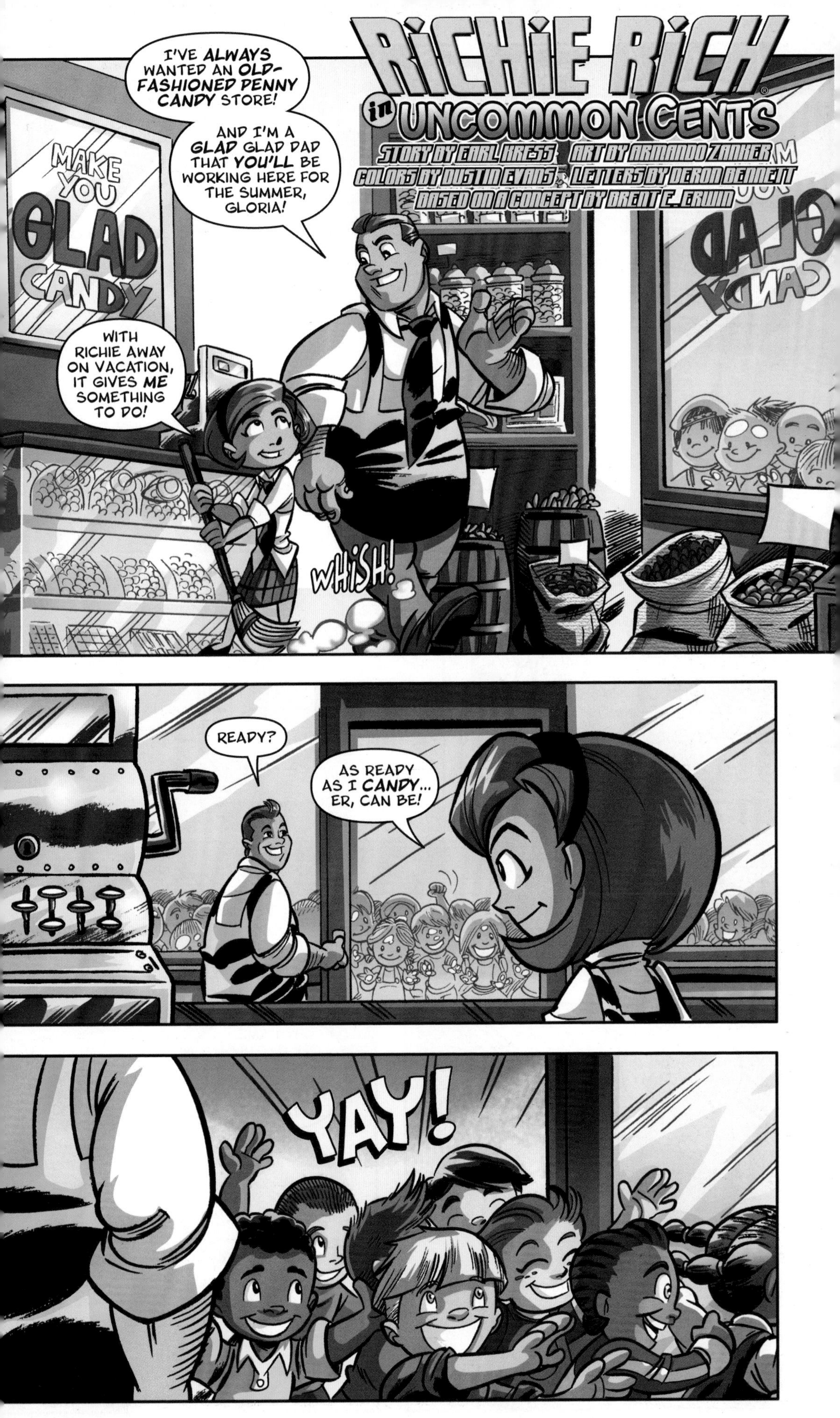
RICHIE RICH®
in UNCOMMON CENTS
STORY BY EARL KRESS ART BY ARMANDO ZANKER
COLORS BY DUSTIN EVANS LETTERS BY DERON BENNETT
BASED ON A CONCEPT BY BRENT E. ERWIN
I'VE ALWAYS WANTED AN OLD-FASHIONED PENNY CANDY STORE!
AND I'M A GLAD GLAD DAD THAT YOU'LL BE WORKING HERE FOR THE SUMMER, GLORIA!
MAKE YOU GLAD CANDY
WITH RICHIE AWAY ON VACATION, IT GIVES ME SOMETHING TO DO!
WHISH!
READY?
AS READY AS I CANDY... ER, CAN BE!
YAY!

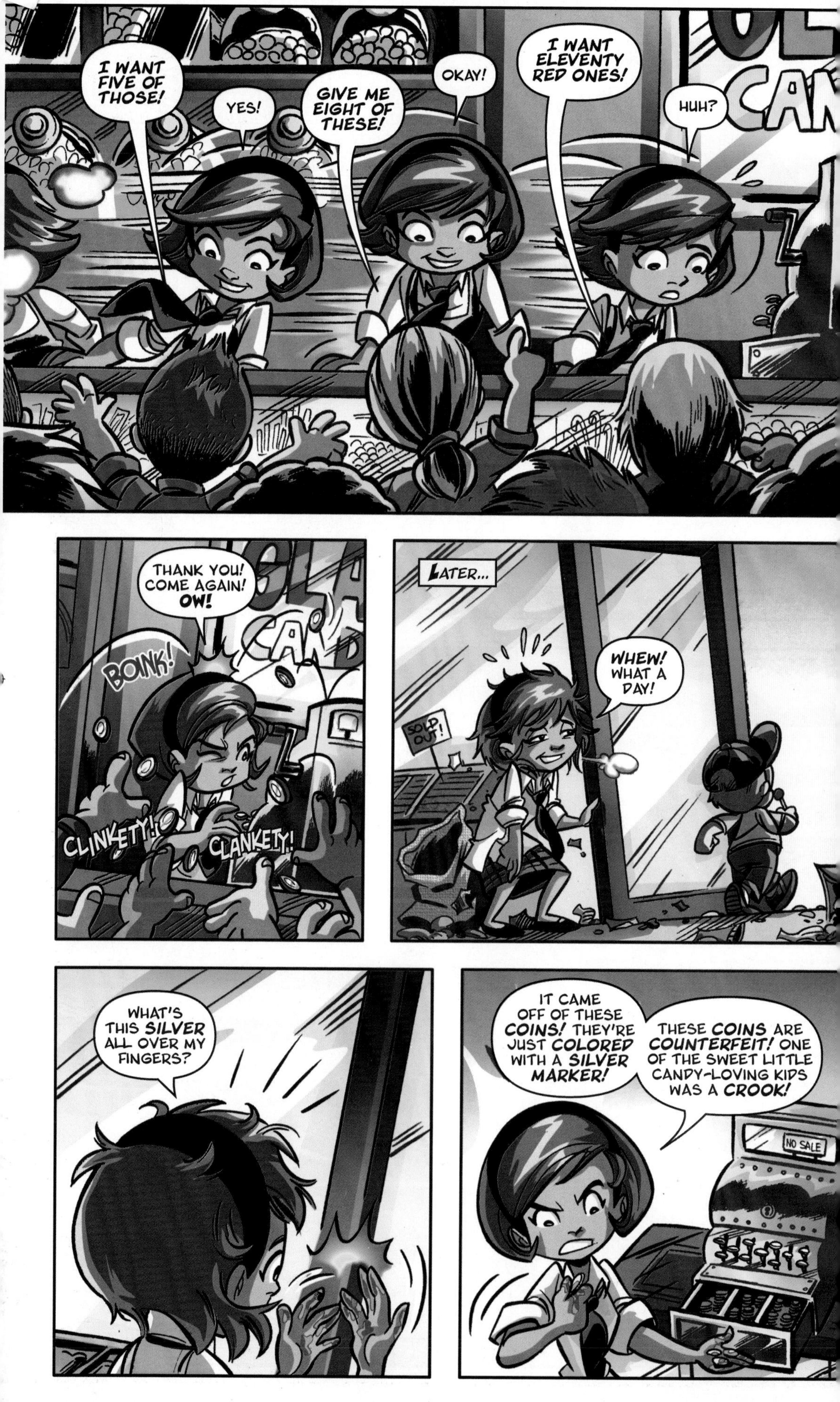
I WANT FIVE OF THOSE!
YES!
GIVE ME EIGHT OF THESE!
OKAY!
I WANT ELEVENTY RED ONES!
HUH?
THANK YOU! COME AGAIN! OW!
BOINK!
CLINKETY!
CLANKETY!
LATER...
WHEW! WHAT A DAY!
SOLD OUT!
WHAT'S THIS SILVER ALL OVER MY FINGERS?
IT CAME OFF OF THESE COINS! THEY'RE JUST COLORED WITH A SILVER MARKER!
THESE COINS ARE COUNTERFEIT! ONE OF THE SWEET LITTLE CANDY-LOVING KIDS WAS A CROOK!
NO SALE

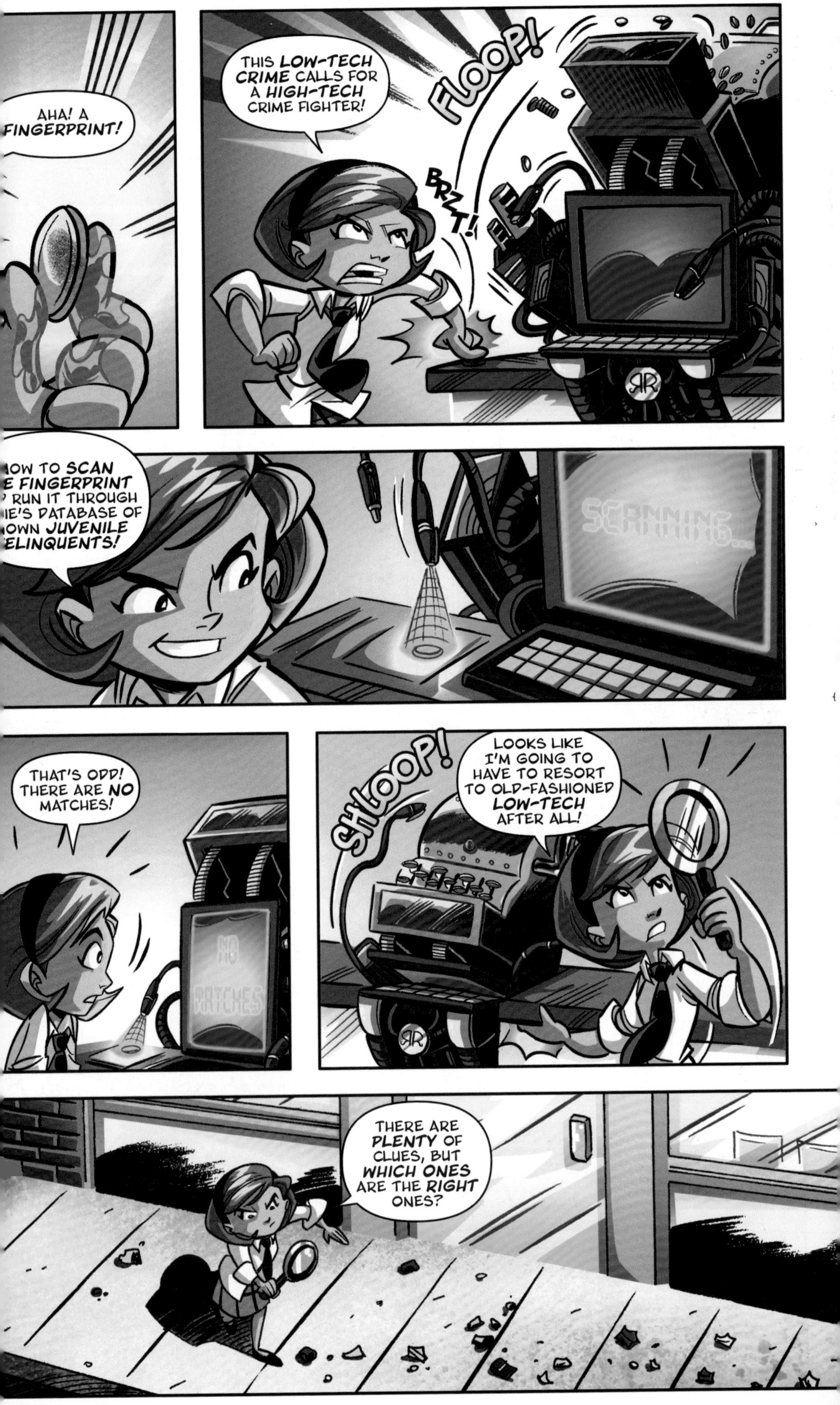
AHA! A FINGERPRINT!
THIS LOW-TECH CRIME CALLS FOR A HIGH-TECH CRIME FIGHTER!
FLOOP!
BRZZT!
OW TO SCAN E FINGERPRINT RUN IT THROUGH IE'S DATABASE OF OWN JUVENILE ELINQUENTS!
SCANNING...
THAT'S ODD! THERE ARE NO MATCHES!
NO MATCHES
SHLOOP!
LOOKS LIKE I'M GOING TO HAVE TO RESORT TO OLD-FASHIONED LOW-TECH AFTER ALL!
THERE ARE PLENTY OF CLUES, BUT WHICH ONES ARE THE RIGHT ONES?

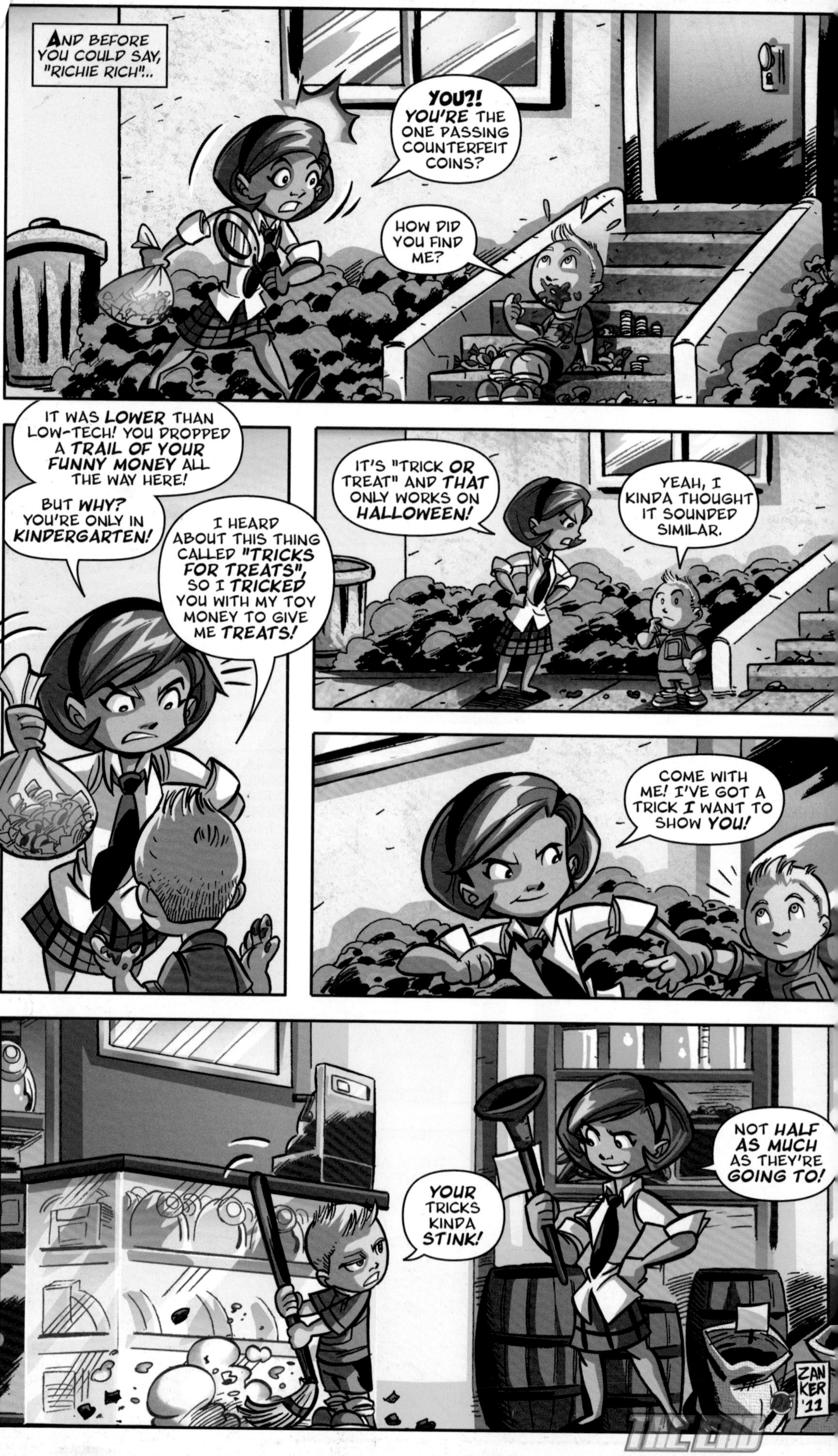

AND BEFORE YOU COULD SAY, "RICHIE RICH"...
YOU?! YOU'RE THE ONE PASSING COUNTERFEIT COINS?
HOW DID YOU FIND ME?
IT WAS LOWER THAN LOW-TECH! YOU DROPPED A TRAIL OF YOUR FUNNY MONEY ALL THE WAY HERE!
BUT WHY? YOU'RE ONLY IN KINDERGARTEN!
I HEARD ABOUT THIS THING CALLED "TRICKS FOR TREATS", SO I TRICKED YOU WITH MY TOY MONEY TO GIVE ME TREATS!
IT'S "TRICK OR TREAT" AND THAT ONLY WORKS ON HALLOWEEN!
YEAH, I KINDA THOUGHT IT SOUNDED SIMILAR.
COME WITH ME! I'VE GOT A TRICK I WANT TO SHOW YOU!
YOUR TRICKS KINDA STINK!
NOT HALF AS MUCH AS THEY'RE GOING TO!
ZANKER '11

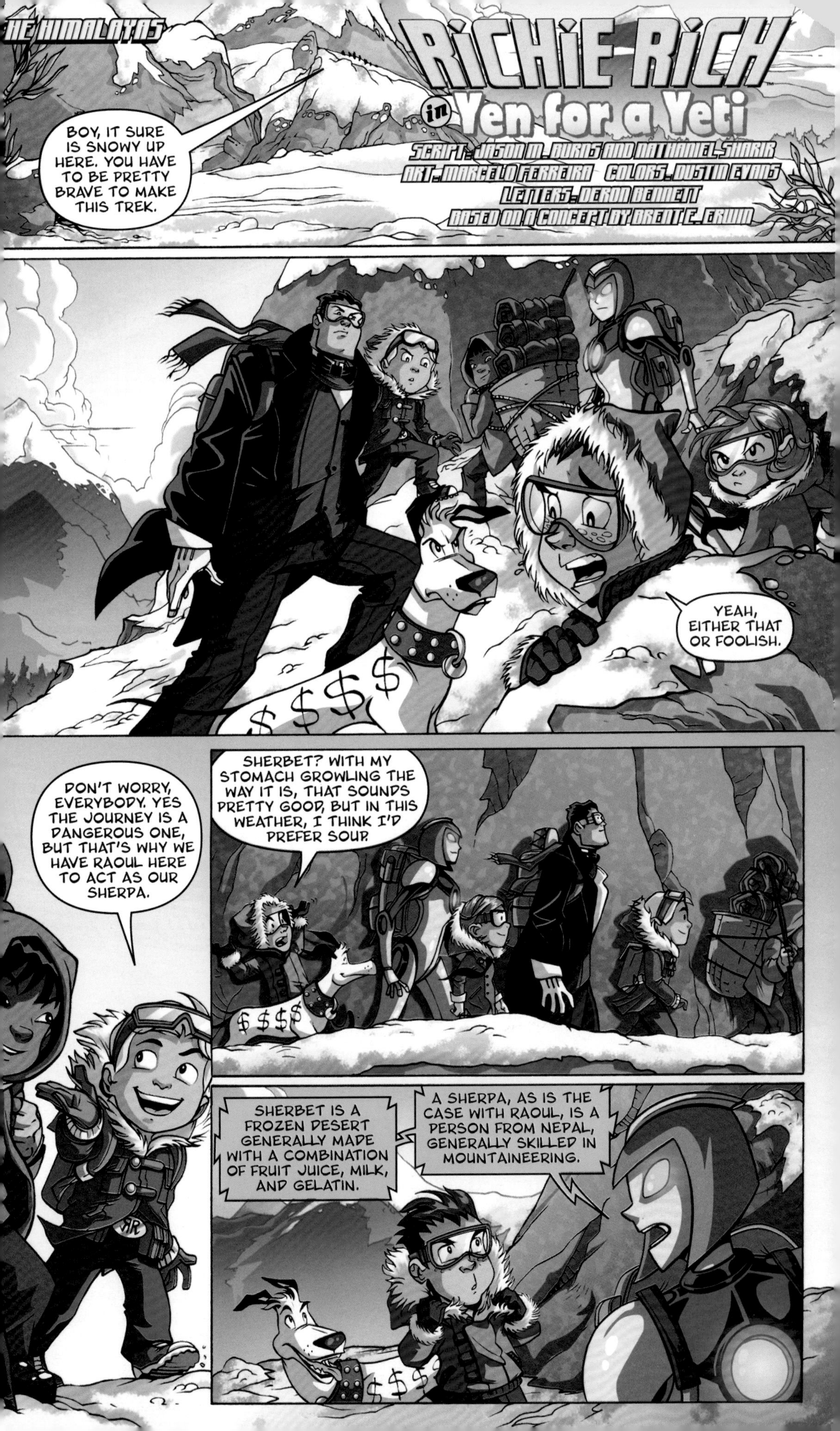
HE HIMALAYAS
RICHIE RICH™
in Yen for a Yeti
SCRIPT - JASON M. BURNS AND NATHANIEL SHARIR
ART - MARCELO FERREIRA   COLORS - DUSTIN EVANS
LETTERS - DERON BENNETT
BASED ON A CONCEPT BY BRENT E. ERWIN
BOY, IT SURE IS SNOWY UP HERE. YOU HAVE TO BE PRETTY BRAVE TO MAKE THIS TREK.
YEAH, EITHER THAT OR FOOLISH.
DON'T WORRY, EVERYBODY. YES THE JOURNEY IS A DANGEROUS ONE, BUT THAT'S WHY WE HAVE RAOUL HERE TO ACT AS OUR SHERPA.
SHERBET? WITH MY STOMACH GROWLING THE WAY IT IS, THAT SOUNDS PRETTY GOOD, BUT IN THIS WEATHER, I THINK I'D PREFER SOUP.
SHERBET IS A FROZEN DESERT GENERALLY MADE WITH A COMBINATION OF FRUIT JUICE, MILK, AND GELATIN.
A SHERPA, AS IS THE CASE WITH RAOUL, IS A PERSON FROM NEPAL, GENERALLY SKILLED IN MOUNTAINEERING.

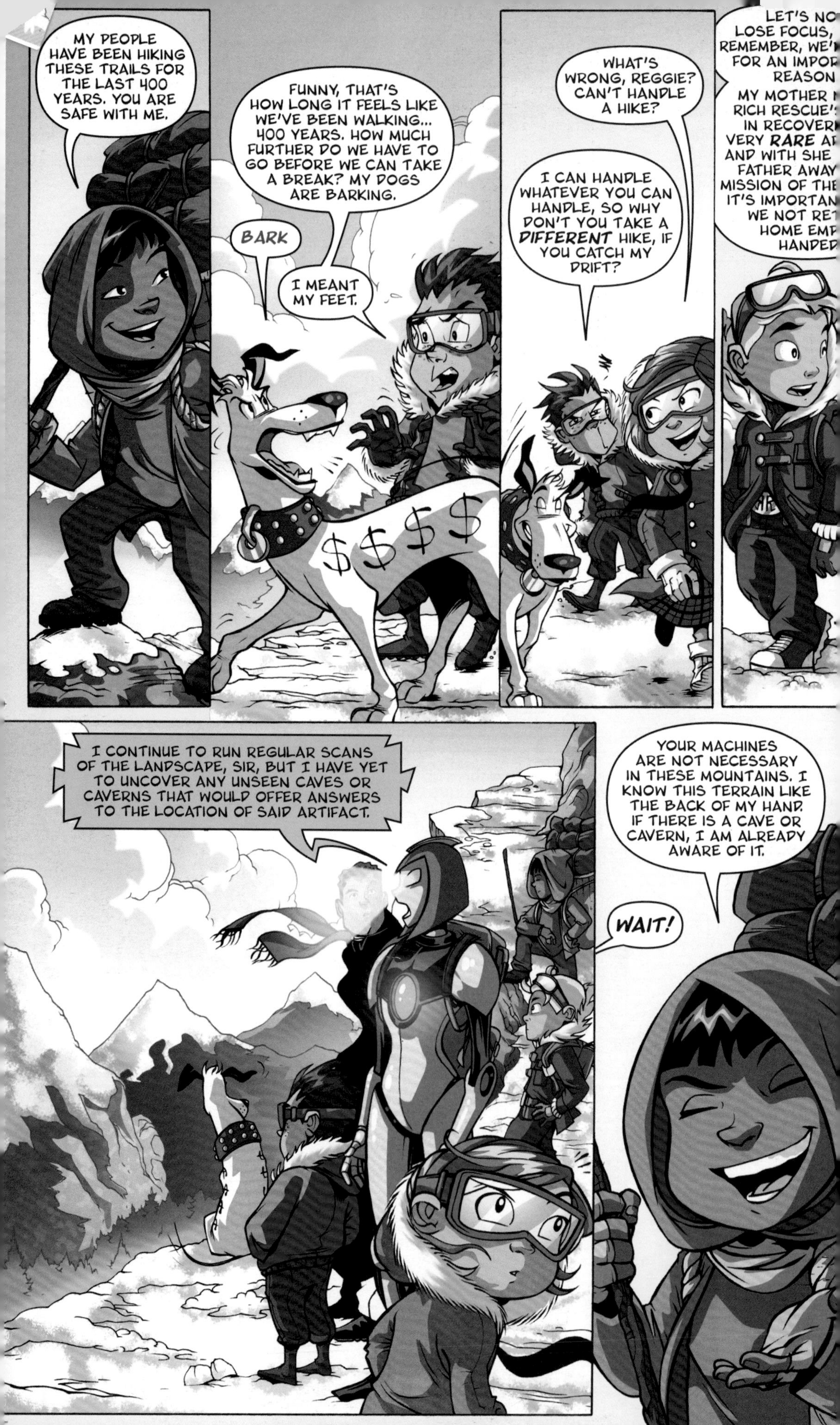
MY PEOPLE HAVE BEEN HIKING THESE TRAILS FOR THE LAST 400 YEARS. YOU ARE SAFE WITH ME.
FUNNY, THAT'S HOW LONG IT FEELS LIKE WE'VE BEEN WALKING... 400 YEARS. HOW MUCH FURTHER DO WE HAVE TO GO BEFORE WE CAN TAKE A BREAK? MY DOGS ARE BARKING.
BARK
I MEANT MY FEET.
WHAT'S WRONG, REGGIE? CAN'T HANDLE A HIKE?
I CAN HANDLE WHATEVER YOU CAN HANDLE, SO WHY DON'T YOU TAKE A DIFFERENT HIKE, IF YOU CATCH MY DRIFT?
LET'S NO LOSE FOCUS, REMEMBER, WE'I FOR AN IMPOR REASON
MY MOTHER RICH RESCUE' IN RECOVER VERY RARE AI AND WITH SHE FATHER AWAY MISSION OF THE IT'S IMPORTAN WE NOT RE HOME EMP HANDED
I CONTINUE TO RUN REGULAR SCANS OF THE LANDSCAPE, SIR, BUT I HAVE YET TO UNCOVER ANY UNSEEN CAVES OR CAVERNS THAT WOULD OFFER ANSWERS TO THE LOCATION OF SAID ARTIFACT.
YOUR MACHINES ARE NOT NECESSARY IN THESE MOUNTAINS. I KNOW THIS TERRAIN LIKE THE BACK OF MY HAND. IF THERE IS A CAVE OR CAVERN, I AM ALREADY AWARE OF IT.
WAIT!

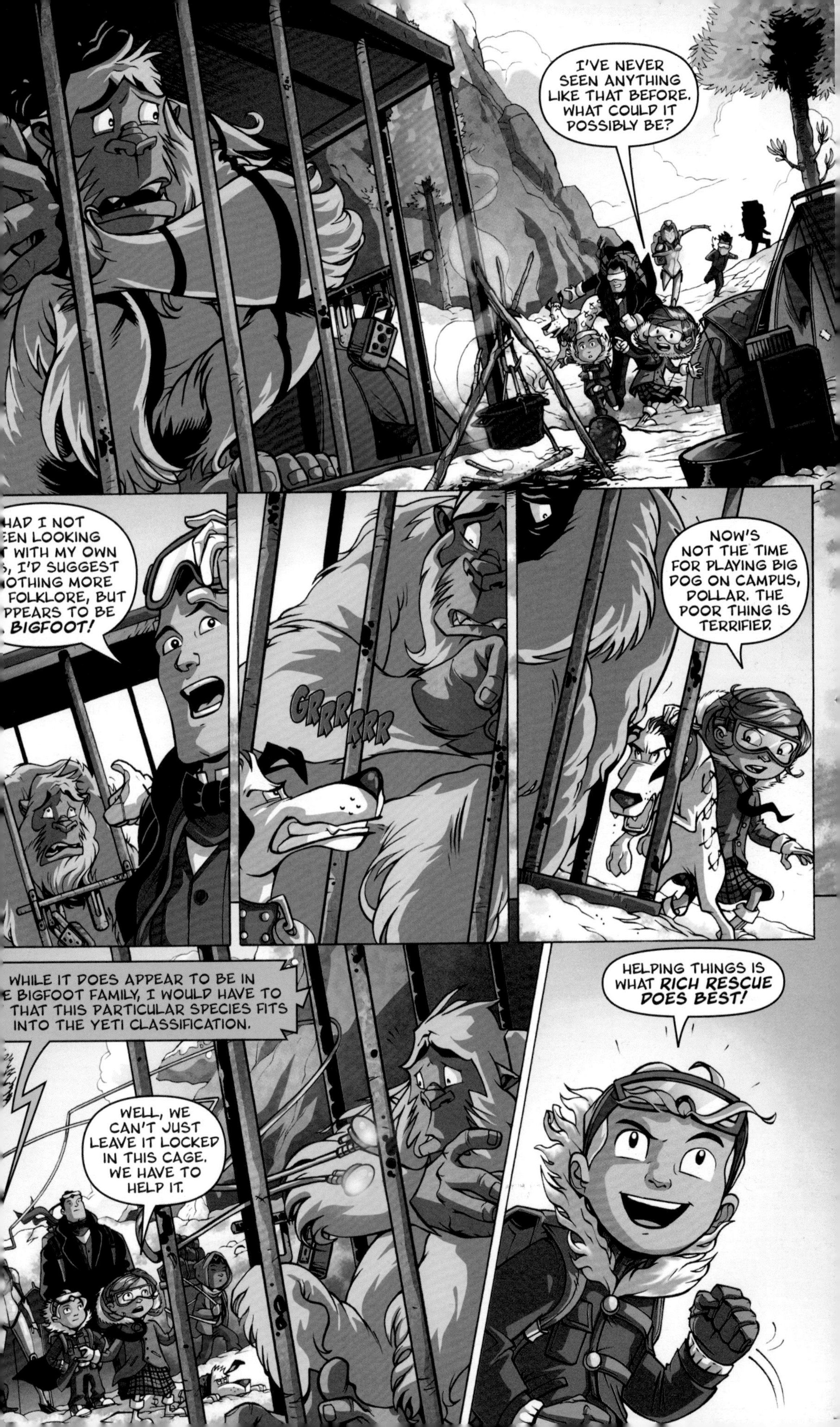
I'VE NEVER SEEN ANYTHING LIKE THAT BEFORE. WHAT COULD IT POSSIBLY BE?
HAD I NOT EEN LOOKING T WITH MY OWN , I'D SUGGEST OTHING MORE FOLKLORE, BUT PPEARS TO BE BIGFOOT!
GRRRRRR
NOW'S NOT THE TIME FOR PLAYING BIG DOG ON CAMPUS, DOLLAR. THE POOR THING IS TERRIFIED.
WHILE IT DOES APPEAR TO BE IN E BIGFOOT FAMILY, I WOULD HAVE TO THAT THIS PARTICULAR SPECIES FITS INTO THE YETI CLASSIFICATION.
WELL, WE CAN'T JUST LEAVE IT LOCKED IN THIS CAGE. WE HAVE TO HELP IT.
HELPING THINGS IS WHAT RICH RESCUE DOES BEST!

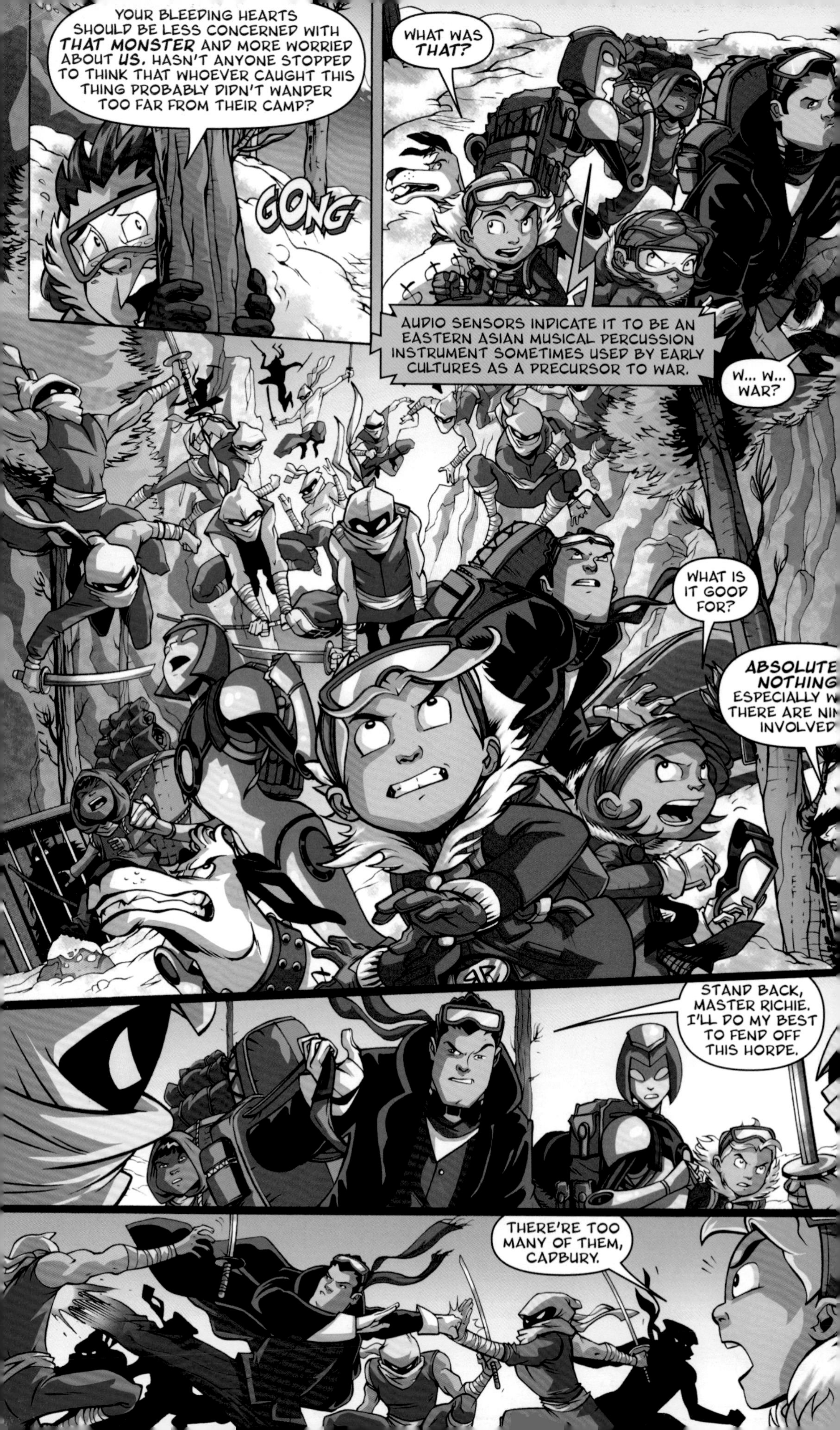
YOUR BLEEDING HEARTS SHOULD BE LESS CONCERNED WITH THAT MONSTER AND MORE WORRIED ABOUT US. HASN'T ANYONE STOPPED TO THINK THAT WHOEVER CAUGHT THIS THING PROBABLY DIDN'T WANDER TOO FAR FROM THEIR CAMP?
GONG
WHAT WAS THAT?
AUDIO SENSORS INDICATE IT TO BE AN EASTERN ASIAN MUSICAL PERCUSSION INSTRUMENT SOMETIMES USED BY EARLY CULTURES AS A PRECURSOR TO WAR.
W... W... WAR?
WHAT IS IT GOOD FOR?
ABSOLUTE NOTHING ESPECIALLY W THERE ARE NIN INVOLVED
STAND BACK, MASTER RICHIE. I'LL DO MY BEST TO FEND OFF THIS HORDE.
THERE'RE TOO MANY OF THEM, CADBURY.

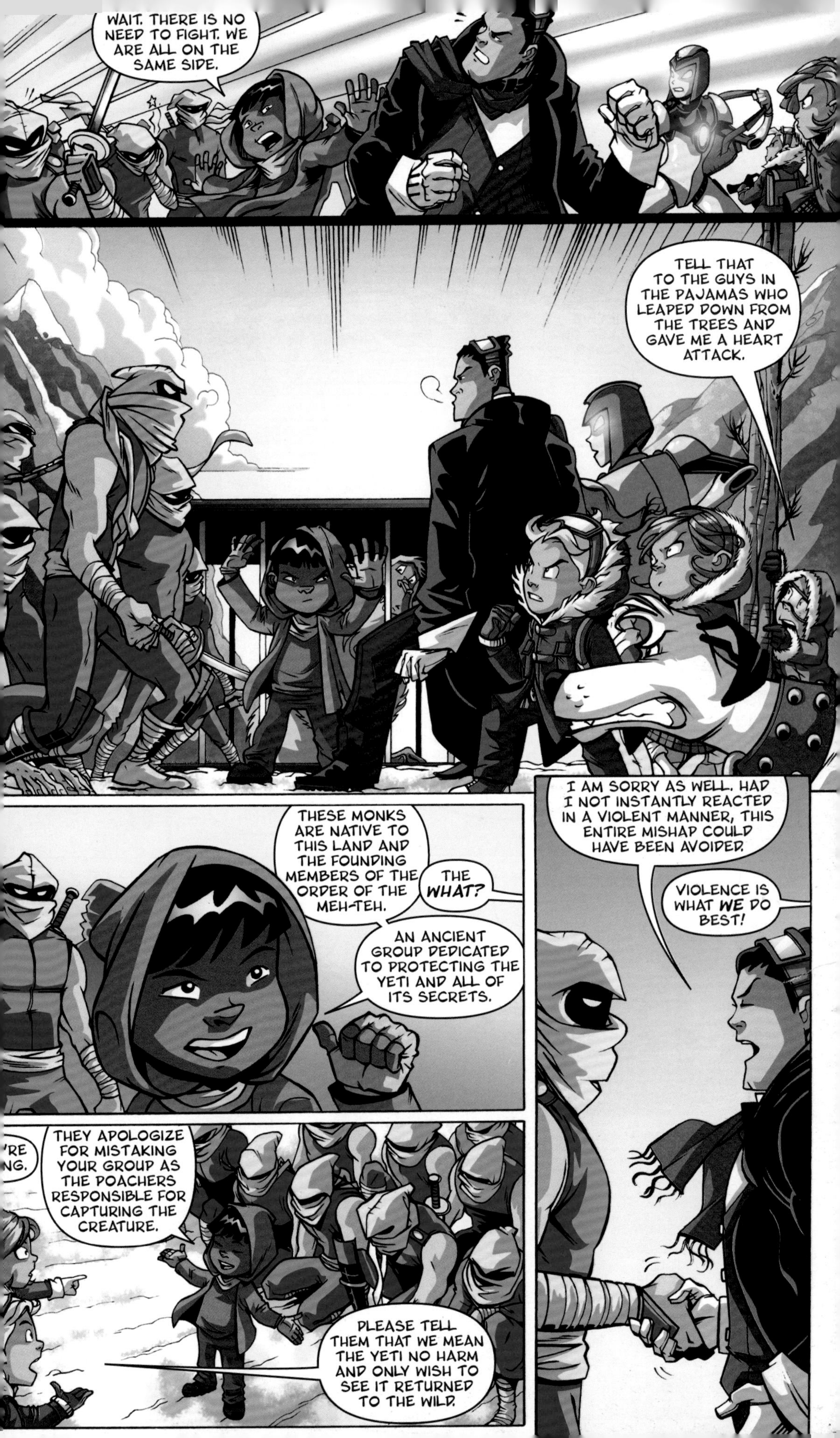
WAIT. THERE IS NO NEED TO FIGHT. WE ARE ALL ON THE SAME SIDE.
TELL THAT TO THE GUYS IN THE PAJAMAS WHO LEAPED DOWN FROM THE TREES AND GAVE ME A HEART ATTACK.
THESE MONKS ARE NATIVE TO THIS LAND AND THE FOUNDING MEMBERS OF THE ORDER OF THE MEH-TEH.
THE *WHAT?*
AN ANCIENT GROUP DEDICATED TO PROTECTING THE YETI AND ALL OF ITS SECRETS.
THEY APOLOGIZE FOR MISTAKING YOUR GROUP AS THE POACHERS RESPONSIBLE FOR CAPTURING THE CREATURE.
PLEASE TELL THEM THAT WE MEAN THE YETI NO HARM AND ONLY WISH TO SEE IT RETURNED TO THE WILD.
I AM SORRY AS WELL. HAD I NOT INSTANTLY REACTED IN A VIOLENT MANNER, THIS ENTIRE MISHAP COULD HAVE BEEN AVOIDED.
VIOLENCE IS WHAT *WE* DO BEST!

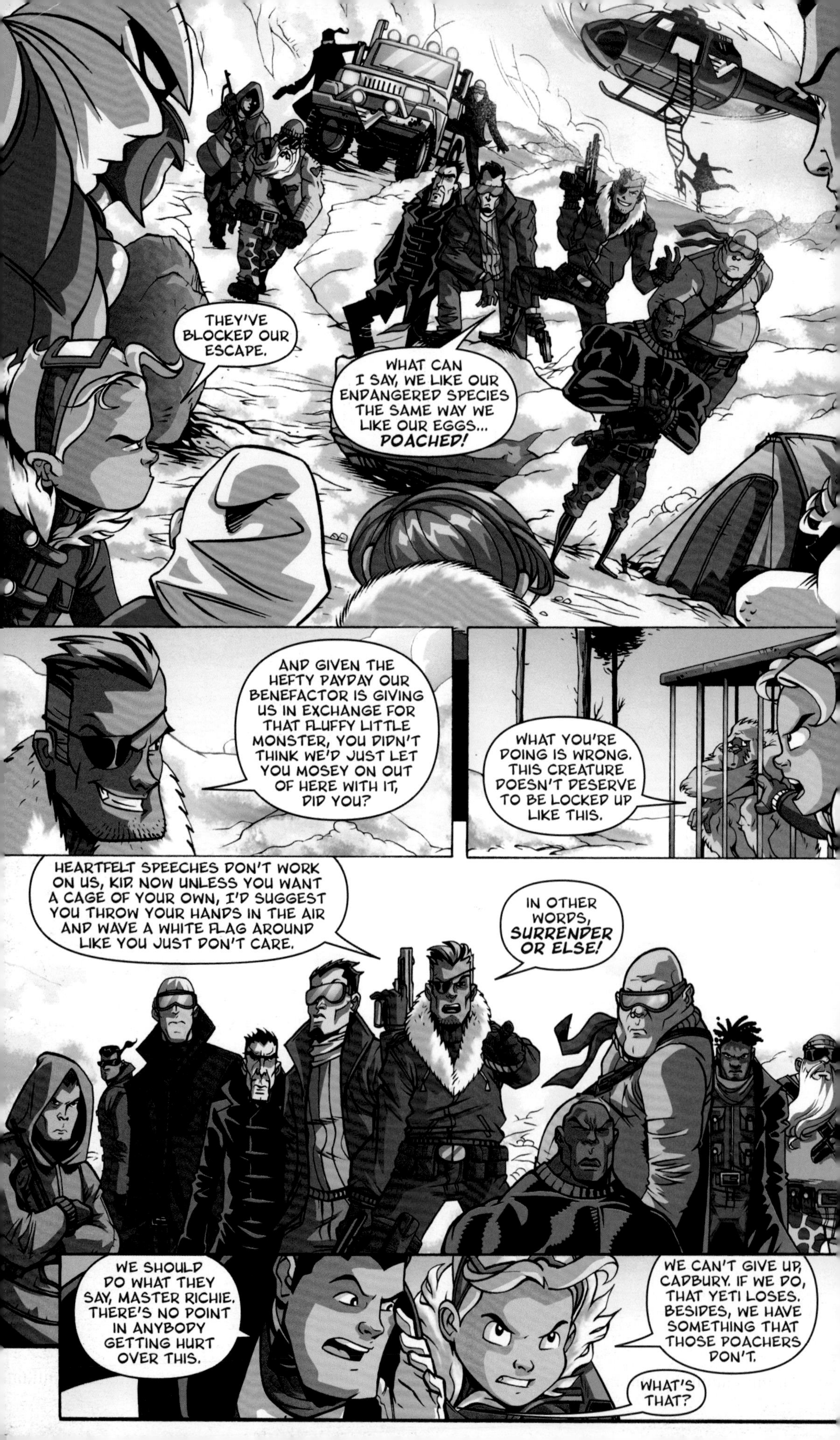
THEY'VE BLOCKED OUR ESCAPE.
WHAT CAN I SAY, WE LIKE OUR ENDANGERED SPECIES THE SAME WAY WE LIKE OUR EGGS... POACHED!
AND GIVEN THE HEFTY PAYDAY OUR BENEFACTOR IS GIVING US IN EXCHANGE FOR THAT FLUFFY LITTLE MONSTER, YOU DIDN'T THINK WE'D JUST LET YOU MOSEY ON OUT OF HERE WITH IT, DID YOU?
WHAT YOU'RE DOING IS WRONG. THIS CREATURE DOESN'T DESERVE TO BE LOCKED UP LIKE THIS.
HEARTFELT SPEECHES DON'T WORK ON US, KID. NOW UNLESS YOU WANT A CAGE OF YOUR OWN, I'D SUGGEST YOU THROW YOUR HANDS IN THE AIR AND WAVE A WHITE FLAG AROUND LIKE YOU JUST DON'T CARE.
IN OTHER WORDS, SURRENDER OR ELSE!
WE SHOULD DO WHAT THEY SAY, MASTER RICHIE. THERE'S NO POINT IN ANYBODY GETTING HURT OVER THIS.
WE CAN'T GIVE UP, CADBURY. IF WE DO, THAT YETI LOSES. BESIDES, WE HAVE SOMETHING THAT THOSE POACHERS DON'T.
WHAT'S THAT?

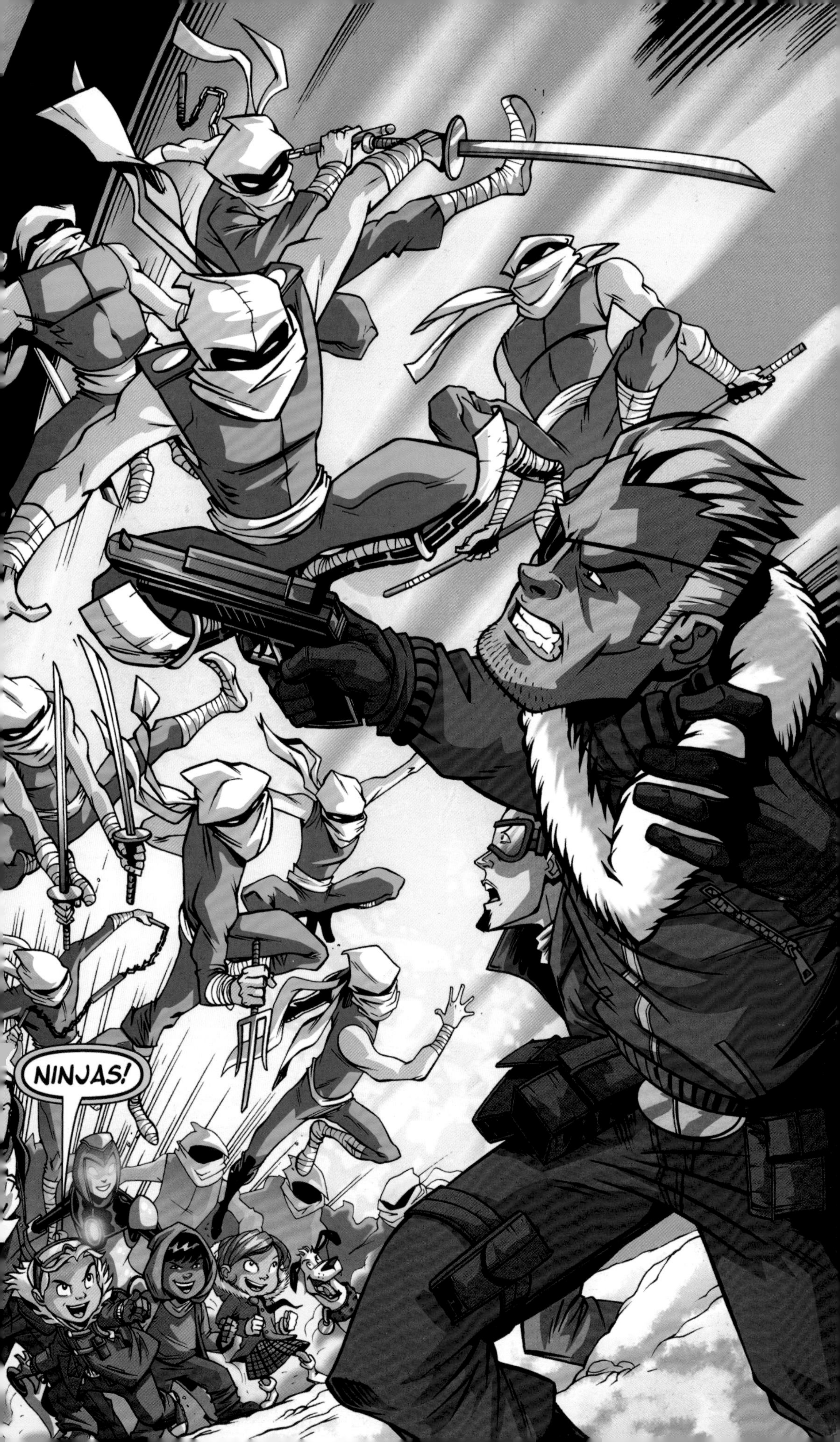
NINJAS!

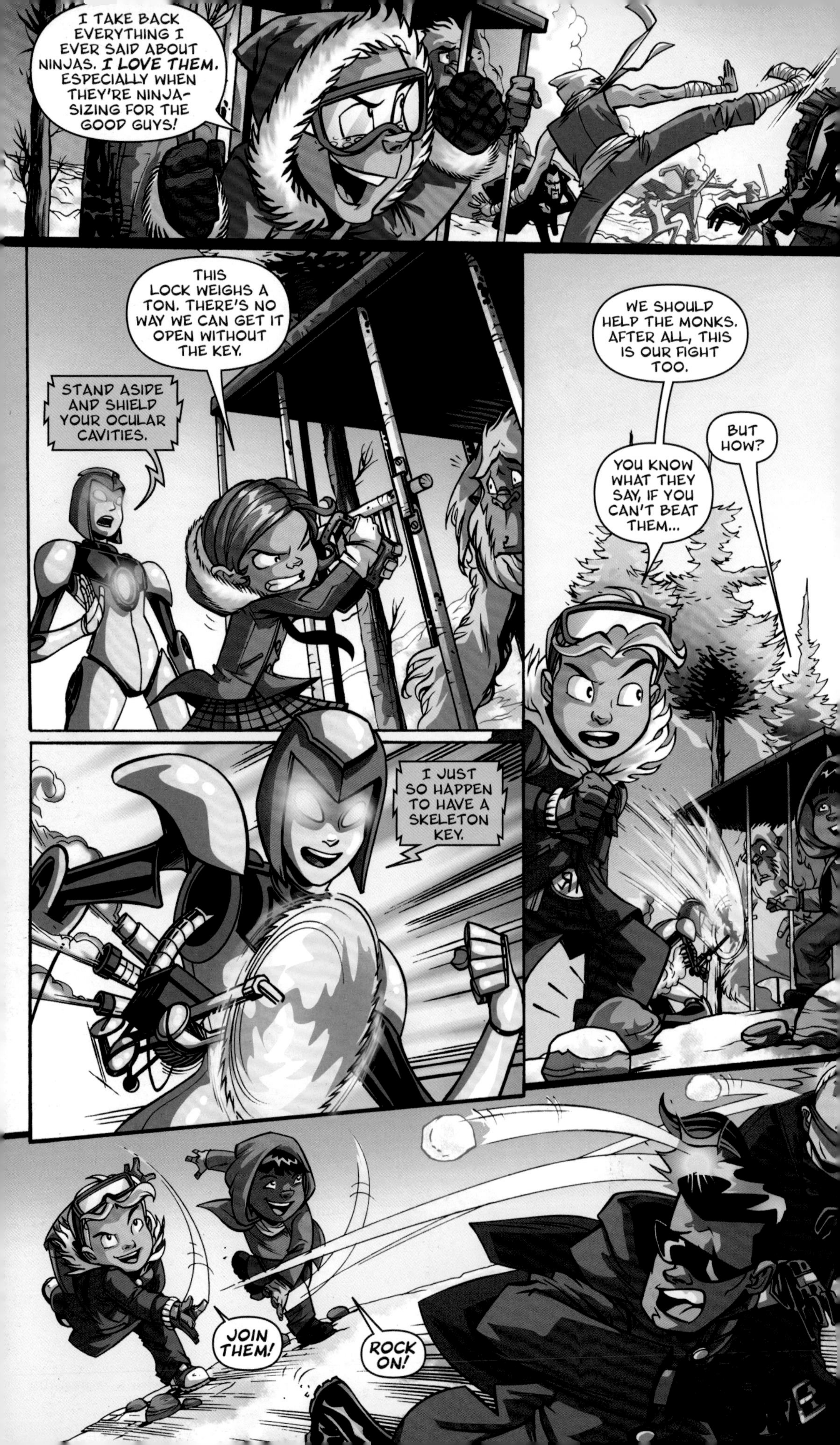

I TAKE BACK EVERYTHING I EVER SAID ABOUT NINJAS. *I LOVE THEM.* ESPECIALLY WHEN THEY'RE NINJA-SIZING FOR THE GOOD GUYS!
THIS LOCK WEIGHS A TON. THERE'S NO WAY WE CAN GET IT OPEN WITHOUT THE KEY.
STAND ASIDE AND SHIELD YOUR OCULAR CAVITIES.
I JUST SO HAPPEN TO HAVE A SKELETON KEY.
WE SHOULD HELP THE MONKS. AFTER ALL, THIS IS OUR FIGHT TOO.
BUT HOW?
YOU KNOW WHAT THEY SAY, IF YOU CAN'T BEAT THEM...
JOIN THEM!
ROCK ON!

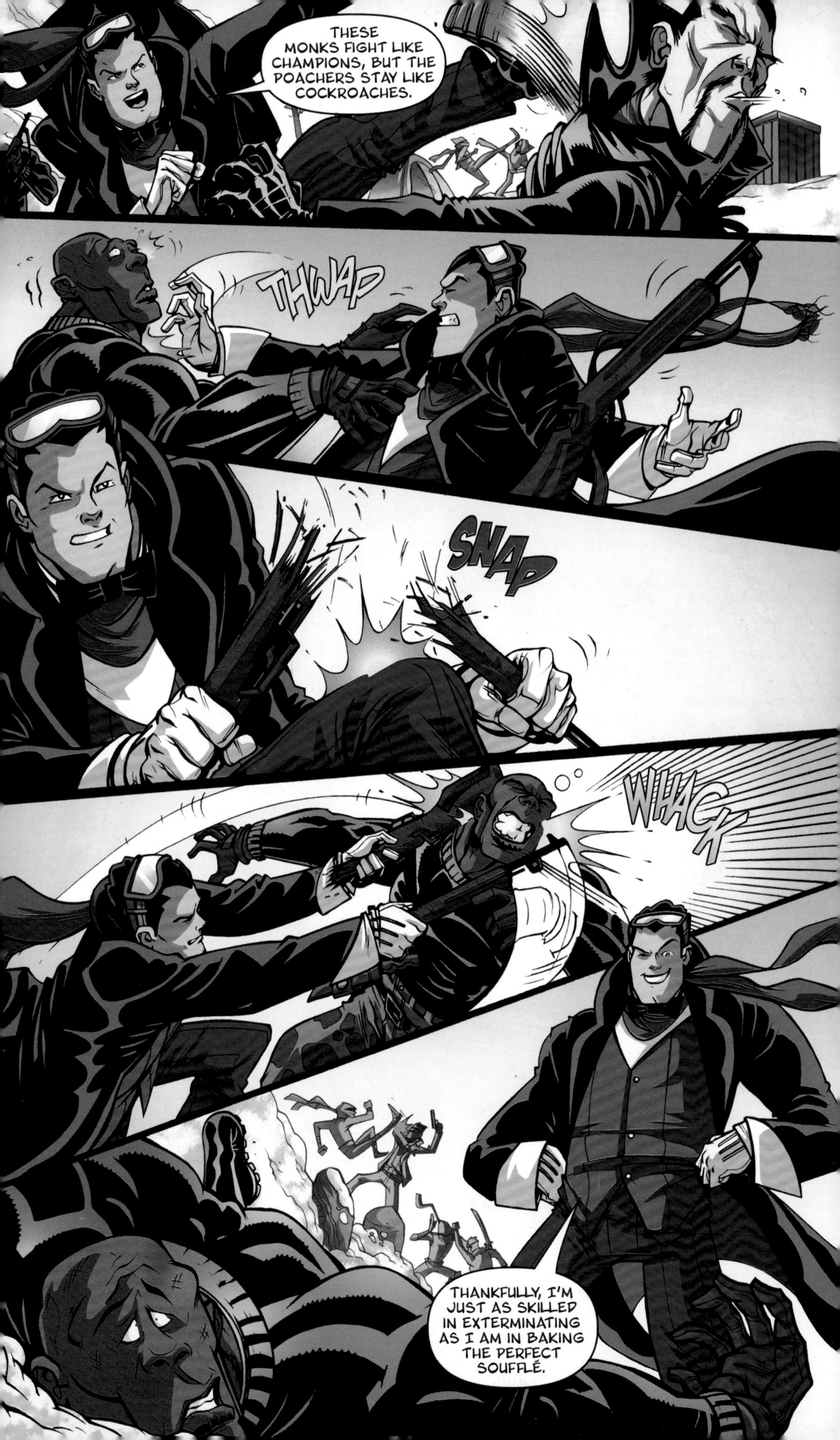
THESE MONKS FIGHT LIKE CHAMPIONS, BUT THE POACHERS STAY LIKE COCKROACHES.
THWAP
SNAP
WHACK
THANKFULLY, I'M JUST AS SKILLED IN EXTERMINATING AS I AM IN BAKING THE PERFECT SOUFFLÉ.

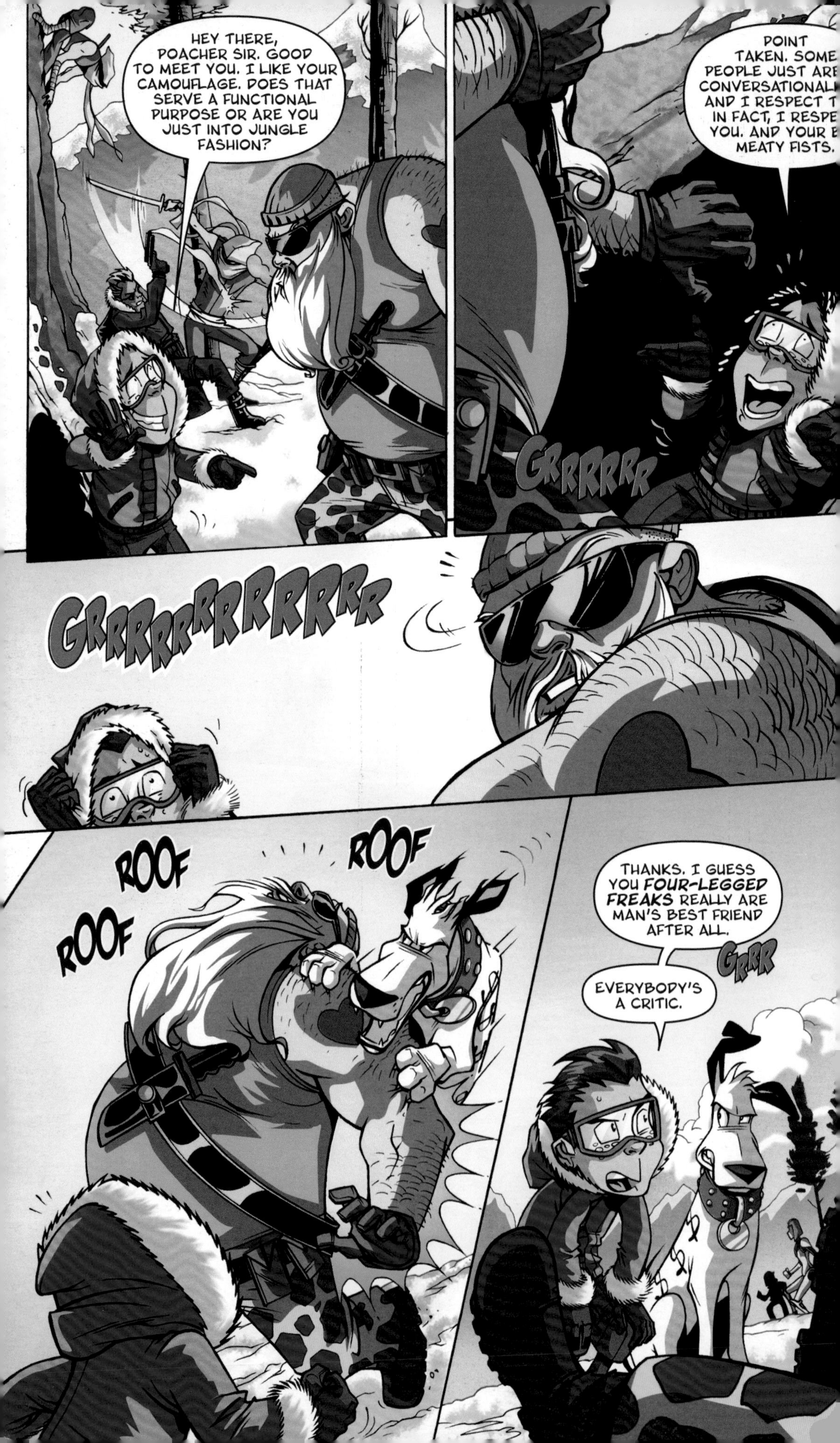
HEY THERE, POACHER SIR. GOOD TO MEET YOU. I LIKE YOUR CAMOUFLAGE. DOES THAT SERVE A FUNCTIONAL PURPOSE OR ARE YOU JUST INTO JUNGLE FASHION?
POINT TAKEN. SOME PEOPLE JUST ARE CONVERSATIONAL AND I RESPECT T IN FACT, I RESPE YOU. AND YOUR MEATY FISTS.
GRRRRRR
GRRRRRRRRRRRR
ROOF
ROOF
ROOF
THANKS. I GUESS YOU FOUR-LEGGED FREAKS REALLY ARE MAN'S BEST FRIEND AFTER ALL.
GRRR
EVERYBODY'S A CRITIC.

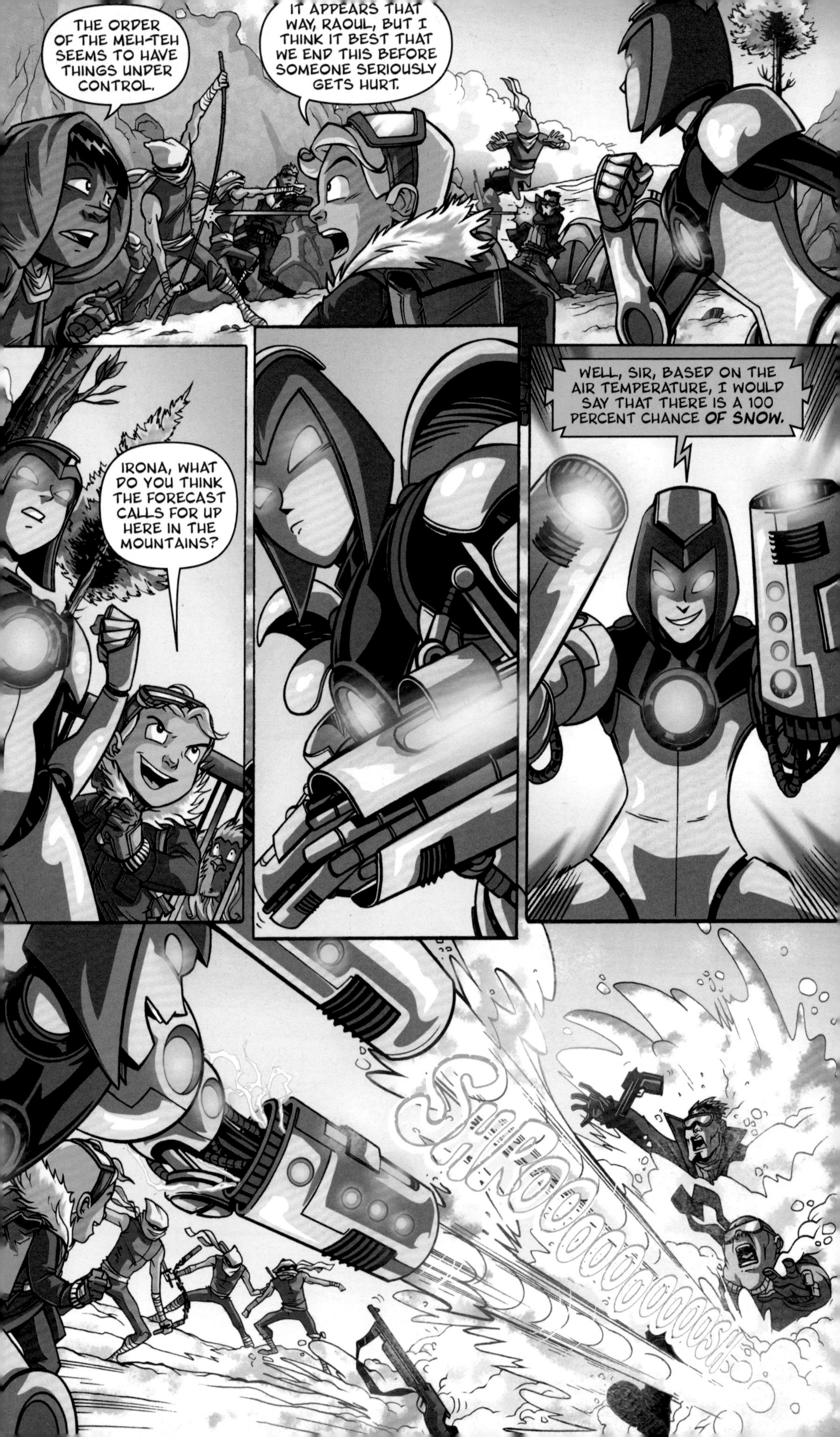
THE ORDER OF THE MEH-TEH SEEMS TO HAVE THINGS UNDER CONTROL.
IT APPEARS THAT WAY, RAOUL, BUT I THINK IT BEST THAT WE END THIS BEFORE SOMEONE SERIOUSLY GETS HURT.
IRONA, WHAT DO YOU THINK THE FORECAST CALLS FOR UP HERE IN THE MOUNTAINS?
WELL, SIR, BASED ON THE AIR TEMPERATURE, I WOULD SAY THAT THERE IS A 100 PERCENT CHANCE **OF SNOW.**
SHOOOOOOOOOSH!

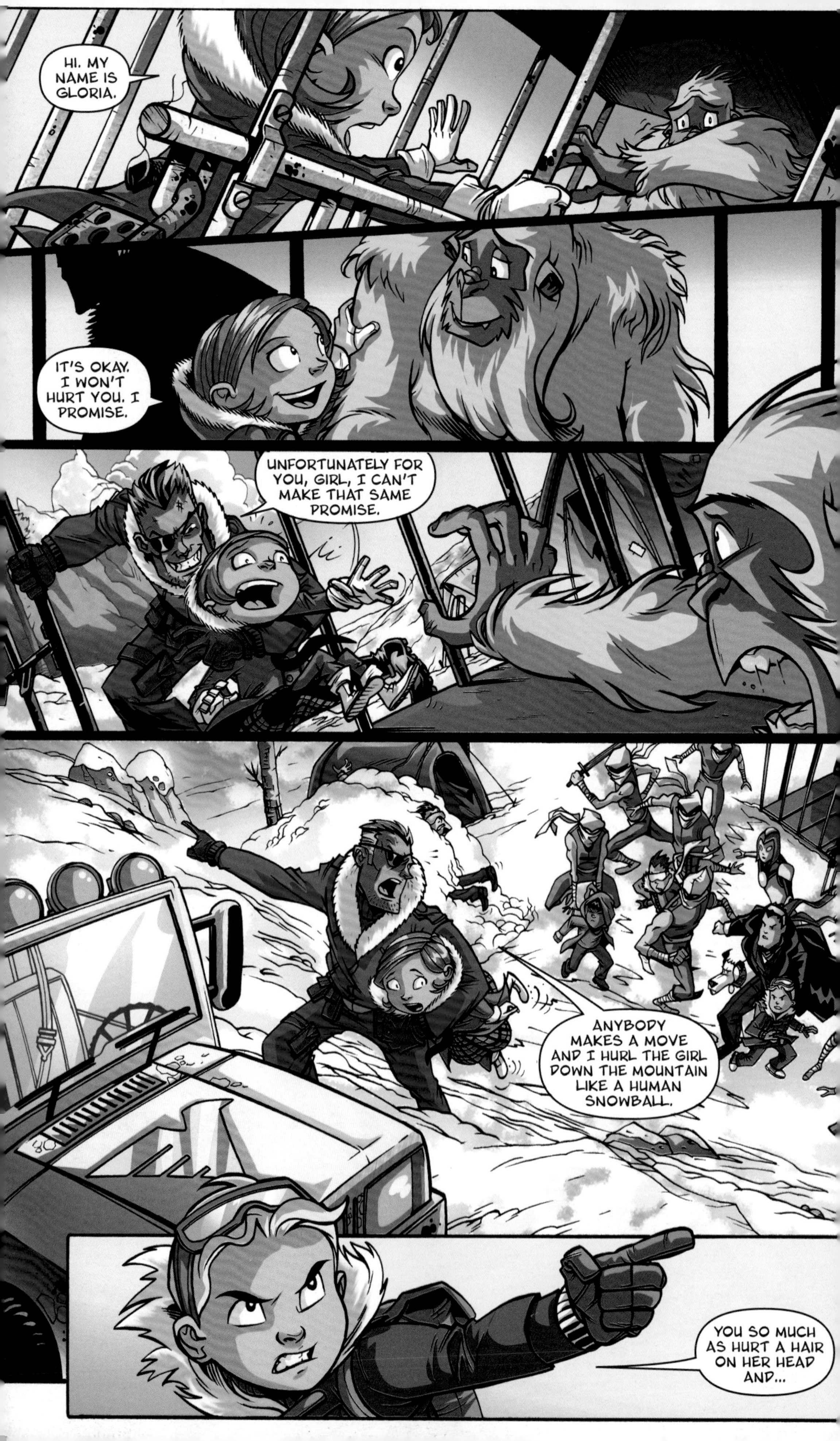
HI. MY NAME IS GLORIA.
IT'S OKAY. I WON'T HURT YOU. I PROMISE.
UNFORTUNATELY FOR YOU, GIRL, I CAN'T MAKE THAT SAME PROMISE.
ANYBODY MAKES A MOVE AND I HURL THE GIRL DOWN THE MOUNTAIN LIKE A HUMAN SNOWBALL.
YOU SO MUCH AS HURT A HAIR ON HER HEAD AND...

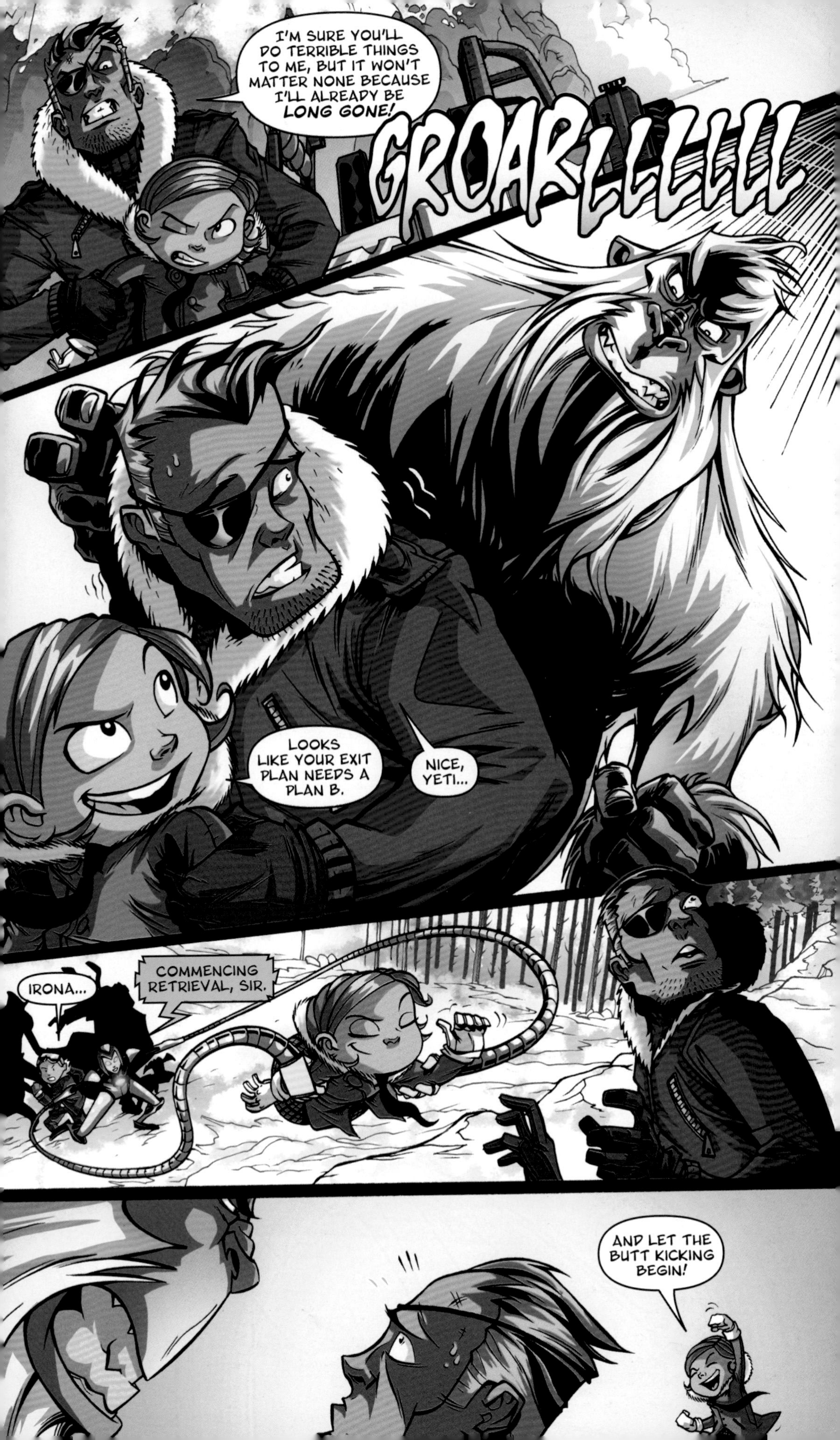
I'M SURE YOU'LL DO TERRIBLE THINGS TO ME, BUT IT WON'T MATTER NONE BECAUSE I'LL ALREADY BE LONG GONE!
GROARLLLLLL
LOOKS LIKE YOUR EXIT PLAN NEEDS A PLAN B.
NICE, YETI...
IRONA...
COMMENCING RETRIEVAL, SIR.
AND LET THE BUTT KICKING BEGIN!

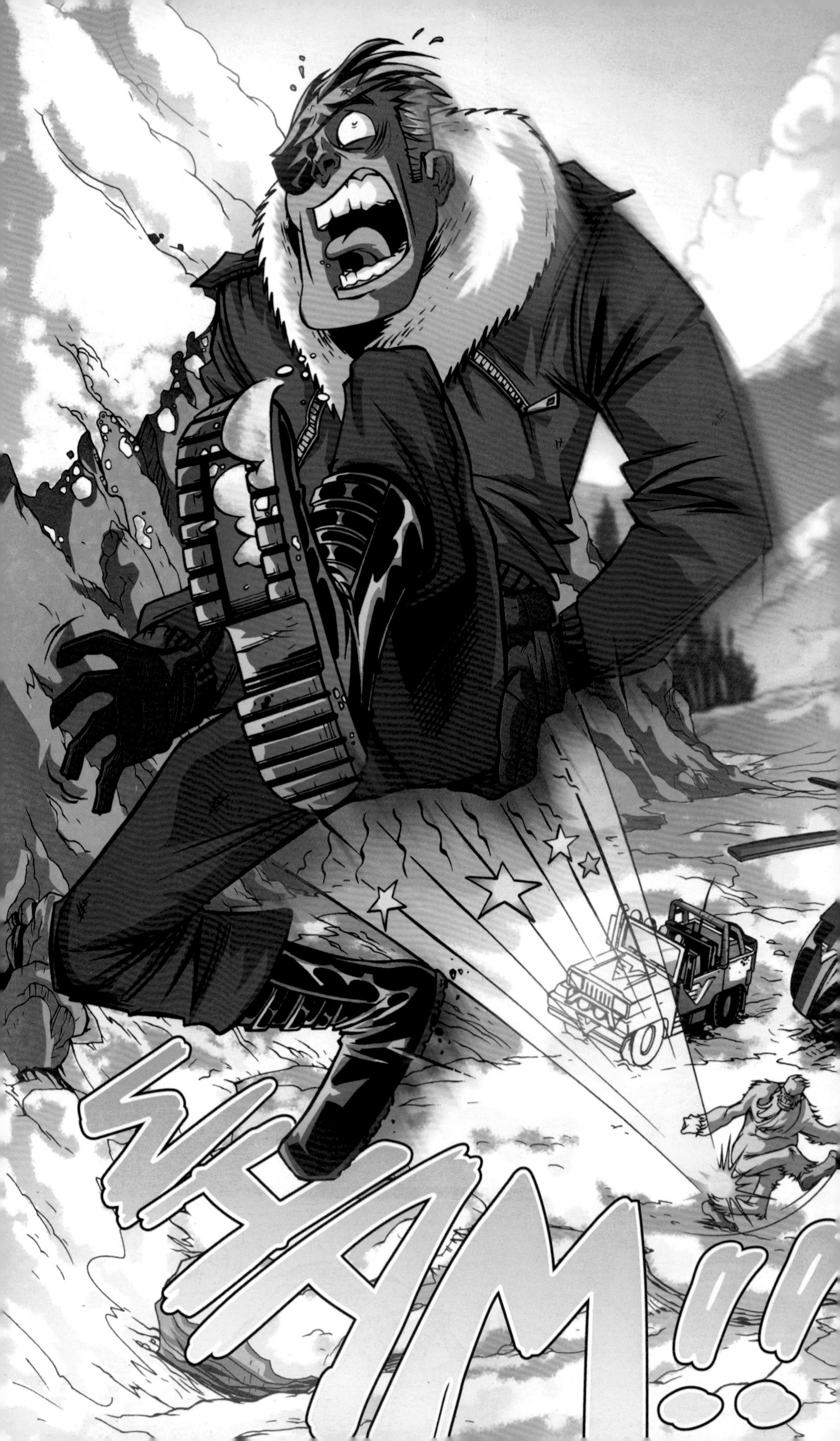
WHAM!!

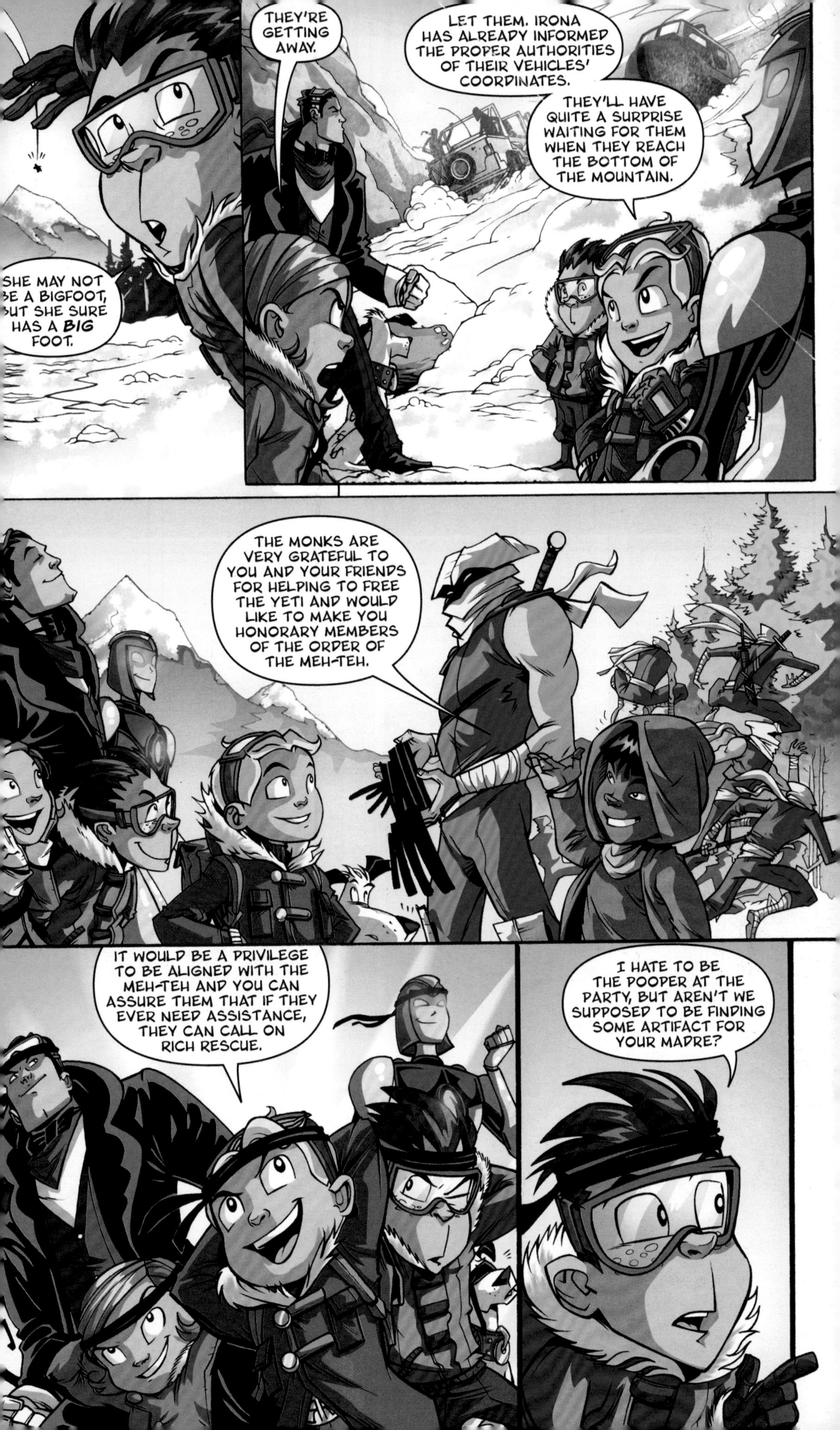
SHE MAY NOT
BE A BIGFOOT,
BUT SHE SURE
HAS A **BIG**
FOOT.
THEY'RE GETTING AWAY.
LET THEM. IRONA HAS ALREADY INFORMED THE PROPER AUTHORITIES OF THEIR VEHICLES' COORDINATES.
THEY'LL HAVE QUITE A SURPRISE WAITING FOR THEM WHEN THEY REACH THE BOTTOM OF THE MOUNTAIN.
THE MONKS ARE VERY GRATEFUL TO YOU AND YOUR FRIENDS FOR HELPING TO FREE THE YETI AND WOULD LIKE TO MAKE YOU HONORARY MEMBERS OF THE ORDER OF THE MEH-TEH.
IT WOULD BE A PRIVILEGE TO BE ALIGNED WITH THE MEH-TEH AND YOU CAN ASSURE THEM THAT IF THEY EVER NEED ASSISTANCE, THEY CAN CALL ON RICH RESCUE.
I HATE TO BE THE POOPER AT THE PARTY, BUT AREN'T WE SUPPOSED TO BE FINDING SOME ARTIFACT FOR YOUR MADRE?

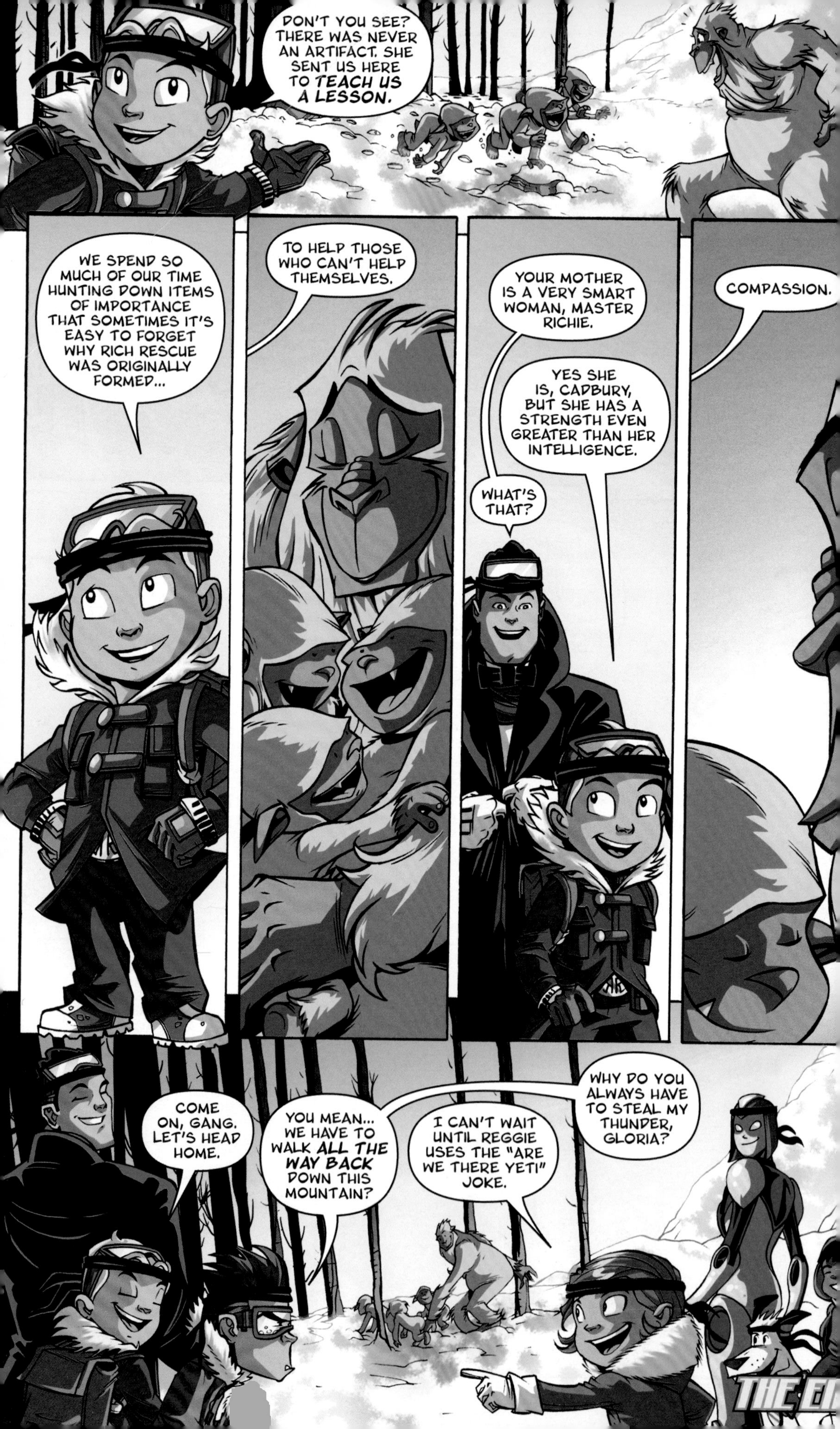
DON'T YOU SEE? THERE WAS NEVER AN ARTIFACT. SHE SENT US HERE TO *TEACH US A LESSON.*
WE SPEND SO MUCH OF OUR TIME HUNTING DOWN ITEMS OF IMPORTANCE THAT SOMETIMES IT'S EASY TO FORGET WHY RICH RESCUE WAS ORIGINALLY FORMED...
TO HELP THOSE WHO CAN'T HELP THEMSELVES.
YOUR MOTHER IS A VERY SMART WOMAN, MASTER RICHIE.
YES SHE IS, CADBURY, BUT SHE HAS A STRENGTH EVEN GREATER THAN HER INTELLIGENCE.
WHAT'S THAT?
COMPASSION.
COME ON, GANG. LET'S HEAD HOME.
YOU MEAN... WE HAVE TO WALK *ALL THE WAY BACK* DOWN THIS MOUNTAIN?
I CAN'T WAIT UNTIL REGGIE USES THE "ARE WE THERE YETI" JOKE.
WHY DO YOU ALWAYS HAVE TO STEAL MY THUNDER, GLORIA?

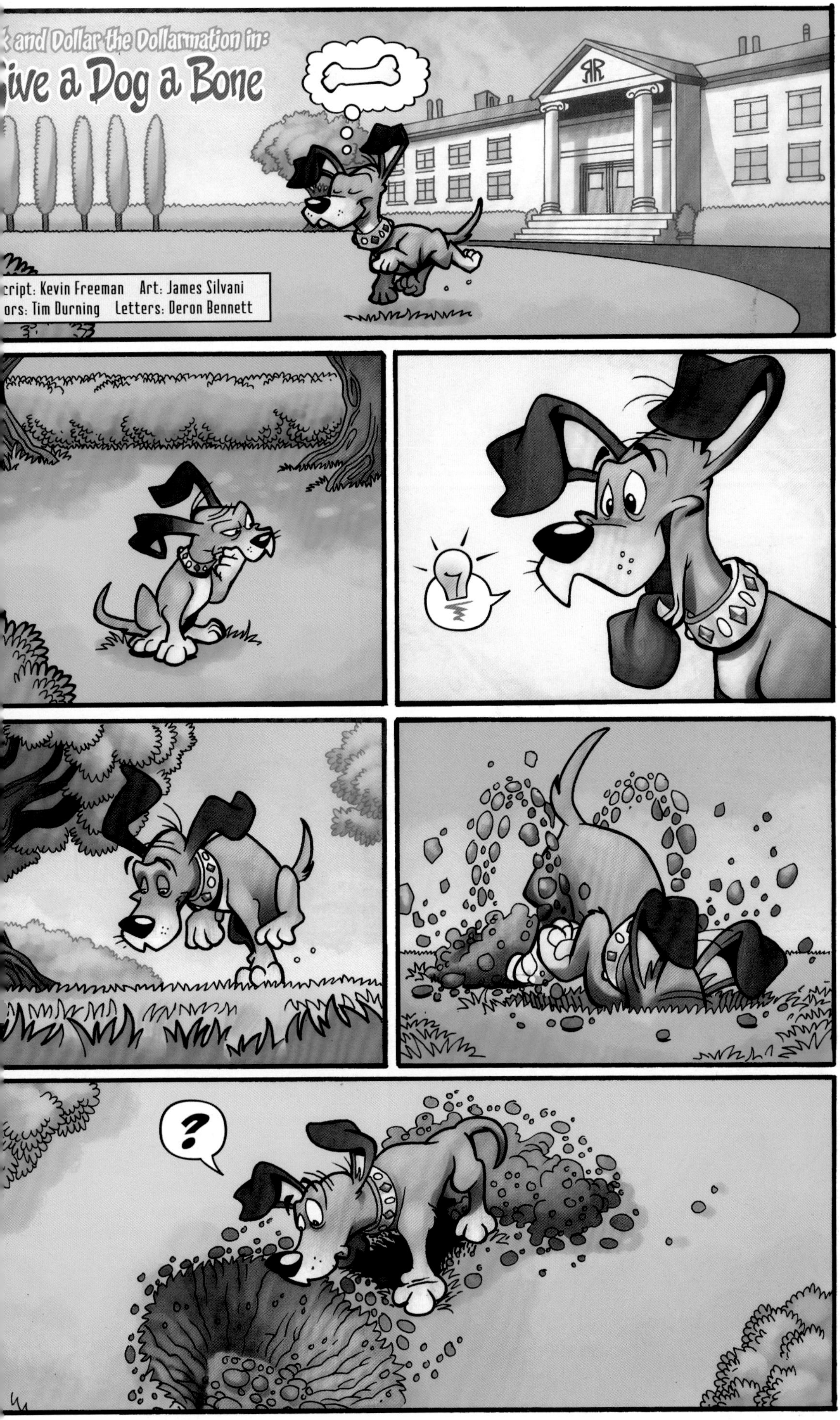
k and Dollar the Dollarmation in:
ive a Dog a Bone
cript: Kevin Freeman Art: James Silvani
ors: Tim Durning Letters: Deron Bennett
?

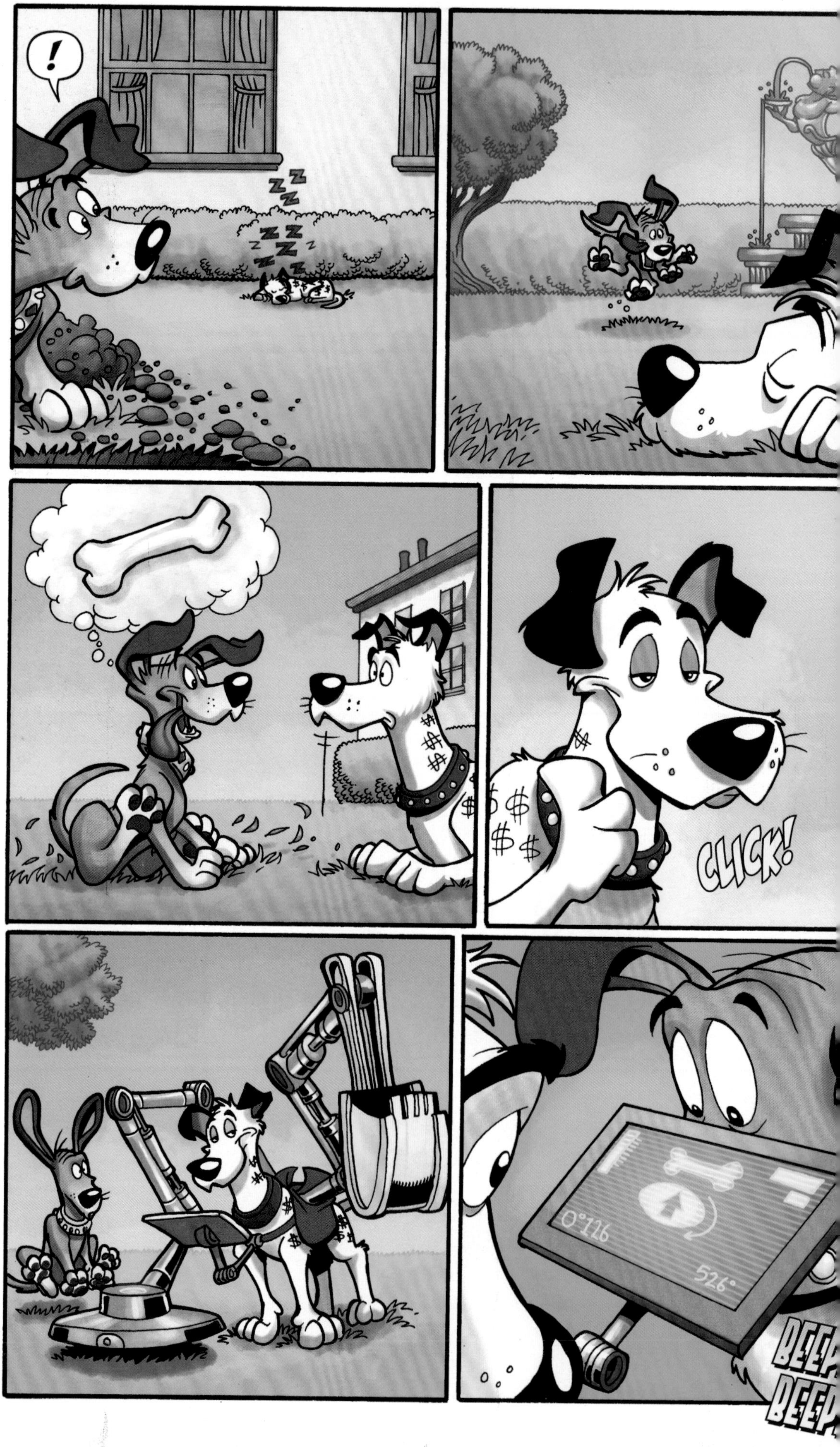
!
CLICK!
0°126
526°

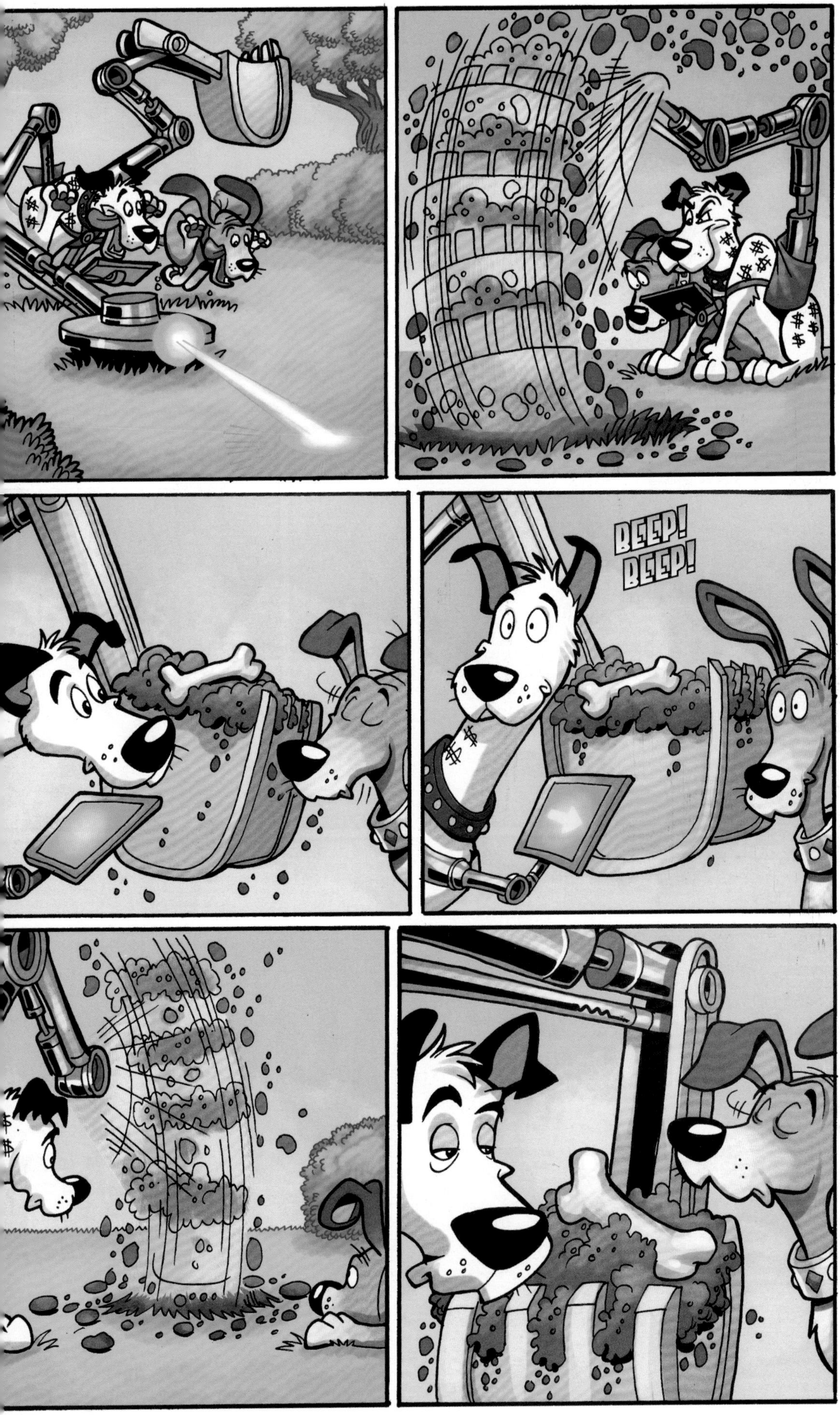
BEEP!
BEEP!

THE END

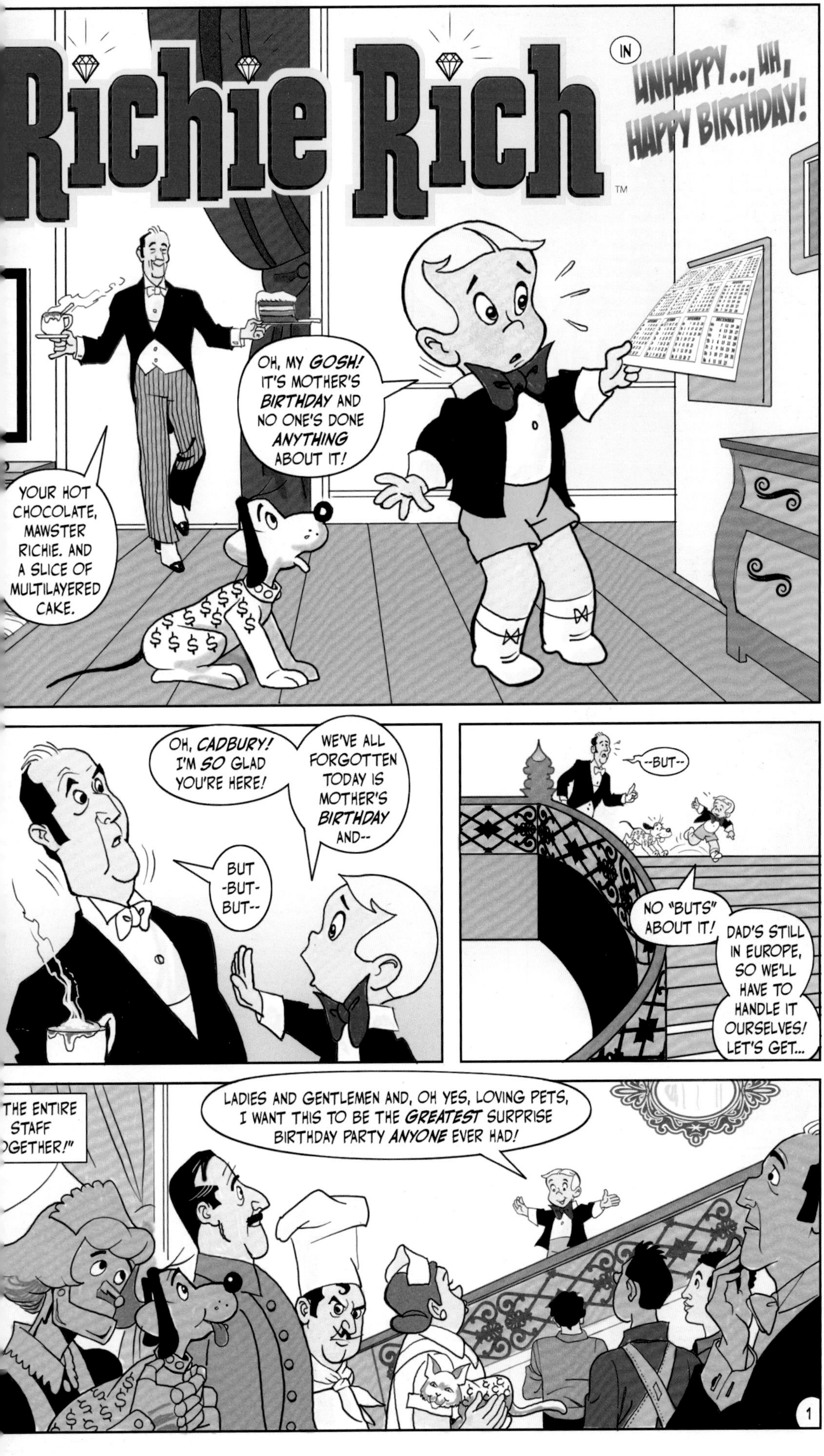
Richie Rich™
IN
UNHAPPY..., UH, HAPPY BIRTHDAY!
OH, MY GOSH! IT'S MOTHER'S BIRTHDAY AND NO ONE'S DONE ANYTHING ABOUT IT!
YOUR HOT CHOCOLATE, MAWSTER RICHIE. AND A SLICE OF MULTILAYERED CAKE.
OH, CADBURY! I'M SO GLAD YOU'RE HERE!
WE'VE ALL FORGOTTEN TODAY IS MOTHER'S BIRTHDAY AND--
BUT -BUT- BUT--
--BUT--
NO "BUTS" ABOUT IT!
DAD'S STILL IN EUROPE, SO WE'LL HAVE TO HANDLE IT OURSELVES! LET'S GET...
THE ENTIRE STAFF TOGETHER!"
LADIES AND GENTLEMEN AND, OH YES, LOVING PETS, I WANT THIS TO BE THE GREATEST SURPRISE BIRTHDAY PARTY ANYONE EVER HAD!

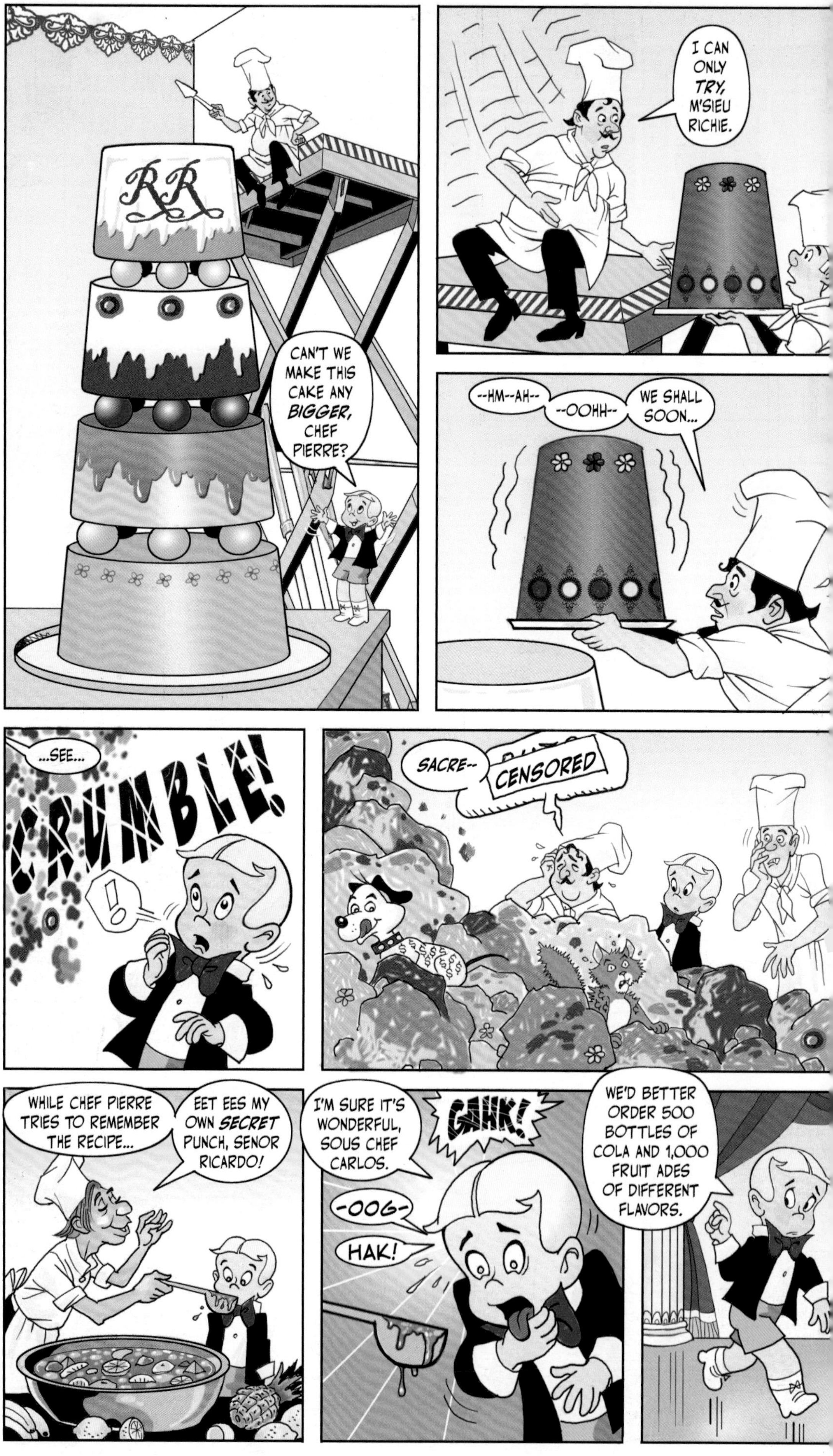
CAN'T WE MAKE THIS CAKE ANY *BIGGER,* CHEF PIERRE?
I CAN ONLY *TRY,* M'SIEU RICHIE.
--HM--AH--
--OOHH--
WE SHALL SOON...
...SEE...
CRUMBLE!
!
SACRE--
CENSORED
WHILE CHEF PIERRE TRIES TO REMEMBER THE RECIPE...
EET EES MY OWN *SECRET* PUNCH, SENOR RICARDO!
I'M SURE IT'S WONDERFUL, SOUS CHEF CARLOS.
GAHK!
-OOG-
HAK!
WE'D BETTER ORDER 500 BOTTLES OF COLA AND 1,000 FRUIT ADES OF DIFFERENT FLAVORS.

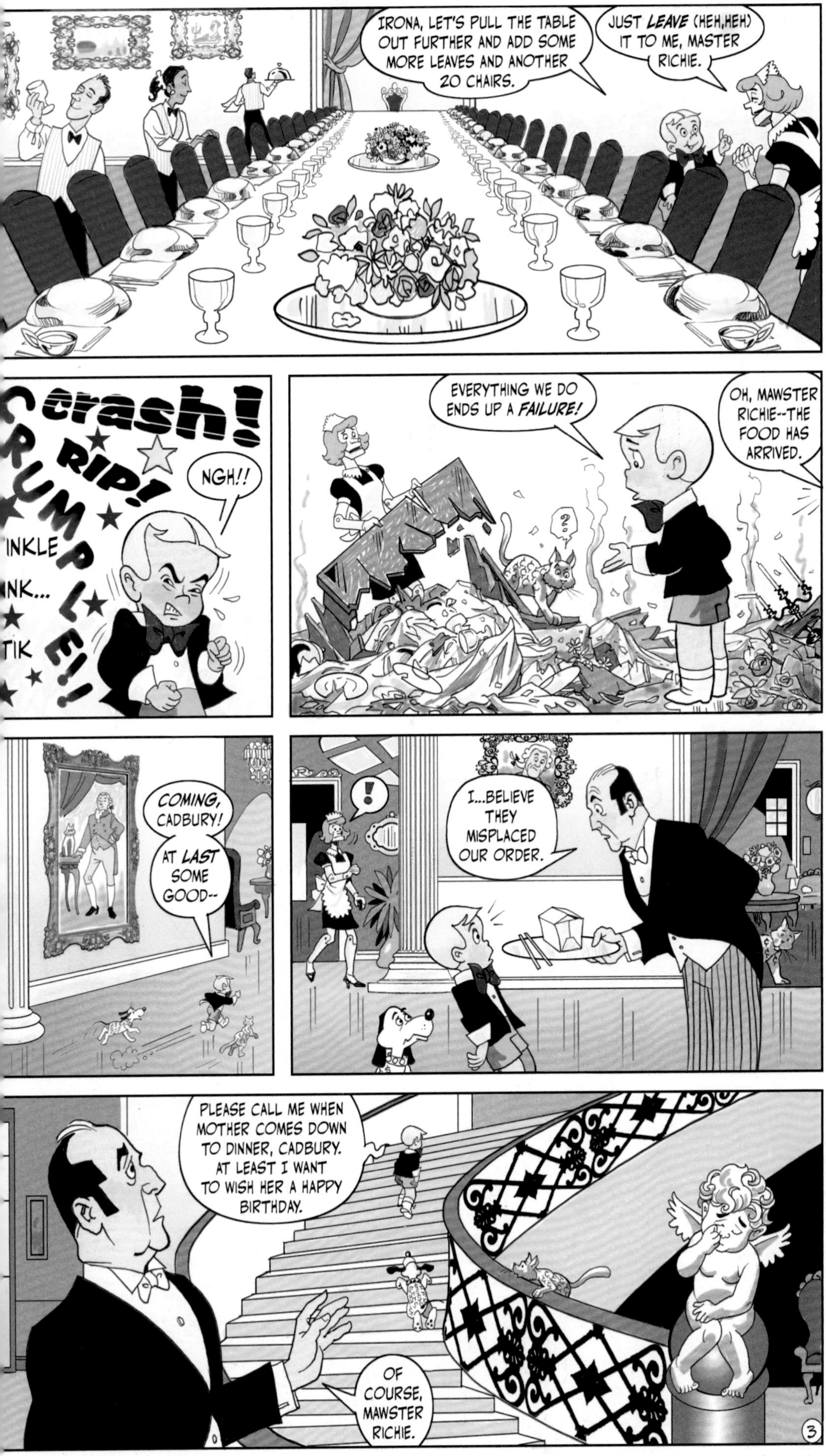
IRONA, LET'S PULL THE TABLE OUT FURTHER AND ADD SOME MORE LEAVES AND ANOTHER 20 CHAIRS.
JUST LEAVE (HEH,HEH) IT TO ME, MASTER RICHIE.
crash!
RIP!
CRUMPLE!!
INKLE
INK...
TIK
NGH!!
EVERYTHING WE DO ENDS UP A FAILURE!
OH, MAWSTER RICHIE--THE FOOD HAS ARRIVED.
COMING, CADBURY!
AT LAST SOME GOOD--
I...BELIEVE THEY MISPLACED OUR ORDER.
PLEASE CALL ME WHEN MOTHER COMES DOWN TO DINNER, CADBURY. AT LEAST I WANT TO WISH HER A HAPPY BIRTHDAY.
OF COURSE, MAWSTER RICHIE.

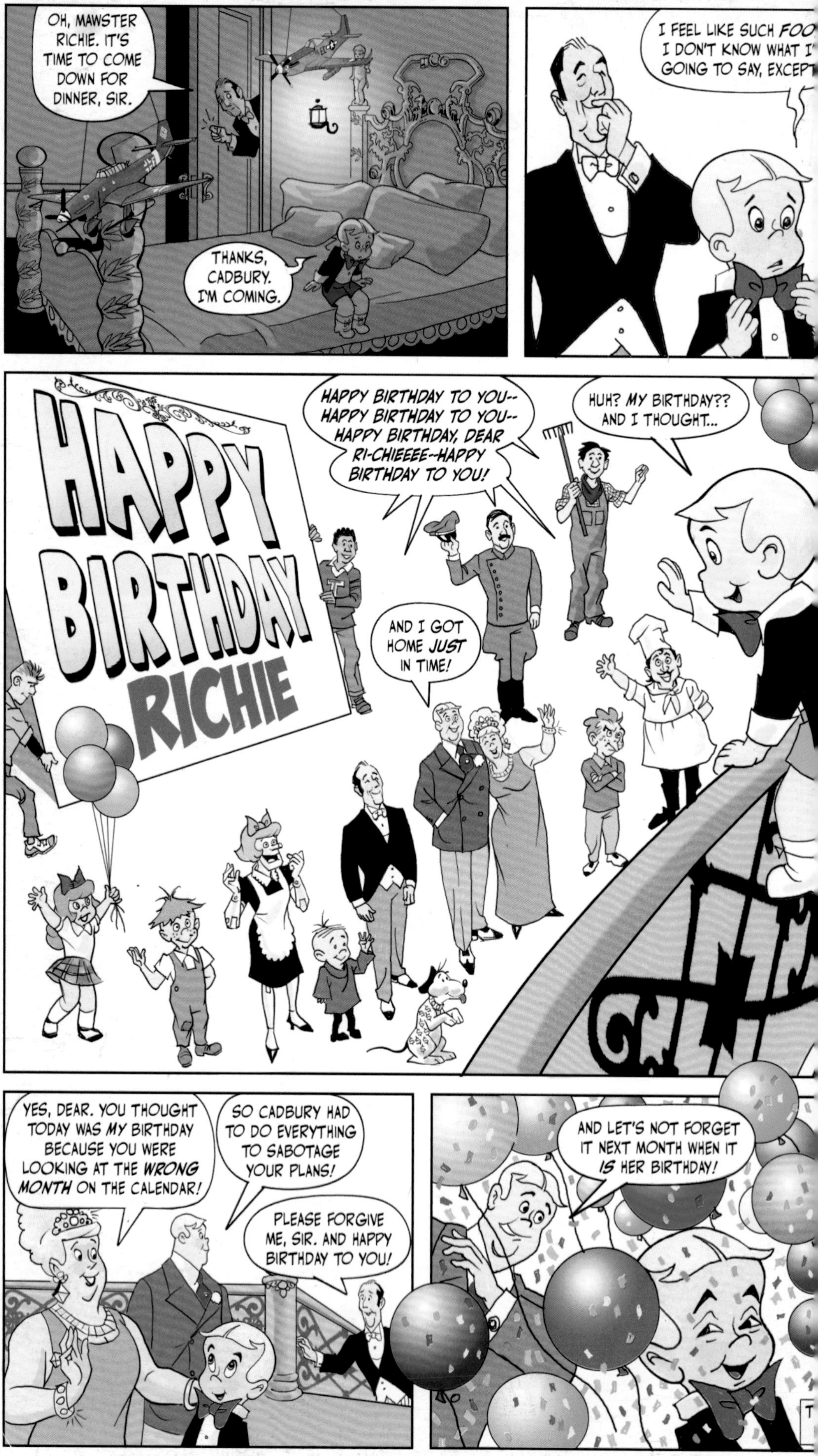
OH, MAWSTER RICHIE. IT'S TIME TO COME DOWN FOR DINNER, SIR.
THANKS, CADBURY. I'M COMING.
I FEEL LIKE SUCH FOO
I DON'T KNOW WHAT I'
GOING TO SAY, EXCEPT
HAPPY BIRTHDAY RICHIE
HAPPY BIRTHDAY TO YOU-- HAPPY BIRTHDAY TO YOU-- HAPPY BIRTHDAY, DEAR RI-CHIEEEE--HAPPY BIRTHDAY TO YOU!
HUH? MY BIRTHDAY?? AND I THOUGHT...
AND I GOT HOME JUST IN TIME!
YES, DEAR. YOU THOUGHT TODAY WAS MY BIRTHDAY BECAUSE YOU WERE LOOKING AT THE WRONG MONTH ON THE CALENDAR!
SO CADBURY HAD TO DO EVERYTHING TO SABOTAGE YOUR PLANS!
PLEASE FORGIVE ME, SIR. AND HAPPY BIRTHDAY TO YOU!
AND LET'S NOT FORGET IT NEXT MONTH WHEN IT IS HER BIRTHDAY!

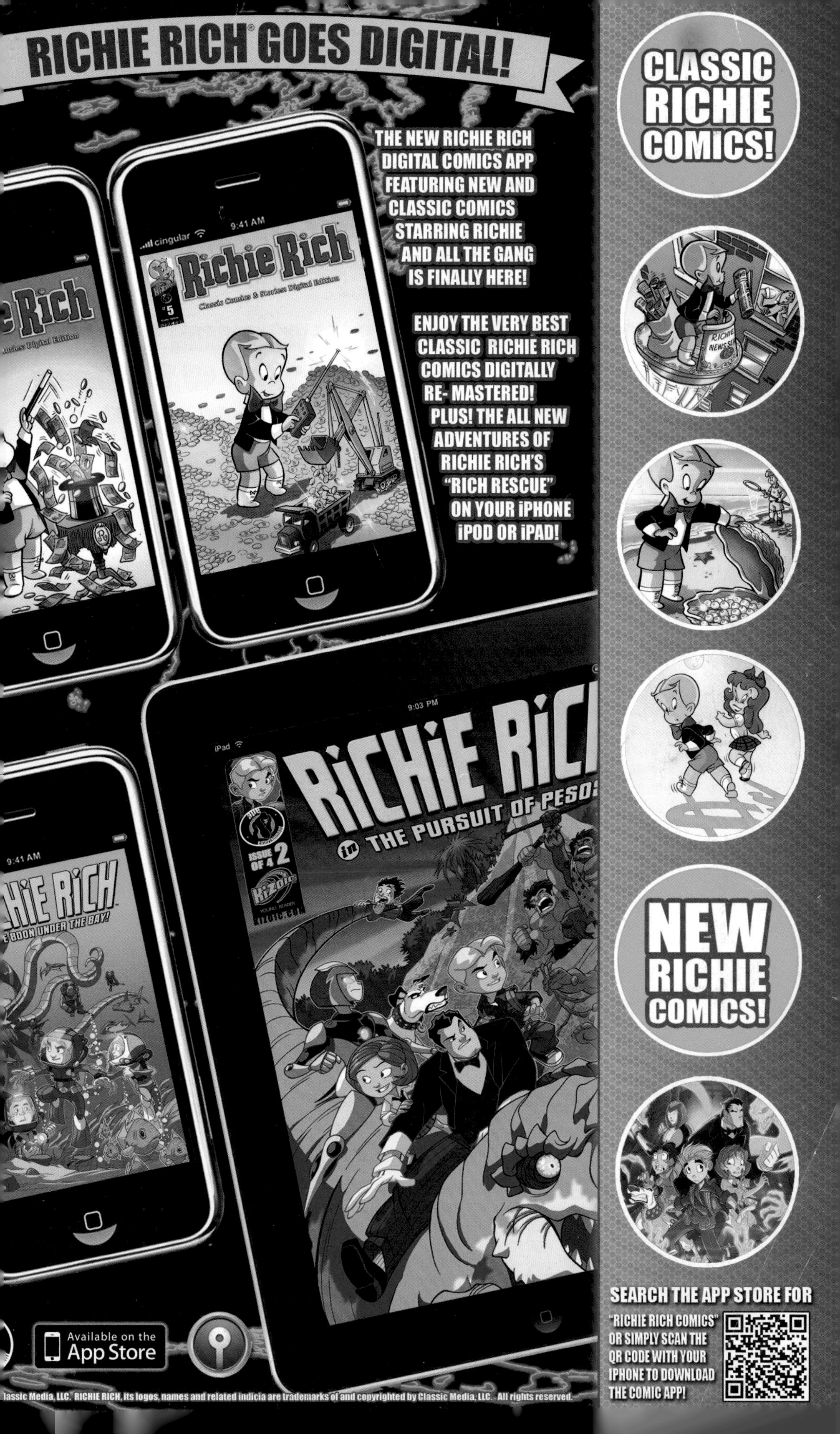
RICHIE RICH® GOES DIGITAL!
THE NEW RICHIE RICH DIGITAL COMICS APP FEATURING NEW AND CLASSIC COMICS STARRING RICHIE AND ALL THE GANG IS FINALLY HERE!
ENJOY THE VERY BEST CLASSIC RICHIE RICH COMICS DIGITALLY RE- MASTERED! PLUS! THE ALL NEW ADVENTURES OF RICHIE RICH'S "RICH RESCUE" ON YOUR iPHONE iPOD OR iPAD!
9:41 AM
cingular
Richie Rich
Classic Comics & Stories: Digital Edition
9:03 PM
iPad
RICHIE RICH
in THE PURSUIT OF PESOS
ISSUE OF 4 2
RICHIE RICH
BOON UNDER THE BAY!
Available on the App Store
CLASSIC RICHIE COMICS!
NEW RICHIE COMICS!
SEARCH THE APP STORE FOR
"RICHIE RICH COMICS" OR SIMPLY SCAN THE QR CODE WITH YOUR IPHONE TO DOWNLOAD THE COMIC APP!
lassic Media, LLC. RICHIE RICH, its logos, names and related indicia are trademarks of and copyrighted by Classic Media, LLC. All rights reserved.

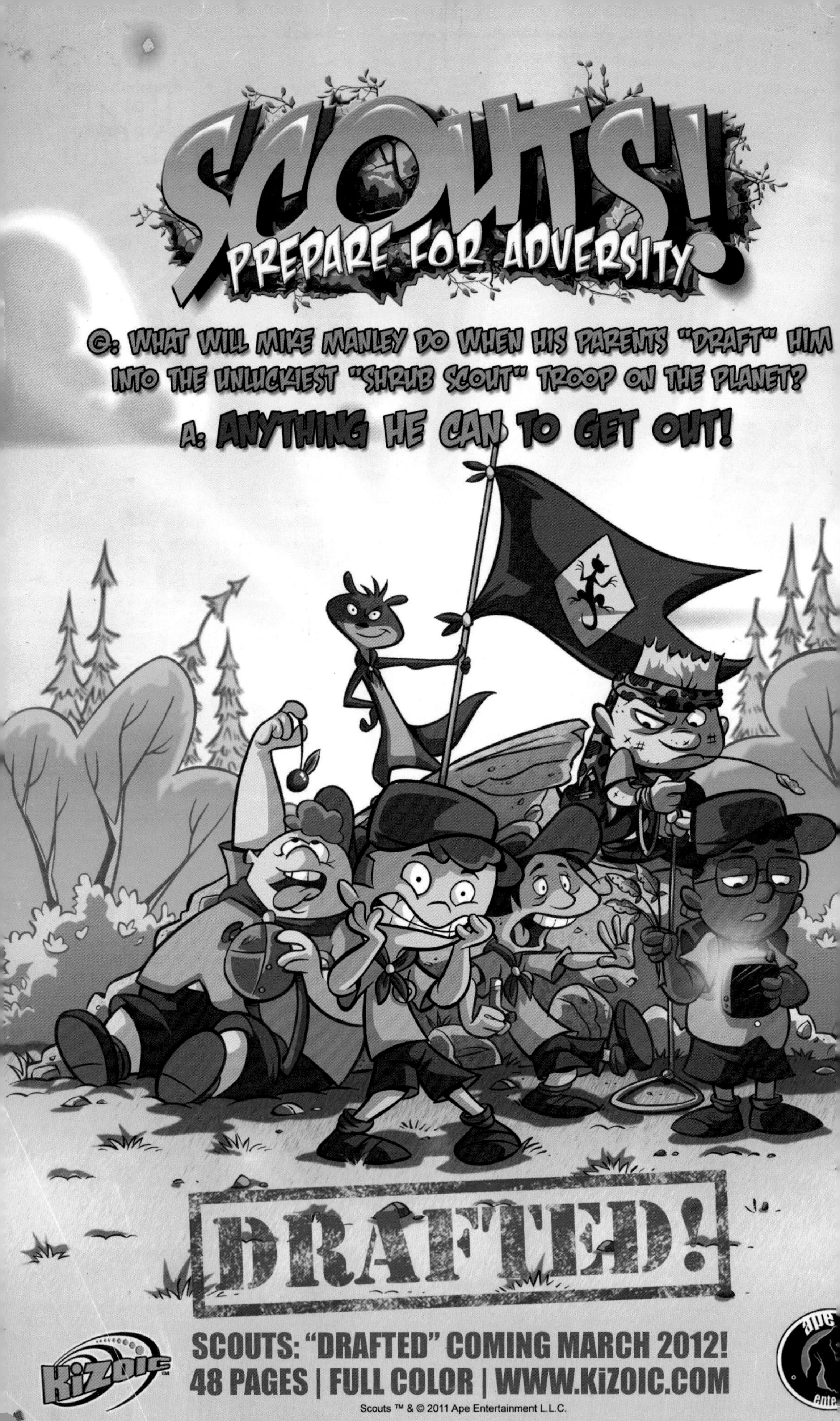
SCOUTS!
PREPARE FOR ADVERSITY
Q: WHAT WILL MIKE MANLEY DO WHEN HIS PARENTS "DRAFT" HIM INTO THE UNLUCKIEST "SHRUB SCOUT" TROOP ON THE PLANET?
A: ANYTHING HE CAN TO GET OUT!
DRAFTED!
SCOUTS: "DRAFTED" COMING MARCH 2012!
48 PAGES | FULL COLOR | WWW.KIZOIC.COM
KiZOIC